Simple Lessons
for
A Better Life

Simple Lessons
for
A Better Life

Unexpected Inspiration from
Inside the Nursing Home

Charles E. Dodgen

(PB) Prometheus Books
59 John Glenn Drive
Amherst, New York 14228

Published 2015 by Prometheus Books

Cover image © Media Bakery
Cover design by Grace M. Conti-Zilsberger

Inquiries should be addressed to
Prometheus Books
59 John Glenn Drive
Amherst, New York 14228
VOICE: 716–691–0133
FAX: 716–691–0137
WWW.PROMETHEUSBOOKS.COM

19 18 17 16 15   5 4 3 2 1

Library of Congress Cataloging-in-Publication Data Pending

ISBN 978-1-63388-016-0 (Pbk)
ISBN 978-1-63388-017-1 (ebook)

Printed in the United States of America

*In loving memory of my sister Sandra K. Dodgen
and mother, Shirley A. Dodgen*

CONTENTS

ACKNOWLEDGMENTS

I wish to express my heartiest appreciation to Dr. Lynne Sacher and Dr. Diane Klein; I am most fortunate to know these estimable women, both of whom are superb psychologists and gifted writer-editors. A valued mentor, Dr. Sacher generously provided her talents from start to finish. In addition to the technical-writing assistance she brought, the encouragement she offered helped sustain my efforts through a challenging work schedule. Dr. Klein, a gracious and trusted friend and colleague, was supportive from the inception of this project and contributed significantly to early versions of the manuscript.

My incredible personal support system maintained a consistently positive presence throughout the writing process. In addition to providing emotional sustenance, my wife, Lisa, offered helpful feedback on the manuscript. My daughter, Danielle, assisted in these ways as well. My son, Christopher, and in-laws Joseph and Annette Calabrese were enthusiastic supporters all along the way. Close friends John King and Rand Harris were ever ready with inspiring words.

It is a privilege to provide services at the nursing home, one that I could not enjoy without administrative approval. I am thankful for the administrative support that I received (and continue to receive) at the nursing home from Michael Duffy and Kenneth Bittman. Social workers Linda Cohen and Fay Ross have been wonderful colleagues; both also read an early version of the manuscript and offered helpful feedback and support. I want to thank all those who provide services at the nursing home and who make it the special care center that it is, including the medical staff; those in admissions, nursing, physical therapy, occupational therapy, speech therapy, dietary, food services, housekeeping, and maintenance departments; and those in the business office.

Thanks also go to Steven L. Mitchell at Prometheus Books for providing this opportunity to publish my work, and to my agent, Joyce Hart, for her kind and gentle assistance with this project. I would like to additionally acknowledge the work of Jade Zora Scibilia, my editor at Prometheus Books who helped considerably to improve the manuscript.

Finally, I am forever grateful to the residents and families at West Caldwell Care Center for the opportunity to work with and learn from them.

INTRODUCTION

We live in a dangerous and disturbing world. As proof of this bold assertion, I'll share an experience I had recently: while standing in line to get an iced coffee at my favorite store, I watched the news on the large television screen mounted above the counter. In less than five minutes, I was barraged by negative images and reports on the following: escalating concerns about threats of international terrorism; the outbreak of the deadly Ebola virus disease; intractable unemployment; financial hardship; climate change and extreme weather events like Superstorm Sandy; revolution in the Middle East; wars; domestic healthcare worries; and crooked and inept politicians in our government. In short, grave concerns were reported about our health, finances, safety, and government.

My experience in the coffee shop is remarkable not because it is exceptional but because it happens all the time. To make matters worse, so many of us also worry about health, family, work, and finances. Against such seemingly insurmountable problems, a person could start to feel awfully puny and helpless about surviving, never mind thriving and feeling happy. Is life getting worse by the day, or does it only feel that way?

As a clinical psychologist practicing for over twenty-eight years, I often ask, How can we cope with all our concerns so that we do not exist in a perpetual state of fear and misery? In order to achieve some peace of mind, it might seem that the answer would be to consult with experts for solutions to the serious challenges that threaten our serenity and security every day. To whom do we turn? Who even possesses the requisite knowledge that could be of benefit? Doctors? Religious leaders? Academicians? Scientists? Politicians? Economists? Military leaders? Believe it or not, I have determined that a valuable source of guidance can be found by looking in a totally unexpected direction: nursing-home residents. Not world beaters, more like the world's beaten. Talk about your unsung heroes!

How did I arrive at the conclusion that nursing-home residents can provide useful counsel at what appears to be such a critical time in history? The nursing home, also known euphemistically as "God's Waiting Room," where people are much closer to the end of life than the beginning, may appear to be an unlikely setting in which to find answers about how to cope with modern problems. That's only because it is. It is an environment that can be unsettling, even offensive, to the newcomer. Unpleasant sights, sounds, and smells can be the greetings one receives at the door. The nursing home does not seem like a place to find enlightenment and wisdom; it can be a morose environment that many people find downright depressing. Even mental-health professionals may resist working in this environment: residents comprise an underserved population for multiple reasons, including the natural revulsion some feel in this setting, as well as the seeming absence of hope. Psychologists, like members of any other professional group, often prefer to work in more appealing environments with healthier, younger patients who show more potential for dramatic improvement.

However, if one looks beyond the initial sensory perceptions and emotional reactions to this setting, observation of the often weak and vulnerable nursing-home resident can reveal valuable lessons for life that are applicable to all of us. Let me be clear, I am not referring to the pearls of wisdom that can be gleaned from an elder with many decades of life experience. Rather, I am intent on revealing what can be learned from interaction with residents who more closely resemble motherless children than they do elder statesmen. The lessons relate less to what particular individuals may say or do and more to what they represent in terms of human beings engaged in the most humble but essential interactions with the world around them. The most critical aspect of this interaction is human relations. People are revealed in their most elementary form—stripped of surface features, in the nursing-home resident, we see the heart and soul of everyman. Timeless, universal aspects of human existence are uncovered. In this setting the essential nature of personhood is distilled and revealed.

Consider the case of Nina, a seventy-four-year-old Italian American widow and mother of one daughter. Her husband had died of a heart attack several years prior to her admission to the nursing home. She had lived independently with some assistance from her daughter and son-in-law until she suffered a stroke. Nina was treated in a hospital and sent to the nursing home for rehabilitation. A hemiplegic, Nina had lost use of the right side of her body. She was referred to me for psychological evaluation due to staff concerns about her mood.

My first several meetings with Nina were memorable. Within seconds of meeting me, Nina was sobbing. She was overweight and sat up crookedly in her bed because the stroke caused difficulty in her ability to maneuver. She complained of pain in her right-side limbs, so that it was difficult for aides to groom her well; she would become emotionally and verbally agitated if they moved her, so she developed an unkempt appearance. Although there was no apparent difficulty with verbal comprehension, Nina was aphasic and had trouble organizing and expressing her thoughts clearly. She could respond relatively well to simple questions, but any inquiries requiring a more abstract or elaborate response resulted in a jumbled, often incomprehensible ramble. She was aware of her inability to communicate well, and this was a source of much frustration, embarrassment, and distress. Nevertheless, she possessed a will to connect with me and she found a way to do so. Through facial and hand gestures, eye contact, tone of voice, and fragmented sentences, she made it plain that she was unhappy and wanted to die. That she was profoundly sad and distraught was obvious. However, the exact causes of her extreme distress were unclear initially due to the limitations of her communication.

As a consequence of her somewhat wordless, formless misery, the only interventions that I could offer to her at first were generic, sympathetic ones. Although I was able to provide comfort for the pervasive distress that Nina conveyed using her then-limited cognitive abilities, the identification of more specific sources of her pain would allow for more precise and effective intervention. Fortunately, because of the combined effects of natural healing processes, speech therapy, and psychotherapy, within several weeks there was an observed reconstitution of Nina's mental functioning so that she was better able to describe her experiences. A theme emerged from conversation with her that related to her worries about the well-being of her daughter and her daughter's family, and about being a burden on the family. In articulating her concerns so clearly, Nina was transfigured from a hulking, wretched soul, of twisted body and mind, to a vision of utter beauty, an archetypal Mother. She was, of course, disturbed by losses of her functional abilities and by pain in her body, but the predominant themes of our dialogue related to her role as mother and to her concern for her family. Discussion of her two granddaughters always lifted her mood noticeably, and from that observation it became clear to me that I had found her "heart light"—the source of her motivation to live, despite her desire to end the pain and suffering. Talking about her love for the kids, her anticipation of their visits to the nursing home, and plans for home visits for special events, such as holidays and birthdays, provided a focus that allowed Nina to maintain her spirits for another four years before she suffered a fatal heart attack.

Nina's struggles and triumphs were personal to her but at the same time represent variations on common human themes. For example, the inevitable outcomes of lifestyle choices were painfully evident in Nina's chronically poor dietary and exercise habits, eventuating in diabetes, stroke, and heart attack. The operation of feelings as a powerful yet somewhat crude method of communication was evident. Nina's fear of injury to her sensitive limbs motivated her to push people away in order to maintain a safe distance; expressing her sadness brought people closer to her for emotional comfort. Ultimately, improved cognitive skills added specificity to her expressions of pain. As Nina put words to her feelings, her overwhelming distress became more organized, which allowed her to experience the beneficial effects of understanding and compassion. This contributed to her being able to better manage her emotions and feel a reduction in suffering. Most crucially for Nina, seeing how her identity was so centrally focused on mothering helped guide treatment. Understanding the importance of this dynamic and encouraging her to act on her maternal feelings by maintaining close contact with the family did not erase the hardship in her life. Rather, it served as a reason to endure the challenges and provided meaning in the suffering. When she was particularly disturbed by physical discomfort and sadness I would ask straightforwardly, "What keeps you from just giving up?" Nina would reply, "I got those kids—my daughter and my grandchildren. That's what!"

In spending time with Nina, and the many other residents in the nursing home whose experiences highlighted other universal issues, I was convinced that if I kept my eyes and ears open, and my mind and heart receptive, I was going to learn invaluable lessons in humanity.

The nursing home may be viewed as a natural laboratory where human behavior can be studied. Designed primarily to provide necessary and important care to the elderly and disabled people in need of such care, nursing homes may also be seen as contained, controlled environments that represent a small replica of the world. As such, these facilities provide a rich environment in which to study and understand the spectrum of human behavior and human nature. Seemingly all the important themes in life can be studied in the interactions and transactions that occur in the nursing home. At both ends of the life continuum we are placed in the hands of caretakers, and our life course depends to a great extent on interactions with people. In our initial family environment, we form loving attachments to people, gain mastery of our body, achieve self-control, develop a conscience, and are taught to communicate. By school age, we engage in relationships with peers, contend with competition, work cooperatively in groups and on teams, develop relationships with authority figures such as teachers, coaches, and religious instructors, and engage in formal learning to facilitate competent functioning in the world. Later, we work, find a partner, and become sexual, mature adults. Along the way we have dealt with dependency, love, communication, competence, power, money, sex, disease, and death. All of these themes are encountered in a typical day in the nursing home!

ORIGINAL IDENTITY THEFT

So what makes the nursing-home setting such a unique environment for discovering the answers that we seek to the puzzles of life? The short answer is that in the nursing home we are seeing people in an unusually revealing state of existence. Just about anyone can be happy and comfortable when life experiences are on the upswing. In a typical progression, the early and middle stages of our lives are characterized by growth, expansion, and acquisition. We grow physically, gain knowledge and behavioral competence, and accumulate material possessions. We also tend to identify so strongly with what we have achieved or obtained that these elements become an essential and indispensable part of our identities. People cling to past and present aspects of their lives as if they could not endure without them.

It makes one wonder if it is possible to be happy, content, and secure without every bit of our health, skills, status, beauty, family, friends, and material possessions. Yet removed from familiar surroundings and stripped of many trappings of contemporary life, human beings remain human beings. It can be argued that humanity is never more evident than when it is laid bare. This is my conclusion after working for over eighteen years in a nursing home. My work in this setting has provided me with the chance to observe people at some of their lowest times. What can be seen with unusual clarity in the experiences of people in this simplified, reduced setting of the nursing home is easily obscured by the window dressing of everyday life. People look different when not armored in their usual way or when dispossessed of the material features that defined their identities. The aging process, often with attendant illness, disability, and loss, is the *original identity theft*.

The elderly or infirmed person can be viewed with a jaundiced eye as a pathetic, broken-down symbol of life; or, with another eye, as an unusually clear representative of humanity where basic aspects of life are raw, conspicuous, and undisguised. In this naked form, certain truths about life are plain to see. We discover that the fundamental challenges of human life are independent of place and time. Once the superfluous aspects of daily life are cleared away, it is much easier to find the roads to happiness and serenity. Most nursing-home residents have experienced this clearing-away process naturally due to their life circumstances. Ironically, the clear and convincing truths that become apparent in the nursing-home setting elude most people when they are younger, independent, and vital. Because of the speed and complexity of the modern world, these roads are still present but less obvious; they are there, nonetheless.

Our modern world seems to move at meteoric speed. In my office I frequently hear of people returning from a week's vacation to find six to seven hundred e-mails awaiting them at work. When I talk to nursing-home residents I sometimes feel as if I am talking to denizens from a different world. They grew up *before* TV, automobiles, and air-planes, never mind cell phones, computers, and video games. And yet their stories are remarkably similar to those of the present. To hear the nursing-home resident, Nina, talk about her pride in the achievements of her daughter, does it matter that she is in her seventies and her daughter in her late forties? I could be enjoying the same conversation with a proud mother of school-age children: a mother's pride is a mother's pride. The issues and challenges we confront do not change. However, when the buzz and stimulation of modern life are so dominant, one can easily become distracted, misguided, and off-course.

The needs for food, shelter, clothing, cleanliness, companionship, and safety are the same now as they were one hundred, two hundred, or two thousand years ago. Human beings shape the world to meet their needs and always have. The human body has not changed much in tens of thousands of years. Neither has the psyche. Most of us entertain a somewhat-arrogant view that we are smarter, more sophisticated, and superior to members of previous generations. It is difficult to resist coming to the conclusion that with our formal educations and technological advances we are superior to our predecessors. Aren't we getting progressively smarter? If it were the case that each successive generation is smarter, how did our farmer great-grandparents, with minimal formal education, raise competent human beings and advance civilization? Going back further in time, the same question could be asked about preliterate peasants in Europe, Asia, and Africa.

Are we all captive to the glitz and glitter of technology and all the intriguing products that make life easier and fun in some ways? Certainly, there exists a modern bias for efficiency, order, productivity, and rationality, but real, meaningful life happens in the interpersonal matrix; it always has and always will. Relationships provide the soil that we grow in and that sustains us. We don't require professional expertise or technology in order to be happy and well-adjusted; we need to know ourselves, have good relationships with people, and to modify our environment to achieve our goals. The human drama, reflecting the interplay of animal instincts, spirit, and intellect, is unchanged by time. This is why we still refer to the Bible and other religious documents, as well as great literature such as Shakespeare's plays and Greek mythology, for guidance and inspiration. These important works capture timeless themes about human life, eternal truths—the same themes and truths that can be observed on any given day in the nursing home. This book is not about the wisdom discovered and dispensed by a few exceptionally bright, perceptive individuals whom I have encountered in the nursing home who have the quandaries of life all figured out. Most of the residents whom I see need assistance with getting dressed and operating the television remote. Rather, this is a book about being human, about intrinsic life challenges and the recognition that we all currently possess what we need to have, within reach anytime, anywhere.

Simple Lessons for a Better Life evolved from my original conception of the book. I first thought of writing a nursing-home book; a book to assist residents in their adjustment to life in the nursing home. Additionally, I wanted to provide insights to help family members understand and cope with their concerns about having a loved one placed in the nursing home. Then I considered providing information to guide staff members to better help residents and family members achieve a successful adaptation to the nursing home. In reviewing my notes, I saw that there was a recurrence of themes in the lives of many residents relating to loss; suffering; dependency; powerlessness; best ways to offer help; best ways to receive help; the healing power of love; arranging life to maximize happiness; the value of spirituality; the benefits of acceptance and forgiveness; and more. Eventually, I realized, *"This is not a nursing-home-adjustment book, this is a life-adjustment book."*

The observations and concepts that I discuss in *Simple Lessons for a Better Life* emerged naturally in the course of my work in the nursing home. The material is almost entirely experience-based and did not arise from theoretical or research models of aging or psychotherapy. (But I have included some references where I thought it useful to provide supplementary historical context, additional theoretical perspective, or empirical support of key ideas.)

Through my work in the nursing home I have concluded that, even in a threatening, ever-changing world, we can take comfort from recognizing that there are some constants that make life good. Some of the simple lessons that I have identified in the nursing home and that I discuss in the book are:

- *We are 3-D beings: we exist as body, mind, and spirit at all times. We must attend to all three. Without our bodies, we cease to exist; without mind, we are beating hearts (think of those suffering from severe dementia); and without spirit, we are aimless human beings without the ability to discern right from wrong—truth from lie—and we are vulnerable to anxiety and despair.*
- *Our mind stands at the intersection of our external world, inner world, and spirit. Free choice offers the means to determine the course of our lives.*
- *Love is the most powerful force in the world. Love provides energy and motivation for life.*
- *Intimate relationships with people are the basis for our humanity and are our primary sources of love and security.*
- *There are many ways to express love and other feelings, but the spoken word may be the most important.*
- *Feelings provide a basis for understanding self and others; openness to experience them is crucial for mental health, effective behavior, and fulfilling human relationships.*
- *There are many aspects of life that we cannot control, so we must take an active role in shaping our lives whenever possible.*

- *The value of spirituality can be seen most readily when people experience failure in the material world. There is intrinsic power in virtuous principles. Identifying and acting in concert with these principles provides vitality, energy, motivation, and happiness.*
- *The basic needs for food, water, air, sleep, safety, and companionship underpin human experience.*
- *Defining our goals provides focus, purpose, and meaning to life.*
- *Achieving happiness requires work; it does not happen automatically.*

Simple Lessons for a Better Life is a psychology, self-help book in which I reveal how observation of the humble nursing-home resident, an unwitting everyman, yields nuggets of timeless wisdom. These universal truths about life and humanity, gleaned from experiences in the microcosm of the nursing home, can be employed to guide behavior in our incredibly complex, full-speed, everyday lives. My book is about developing a positive life at any stage. It is not about the elderly or the nursing-home resident per se; the nursing home merely provides the population and setting from which the observations and conclusions were drawn. The elderly are the same as anybody else. The aged person as discussed in my book is you, me, and the child next door; she may be cloaked in a different body and living under different conditions and circumstances, but she is dealing with the same basic challenges—as such, the book may be considered a study of the individual as representative of the whole of human experience. The solutions employed to great benefit in the nursing home can be used successfully by anybody. If the reader is currently old (or caring for a senior citizen), the book applies. However, the insights and advice apply equally well to everybody else.

Replete with anecdotes that will engage the reader's interest, the book also informs on a deeper level with insights obtained from over a quarter-century of clinical work as a practicing psychologist and over a half-century of life experience. *Simple Lessons for a Better Life* is not written to be read like a novel. Instead, chapters offer discrete lessons to promote thoughtful reflection. Each chapter contains examples drawn from current and past nursing-home cases that best illustrate the life lesson being discussed. (Please note that the identities of individuals described in the book are disguised, as required by professional ethics and privacy laws.) Each chapter also presents ways for readers to apply the lesson to improve their lives.

The book confronts key questions related to life in the nursing home:

1. Is it possible to be happy and secure in an apparent sea of negativity?
2. Do nursing-home residents have any control over their quality of life?
3. Can meaning and purpose be found despite the realization that a person will likely remain in the nursing home until the end of his or her life?
4. Is there any reason for hope? Joy?
5. Is it possible to experience love, fellowship, and compassion in the nursing home setting?
6. Are there *human* solutions, beyond medicine and science, to problems faced in the nursing home?

The answer to all these questions is a resounding YES. The lessons learned and applied to the benefit of residents in the dire circumstances of the nursing home can be used to improve the life of the reader.

Benefits to the reader include an enhanced ability to:

• Increase security and serenity for oneself and others
• Identify factors to change in order to maximize happiness
• Improve relationships
• Use words to heal suffering
• Understand and manage feelings more effectively
• Embrace the advantages of acceptance and forgiveness
• Cope well with challenges
• Understand and harness the healing power of love, spirituality, and mind (attitude)
• Simply put, make life better

CHAPTER 1

SUFFERING IS OPTIONAL

Jonathan is a Jamaican-born eighty-seven-year-old who came to this country as a young man. He is married to Claudette, also Jamaican-born, whom he met at a job when both were in their twenties. Jonathan enjoyed a career in sales and supported Claudette and their two daughters well. He came to the nursing home several years ago because of debilitation from chronic obstructive pulmonary disease (COPD) and heart disease. He is chronically weak, tired, and in need of assistance. The couple suffered the death of one daughter several years ago, and the other passed away two months ago. His wife, also a nursing-home resident owing to cancer, recently has been in and out of the hospital. Understandably, the shocking loss of their second child has deeply disturbed both of them.

On one recent visit, Jonathan looked me squarely in the eyes and asked, "How much more am I supposed to be able to take?" His question to me, which was more of a statement ("This is too much for me to take!"), highlighted the difficult reality in the nursing home and in life: There is grievous suffering. Bad things happen that cause us pain, sadness, frustration, torment, and discomfort. We get sick, lose people dear to us, lose jobs due to downsizing, experience personal rejection, have financial pressures, and are confronted by the many problems of daily life. What could I do to alter Jonathan's health or change the devastating circumstance of the premature deaths of his children or improve his wife's terminal medical condition? Not a blessed thing. What could I do to help him? Plenty. I realize that it is impossible to magically change the external circumstances causing Jonathan such profound distress. However, I also know that his *internal* circumstances can change. Pain in life is inevitable. However, suffering, the emotional reaction to pain, is a separate and optional experience.

You may think, "Here comes another psychologist trying to tell me all of my problems are in my head." Well, right, sort of. Many different types of evidence suggest that suffering can be mitigated and that persons enduring devastating situations like Jonathan's can be helped. Researchers investigating the human brain, studying infant development, and working with victims of trauma, confirm my own clinical experience and observations in this area. Neurologists have determined that the perception of pain registers in different areas of the brain than the experience of emotion. Although pain and suffering are strongly linked, these experiences can be separated so that it is possible for the brain to register injury to the body or psychological pain, but to block or minimize the emotional reaction of suffering. A classic example involves the medical condition of trigeminal neuralgia, which can cause intense, debilitating facial pain. For victims of this condition who do not respond to medication, surgeons can destroy neurological connections to the emotion center of the brain. The result of the neurosurgery is that patients will still describe a sense of the pain, but they feel subjectively indifferent to it. In other words, they are no longer suffering because they do not experience the emotional reaction to their pain.[1]

Careful observation of infants has revealed interesting data concerning emotional development and health. Of particular relevance are the observations relating to caretaker-child interactions. Studies reveal that infants who are upset can be comforted when the caretaker responds in a manner sensitive to the child's emotional state. An accurately attuned response by the caretaker results in beneficial changes in brain neurotransmitter activity, hormones, heart rate, and feelings; negative emotional states are reduced and supplanted by positive emotions.[2] In other words, an empathic response mitigates suffering in the infant even in the absence of language capacity and even if the cause of the upset is unchanged. Of course, if an infant is hungry or wet, for example, feeding or changing the baby will be helpful. But sometimes an infant is upset for no obvious reason. Nevertheless, whether or not the cause is apparent, comforting is often necessary to calm the baby. Have you ever tried to change the diaper of a distressed, thrashing infant? Every parent knows that a tender, loving response can help soothe a crying baby, but who knew that such ministrations affect the deepest levels of the body? Not only do the visible signs of distress diminish with tender care, but biological systems change as well. A loving human response results in positive emotional, behavioral, and physiological changes *regardless of the source of distress.*

Emotional attunement between the caretaker and infant is communicated mainly through gaze and facial expression, but also through the caretaker's tone of voice and manner of touching and holding the infant. The message that appears to be communicated is, "I know you are upset. I am here for you. You will be all right." Infants handled in this manner tend to grow up to become more emotionally stable, secure, and resilient children. The caretaker does not try merely to stop or stifle the infant's reaction; the presence, acceptance, and loving concern of the caretaker are what appear to be beneficial. In this way, infants learn that negative feelings are tolerable and temporary.

In trauma research, much attention is given to personal factors that promote recovery. Of course, it would be best if all traumatic occurrences could be prevented. However, as this is impossible, it is helpful to isolate factors that facilitate successful recovery after a trauma is experienced. In many studies of trauma victims, one of the most powerful factors associated with successful recovery is the presence of a support system, such as a loving family and friends.[3]

Evidence from my work in the nursing home is consistent with this research. Many residents, such as Jonathan, have experienced irreversible negative life events. Through the proper response, a significant portion of their suffering can be reduced. So what was the proper response for Jonathan when he asked me how much more he was supposed to be able to take? I said to him, "This is too much for one man to bear." He looked at me with an expression of surprise that I interpreted to reflect amazement at two things: that I clearly understood the extent of his burden and that I would state this so bluntly. In my experience, people often deny, minimize, or sugarcoat such unpleasant realities (to protect either themselves or others), and in so doing, they invalidate their feelings or fail to acknowledge them. His response? Jonathan sobbed. And he sobbed some more. And it was good. The two of us experienced a deeply felt sense of closeness based on the ingredients that help to heal suffering: the honest expression of emotion in the context of an intimate, trusting relationship. On this occasion, Jonathan expressed his sadness; at other times, he revealed his anger, hopelessness, and sense of helplessness. In a time when fake reality dominates public interest, this is the real stuff. I demonstrated my understanding, acceptance, and desire to be with him even at his lowest point. I was unafraid of his sorrow, and of my feelings stimulated by his intense emotion. The tragic causes of Jonathan's pain remained unchanged; however, Jonathan experienced some relief from his suffering.

Contrast my response to Jonathan to a situation I saw on the evening news a few years ago. I was watching a live broadcast of a house fire in a suburban neighborhood. In the picture I could see two men. One man, presumably the homeowner, was crying and obviously distraught. Another man stood next to him, patting him sharply on the back in an effort to soothe his grief. It seemed to me that in his response the second man was in some way trying to put out the fire! Whereas his intention was to provide comfort, he reacted to the show of emotion as an out-of-control, destructive force that had to be tamped down.

In my practice I often use the following example from everyday life to illustrate the difference between pain and suffering and to show how suffering can be reduced without stopping the pain. Think of this not-unfamiliar scene: a four-year-old child running toward her mother on the blacktop, falls, ends up crying, and gets a skinned knee. When the mother picks up the child, the crying stops immediately, and the child is comforted, *even though nothing has been done to fix the injured knee.*

When a person we care about is in distress, we mistakenly believe we must *do* something about it. The dual assumptions are that doing something must consist of changing the situation in order to stop the pain, and that just holding, comforting, and loving is not doing anything. We tend to think that we are inadequate if we are unable to stop the pain, fix the problem, or quickly alleviate any emotional suffering. Emotions that accompany pain demand our attention and motivate us to take corrective action. But the truth is that we can't eliminate all suffering, nor should we want to. We cannot change the inevitability of pain and suffering in life; we can help, however, to mitigate suffering. Even people who experience extreme distress like that suffered by Jonathan, who have premature losses, disability, poor health, and the imminent loss of a spouse, can be helped to suffer less. The best part is that anybody can help to heal suffering. All that is required is compassion. No medical or religious training or any other special type of education is necessary. This is why your grandmother with a tenth-grade education could do it.

Lesson: Although suffering in life is inevitable, we can mitigate it.

Applying the Lesson to Your Life

- When you are suffering with emotional distress, reach out to family and friends. Seek practical assistance for problems that may be solvable, and get emotional support even if practical solutions are not possible.
- If you do not have a support system to provide comfort, try religious institutions, support groups, or self-help groups, or seek professional help. Just as Jonathan needed social reinforcement of his pain to move past suffering, others might find strength in having their pain acknowledged. This is why support groups, for instance, are so helpful. An alcoholic might feel alone in dealing with his addiction, and maybe he pushed away family members and friends. But through participation in a recovery network, he can attend meetings where he is surrounded by peers who are struggling with the same problems that he is. Finding strength in a group—and seeing how other alcoholics are remaining

determined and becoming successful—can reduce his emotional upheaval and give him the courage he needs to begin tackling his personal issues and to overcome the obstacles he is facing.

- If you know someone who is distressed, extend practical assistance if possible. Offer compassion, love, and emotional support even if you cannot help solve the problem. Do not underestimate the healing power of loving, concerned support for a person in distress.

CHAPTER 2

SOCIAL SECURITY

Only in the twentieth century did we come to fully appreciate the insulative and protective powers of loving relationships. The experiences of World War II provided us with some very surprising knowledge about the needs of human beings. In England during the war, many children were sent to orphanages and nurseries. Because of the relentless bombing of London, in particular, parents were advised to send their children away for their protection. What was discovered was that many of the children living away from home suffered emotionally despite having received what were considered the necessities of life: they were clothed, fed, cleaned, and kept warm and safe. Observers eventually determined that the displaced children suffered from not having their emotional needs met.[1] For some, there were no regular caretakers with whom the babies could attach emotionally, bond, and form relationships. Although competent care may have been provided to meet physical needs, this was clearly insufficient to sustain healthy emotional development and the ability to thrive.

MOTHER'S LOVE WAS MORE POWERFUL THAN WARTIME BOMBS

The experience in the World War II–era childcare arrangements in London made it plain that human beings require more than the satisfaction of their most basic physical needs to be healthy. Love, affection, and special relationships are vital ingredients to happy, healthy, successful life. One especially powerful observation emerged clearly: children who remained with their mothers in bombed-out homes, vulnerable to further bombing and exposure to other traumatic experiences (burning buildings, witnessing of people with war injuries or death) appeared to do better than children in nurseries who were separated from home and family! In terms of the emotional well-being of a child, *the mother's love was more powerful than wartime bombs. Subjective safety trumped objective danger.* Thus it was established that our primary relationships are the principal components of the origins of our "social security."

We are accustomed nowadays to hearing about the use of "human shields" by terrorists. In conventional warfare, soldiers are kept away from noncombatant citizens to minimize collateral damage. The amoral terrorist tactic is intended as a deterrent force—the possibility of killing innocent citizens places attackers in a moral bind; if in attacking they kill private citizens, they will have committed a devastating atrocity and the terrorists might gain political currency. There have been positive human shields, though, in other wartime situations. Being enveloped in familiar surroundings with loving parents and family members is solid insulation. Some children in London who were subjected to repeated bombings were at times literally buried in rubble; there were reports that children played amidst unexploded bombs and in craters and showed no signs of distress when under the protective shield of the family. The loving relationships allowed them to feel secure, suffer no unusual distress, and remain happy, playful, and able to enjoy other children and activities. That is, they behaved as normal children despite the extraordinarily dangerous and abnormal conditions and circumstances. Interestingly, the degree of emotional protection experienced by the children related to the condition of the protectors—their mothers. If a mother was experiencing psychological distress and emotional disturbance, this negatively affected the emotional well-being of her children. The psychological-emotional state of mother had a greater impact on the child's well-being than the conditions of wartime England.

NURSING HOME AS ADULT ORPHANAGE

The importance of the stable provision of love is obvious with young children who would surely perish without loving caretakers. As they grow more independent and competent and develop ever more important additional relationships outside the home, it may appear that love is less important to them. But this is a false assumption; actually they are diversifying the sources of love and getting it from different people. As children grow and experience a range of relationships and develop greater emotional understanding and cognitive skills, they become attuned to the expression of love in more symbolic form. For example, a thoughtful word from a friend can mean a lot to a twelve-year-old; it is not necessary for caring to be expressed in the physical manner or explicitly reassuring way that a small child would require. As people age and begin to lose both mental and physical abilities, they understandably become more helpless and dependent and lose self-confidence. In the absence of gratifying interactions from other spheres of their previous lives, they may need to have love demonstrated in more concrete terms again.

The life-inspiring power of positive relationships can be seen in nursing homes by watching residents interact with family and close friends from the community, as well as in their relationships within the nursing home. Aides, who tend to have the most frequent, and the most physically intimate contact with residents, play a crucial role in maintaining positive relationships.

Frank, a sixty-seven-year-old resident with amyotrophic lateral sclerosis (ALS; Lou Gehrig's disease), is widowed with two adult children (a son and a daughter). His needs for care became so excessive that he could not be safely and comfortably maintained in his own home, despite his family's desires. Frank is fully mentally competent but is unable to move his body. Family members and friends visit him frequently. Despite his grave future, Frank's spirits are surprisingly high.

Angelo, on the other hand, has a different relationship with his family, and his spirits reflect it. Angelo, seventy-eight years of age, also has a dreaded condition, Parkinson's disease, which carries its own bleak forecast. He is currently capable of doing much more than Frank can, but he shares the same gloomy future of progressive debilitation and death. Angelo has two sons. His wife is long deceased. Often angry, he speaks with bitterness about being "dumped" in the nursing home by his sons; he always complains to them and demands that they see him more or insists that they bring him home. When I hear him speak with his sons, it is clear to me that they visit their father out of obligation and resent his demands. They take turns visiting on weekends.

There are two points I want to make about Frank and Angelo, one concerning family relationships, and the other regarding extrafamilial relationships. Frank's good relationship with his family ensures a healthy supply of love and support from them. Frank feels cared about and loved; despite the gruesome reality of his medical condition, he is generally able to maintain good spirits. Angelo's negative relationship with his family confers no benefit to his emotional adjustment. Even when his sons are present, or talking with him on the telephone, his negativity and resentment ruin the contact.

Regarding his relationships in the nursing home, Frank's attitude allows him to connect with caretakers, his roommate, and other residents at the nursing home, which contributes to even more emotional "feeding." Because Angelo is so bitter, and despite the fact that he desperately needs positive relationships since he extracts little support from his family, he chases away potential opportunities for positive relationships in the nursing home. Angelo requires that a trained professional work with him regularly in order to receive the benefit of interaction and personal contact because others find him intolerable to be with. Residents at the nursing home sometimes have no outside support system—perhaps they never had children, have outlived siblings, or are alienated from family because of past history—but such situations are not necessarily terminal for them. Residents can develop relationships with staff members and other residents in order to build a supply line of love, unless they drive others away the way Angelo does.

The crucial impact of relationships on the sense of well-being can be seen in the interaction of residents with their aides, who attend to their most personal and physically intimate needs. Residents become very disturbed when their regular aides are away because of illness, vacation, or turnover. Residents do not think of their aides as interchangeable or generic. Lack of consistency of care and contact with a resident's personal aide is a common source of unhappiness. Moreover, the attitude of the aide is as important as her physical handling of the resident, if not more so. Even competent physical care will not be well received if the caretaker is out of sync with the resident. If the aide is businesslike when the resident is chatty and upbeat, the resident will perceive the aide as cold, uncaring. If the aide is playful when the resident is upset, the resident will feel mocked. It is critically important for the aide to match attitudes with the resident. These two factors— regular availability and emotional attunement of the caretaker—contribute to much of the quality of the relationship. Physical needs will be met every day, and the aides are always working so that residents will be cleaned, dressed, and fed. Sound familiar? Like the findings from the British nurseries in World War II demonstrate, relationships matter. Building on this research from the 1940s, psychologists have been able to show that ideal circumstances for the development of mental health are established within the context of a loving relationship with a caretaker who provides a trusted, reliable presence and the opportunity for secure attachment.[2] In addition, the caretaker must show the capacity for attunement, to be able to match attitude and behavior to those of the child. The nursing home can be thought of as an adult orphanage, and the data from the orphan studies is directly applicable. People seek trusted figures for emotional protection when frightened, tired, or ill— the typical day in the life of a nursing-home resident.

CAN BUY ME LOVE

When love is understood to be a vital emotional nutrient, several implications follow. First, the need is universal. Everyone requires love, affection. Second, the need is lifelong. It must be supplied regularly or we suffer, usually in the form of anxiety, depression, demoralization, loss of motivation, and disinterest in life. You cannot ever eat so much food or breathe so much air that you will never need to eat or breathe again. Likewise, you never outgrow the need for TLC. In the nursing home there is no such thing as spoiling. If family and friends are ready, willing, and able to visit, they should. Frequent visitation only becomes a problem if it interferes with the resident's care or adjustment to the facility.

Third, love is love. What I mean by this is that there are many different potential sources of this emotional nutrient. Family and longtime friends can provide good sustaining supplies of attention and affection when they are present in a resident's life. However, if I am hungry, it really makes no difference if I eat an apple given to me by a close friend, picked from a tree, or bought from a stranger at a store—every apple has the same nutritional value. Yet, trust of the source of the apple is important. I would not take an apple from a sworn enemy; I might also hesitate to take it from an unknown grocer or a random tree because of the possibility of pesticides. I must trust the source before I accept the apple. Relationships provide the context for trust in what is received. New friends, aides, and other professionals at the nursing home can provide residents with loving care too, so that residents without outside supplies are not doomed. However, people like Angelo, who because of their personal difficulties are unable to develop new, positive relationships, experience additional vulnerability and deprivation instead of emotional sustenance. Compassion, care, and concern from professional staff provide strong emotional nutrition to residents when trusting relationships are established. These experiences of loving care, supplied by professional staff workers, can become as vital and beneficial as loving interactions from family and friends. The genuine expression of care and concern helps to nurture and sustain residents in the nursing home. That the person providing the care with love and attentiveness is a paid professional does not diminish its significance. The fact of the matter is that I *can buy me love*.

Loving care can be expressed in myriad ways. Of course, the nature of a relationship largely determines how these feelings should be expressed. The personal and intimate relationships a resident shares with family and friends allow for physical contact and overt expressions of affection. However, nursing-home staff members must always be mindful to interact in a manner consistent with the ethical codes of their respective professions so as to maintain proper boundaries and respect for residents. For example, I have seen aides, who render physical care, appropriately convey their compassion by singing while engaging in the gentle dressing of residents. I have also observed nurses who demonstrate caring by remembering that a resident prefers crushed pills served in applesauce and with a smile. As a psychotherapist I do not render any physical care, so that compassion is expressed in some nonverbal forms (e.g., conveying an attitude of concern; giving regular attention through appointments with residents), but primarily it is expressed with words. Verbally, concern may be demonstrated by an understanding and sensitive response to complaints, by the offering of supportive statements, through assisting with the resolution of practical challenges (e.g., improving relations with a vexing resident), and the remembering of prior discussions. The latter form is a surprisingly potent way to demonstrate to someone that she is important. It has been suggested that holding someone in mind by recalling her prior conversations can induce in her an emotional experience of being held.[3] To appreciate the validity of this concept one need only to witness the family members of residents with dementia: such unfortunate residents are unable to retain prior conversations and family members often feel forgotten and unimportant, in addition to the more obvious frustration, anger, and sadness they express.

Finally, some aspects of life must be experienced directly to be beneficial. We can read about food, be told about it, understand its importance and the pleasure it can provide, but food must be consumed in order to be of use to us. It is the same with emotional nutrition. Nurturance, caring, and love must be experienced in the relationships formed between nursing-home residents and caretakers for healthy living and fulfilment.

*Lesson: Love is an irreducible, lifelong requirement
for health and well-being.*

Applying the Lesson to Your Life

- Recognize your need for love and fellowship. A sufficient supply of love is necessary to maintain energy and motivation for life. Acknowledging this need does not make you dependent, needy, or anything else negative; it just makes you human. For no apparent reason, there seems to be a prevailing negative view of our requirement for affiliation. It should be obvious that the support of a good friend is invaluable when experiencing the travails of a challenging life event, such as a divorce or a job change. There might also be no greater source of enjoyment than to attend a sporting event, share a drink and a meal, or vacation with friends.
- If an insufficient supply of love exists in your life, consider developing new relationships or seeking professional assistance.
- Sometimes relationships with family and friends are available but not accepted. Are you allowing love in?
- As a source of love for others, are you maximizing your output to the people with whom you interact? Not only is it pleasing to spread some love, but it often results in bringing more love back your way (what goes around, comes around).

CHAPTER 3

HUMPTY DUMPTY
OR BIONIC MAN?

Whenever we are sick or injured, we suffer a psychological blow, too. We ponder the difficult question, Will I get better? In effect, we vacillate between, "Am I Humpty Dumpty?" (broken beyond repair) or "Am I a bionic man?" (made whole again, if not enhanced, through the wonders of modern science and medicine). In essence, the challenges associated with illness and injury create a crisis of faith: we can become demoralized. This is as true for a young, strong, healthy seventeen-year-old who sprains his knee in football practice as it is for a seventy-five-year-old with diabetes who falls and breaks a hip. Recovery requires fortitude. An individual's restoration to health turns to a significant degree on his morale, his fighting spirit.

DR. SHAMAN

Prior to the advent and widespread application of modern medicine, the healing arts were performed by religious and spiritual practitioners. During ancient times, physical disorders were viewed as the result of spiritual problems, and various supernatural remedies were devised to correct them. Although science-based medicine has supplanted spiritual healing as the preferred method of treatment for physical maladies, at least in the United States and most developed nations, it has not rendered matters of spirit completely irrelevant. The esprit of someone trying to regain health and functioning is an integral component of her recovery. My work in the nursing home is not only focused on the treatment of traditional psychiatric symptoms and disorders; a large portion of my time is spent with residents addressing their demoralization. In this setting it is crucial to build and maintain their spirits so that they can benefit from the physical and medical care they are receiving. *In the nursing home, I am closer to behaving like a shaman than a scientist-clinician.* I would not suggest for one moment that a resident's high spirits automatically equate to the achievement of total health and wellness. However, I do posit that low spirits will greatly interfere with, and limit, recovery.

Low morale was the chief concern for Tim, a seventy-six-year-old resident at the nursing home who has lived at the care center for about three months. He was transferred to the nursing home from a nearby hospital following hip-replacement surgery. Tim was never married and was living with his older brother, who was also never married, and their younger sister, who was widowed with no children. They were each other's loving support system. It was a mutual decision that following rehabilitation from the surgery, Tim would remain a long-term resident at the facility. He explained that they were all elderly and incapacitated to varying degrees, and functioning like "three blind mice."

Tim maintained good command of his faculties. He was always easy to involve in conversation; he was friendly and verbally facile. Tim was a World War II veteran who worked for the United States Postal Service for many years before retiring as a supervisor. When I met Tim, he was in the subacute unit of the nursing home, where he was receiving the rehabilitative services that typically follow hip-replacement surgery. He was referred to me because staff workers in the physical and occupational therapy departments had noted abnormally high levels of negativity and emotionality and substandard participation in his physical therapies. Tim was sporadically refusing to participate in these therapies, and when he did attend, his efforts appeared halfhearted to staff workers.

Tim freely discussed his complaints and concerns with me. He was unhappy and distressed. He spoke rapidly, with a pressured tone that revealed tension and inner turmoil. Discussion with Tim brought me to the conclusion that he was dispirited, demoralized. It was also clear that he was not depressed, an important distinction I will discuss below. Evidence of his demoralization came from his complaints. Tim expressed disappointment in his surgeon, who he felt had poorly prepared him for the aftermath of the procedure. He reported that the surgeon oversold the benefits and downplayed the pain and discomfort that he would experience after the procedure. Tim also reported anger with the food services department of the nursing home. He focused on the fact that he did not receive the breakfast order that he had requested that day: "How can I trust this place with the big things if they can't even get that right?" In essence, he had little confidence in his surgeon and in the nursing-home caretakers.

When I addressed the concerns about Tim's apparent variable motivation for rehabilitation services, he explained, "I'm too weak and I'm in pain—I don't know if I can do it." He lacked confidence in himself. Tim also stated that he did not see much of a point to even trying to get better. He and his siblings had already decided that he would remain in the nursing home for the long term. Since he was not going home, he questioned if it even mattered what kind of a condition he was in. His questions exhibited a loss of purpose.

Other comments indicated a loss of self-worth. For example, Tim admitted, "I'm just a sick, broken-down old man. Nobody wants me or cares about me. I don't even know if I care about myself." Comments connoting that he was junk and damaged goods revealed shame, worthlessness. Another facet of demoralization that Tim evidenced was related to feelings of helplessness and hopelessness. He reported, "Even when I go down there [to the rehabilitation department], I don't get anywhere. I'm not making progress, so why put myself through the pain and effort? I'm never going to get better."

Tim's lack of faith in his caretakers, flagging self-confidence, low self-esteem, loss of a sense of purpose, and feelings of helplessness and hopelessness highlight the classic features of demoralization. Demoralization is a growing topic of interest among mental-health and medical researchers because if it is unrecognized and unaddressed, it can seriously undermine a patient's motivation for treatment, which makes it a risk factor for physical and mental illness, especially depression.[1] Whereas demoralization and depression may appear similar, they are two distinct conditions requiring different treatment strategies. The defining features of depression include apathy, anhedonia (a loss of pleasure and interest in things previously enjoyed), and low motivation. The key distinguishing features of demoralization appear to be a sense of futility or helplessness and a loss of purpose or meaning. Treatment plans for depression usually involve psychotherapy and psychotropic medication; pharmaceutical products are less effective in the treatment of demoralization, which is more responsive to psychotherapeutic interventions that aim to restore hope, self-efficacy, meaning/purpose, and connection with others.[2]

In the nursing home, re-moralizing residents and reinforcing their motivation are of the highest priority. Residents must be assisted to find renewed faith in the rehabilitation and medical staff and in themselves. Otherwise, they tend to react with suboptimal effort and handicap their own recovery. Yet, in my experience, serving as a cheerleader is of limited benefit; instead, reviewing a resident's history of accomplishments is usually more beneficial. Residents often forget that they have overcome many challenges in their lives: discussing relevant personal history with them can help to reestablish their self-confidence. Being reminded that they possess the personal skills to battle through the current situation is uplifting. I also find it helpful to review the actual measures of current progress in their rehabilitation. Residents tend to compare how they are at the moment to how they were when completely healthy and fully functional. By this standard, they may feel that they are doing horribly. When reminded of the condition they were in when they first arrived at the nursing home, however, most residents are able to acknowledge their progress.

In Tim's case, across several sessions we addressed individually each complaint that he reported to me. The parceling out of his concerns was an intervention in and of itself: to reduce the deluge of emotion and consequent confusion, we considered his problems separately, one at a time. To ease Tim's low confidence in his surgeon, I inquired about how he came to use this particular doctor. It turned out that the surgeon had performed a procedure on Tim's brother several years prior and that Tim felt a sense of trust in him from that experience. When Tim and I discussed the matter, he offered the thought that maybe the doctor knew it would be best for him to have the surgery and did not want to scare him off with a more realistic depiction of the recovery process. It provided reassurance to Tim to remind him that trust of his doctor was the basis for his original selection of him to perform the surgery.

I challenged Tim's disappointment with his meal by giving him the name of the director of food services in the facility and the name of the social worker who was involved in his care. In doing so I was attempting to empower Tim to correct the errors with his meal. I offered to assist him by contacting the staff members for him, but he did not think it was necessary.

I confronted Tim's minimal self-confidence in his ability to persevere in his physical therapies by referencing prior acts of courage and triumph. Tim told me multiple times about his days as an army-tank driver in Europe during World War II. He shared stories demonstrating impressive toughness, such as when he endured bitter-cold nights in the field while subsisting on minimal food rations. Tim also discussed the losses of his parents as difficult times he had braved, as well as some hardships he had overcome in romantic relationships and at work. Recalling with Tim his past triumphs helped him summon up personal strengths he had taken for granted or forgotten about. This battle-tested war veteran had survived more grueling times than the present. We both knew that. Tim just needed some reminding.

That he was not going home after he completed his rehabilitation initially resulted in a loss of purpose for Tim. Essentially, he felt as though there was no point in doing anything if he was not going home. Despite what he was saying, though, Tim was not giving up on himself altogether. An intervention that I employ in situations where there is a possible loss of purpose is to directly inquire: "What has stopped you from giving up completely?" I may further state, "I have seen people give up here under less trying circumstances. What keeps you going?"

With Tim I added, "Guys who have given up do not attend therapy sessions and do not complain about the food!" This kind of questioning and discussion enabled Tim to realize that his behavior indicated a will to live, and he was eventually able to identify his reasons to go on: he wanted to experience reduced pain; to recover possibly to the point of walking independently; to be able to enjoy visits with his family; and to enjoy reading again. In my experience, the goals do not have to be grand in order to provide meaning and purpose. Reasons to tolerate pain and suffering need only be personal and relevant to the individual.

Pointing out how devoted his siblings were to him offset the shame and worthlessness Tim expressed. Although elderly themselves, they made it a point to visit Tim several times a week. There were always visible traces of their visits in the forms of food and reading material. Noticing remnants of his sibling's visits, I underscored their faithfulness to him.

Regarding the futility that Tim expressed, it was beneficial to him for us to review comments made to him by staff members and to read his progress notes. Tim reported to me that staff workers were informing him that he was advancing in terms of diminishing pain and improved balance, strength, and walking. Although he challenged the validity of their statements ("They probably tell everyone they are doing well"), I assured him that I knew that not to be the case. Furthermore, I informed him that the progress notes, as official medical records, were required to accurately reflect improvements or the lack thereof.

Having retained good mental functioning, and endowed with excellent verbal skills, Tim was able to work through the demoralization he initially experienced, preventing excess physical and emotional disability. Tim experienced less pain, greater mobility, and a better quality of life than before the surgery. With his new hip and improved adjustment to life in the nursing home Tim was more similar to a bionic man than to Humpty Dumpty.

Predicaments other than physical or medical problems can result in demoralization. In fact, any failure, loss, or frustration carries the potential to damage morale. Stressful situations require coping responses predicated on our marshaling the courage to confront the problem and our feelings rather than avoiding them. For example, early in my career I conducted research on children with the learning disability dyslexia, a reading disorder. Children with dyslexia function with normal intelligence and are otherwise indistinguishable from other children. However, they suffer unexpected difficulty with reading, despite their intelligence and adequate abilities in other academic subjects. In my work with these children I was struck by the consistency of their accounts: by second or third grade it became painfully apparent to these children that no matter how hard they tried, they could not read as casually or effortlessly as their peers. They had a pervasive sense of helplessness and futility. Even worse, their difficulty usually became obvious to their peers and became a source of mortification if they were asked to read before the class. The most common coping method was avoidance—these children often stopped trying, which exacerbated their weakness, generated more failure, raised tension with their parents, and increased their low self-esteem. They reported feeling that something was wrong with them, a sense that something was broken in their brains that could not be fixed.

The good news about learning disabilities is that the brain, mental skills, and behavior are very plastic, or malleable and responsive to intervention: effective treatment strategies can help individuals to deal with dyslexia and other problems in learning. In general, the earlier someone's learning disability is identified and treated, the better the outcome. One significant obstacle is in the engagement of the child. There are no shortcuts in fixing learning disabilities; treatment demands massive practice. The child must participate in order to benefit. Doing large amounts of work that reminds a child of his handicap and makes him feel stupid is not fun; individuals would rather run than stand and fight. Therefore, the success of treatment can hinge on re-moralizing the child in much the same way that I assisted Tim to restore hope and self-confidence; motivation must be sufficient to maintain efforts toward the helpful work.

Lesson: Pain, injury, illness, or setbacks of any kind involve distress and demoralization; recovery requires trust and courage.

Applying the Lesson to Your Life

- Remember that any setback will generate some self-doubt, confusion, and discouragement. Physical or mental illnesses are particularly challenging and are more likely to instigate problematic demoralization. Everyday happenings like giving an incorrect answer in the classroom, having a conflict with a friend, or being challenged by a coworker can generate self-doubt. The response to adversity is only problematic when it results in a persistent state of insecurity and discouragement.

- Be alert to the signs and symptoms of demoralization. If you or anyone you know is experiencing demoralization, seek assistance. The classic features of demoralization include enhanced feelings of helplessness and futility, and the experience of a sense of purposelessness. If a student who felt deflated by calling out an erroneous response in front of his class concluded that he was incapable of ever responding correctly, he would be in danger of becoming demoralized. However, if he was able to recover from the embarrassment and participate the next day, his reaction would be normal and of little concern.

- Think about spirit even when you are not beset by adversity. Engage in activities that inspire you and aim to maintain high motivation for life. In addition to enhancing your life presently, these skills can be a well-developed resource to draw upon when challenges arise.

CHAPTER 4

LOSS: SUBTRACTION AND ADDITION

Loss is part of life and is not all bad. For example, we need to lose baby teeth in order to get our permanent set. The boxes of Legos have to be put away to make room for the TV in the bedroom. We simply must lose things to grow and move forward—we can't take it all with us, forever. Compulsive hoarders try to hold onto everything, with disastrous results. The clutter and chaos visibly evident in the home of a hoarder could quite accurately reflect the inner workings of our minds if we did not let go of things and progress in life. However, loss often takes on a sinister feeling as we age. It seems only bad, dark, and sad. And it is inevitable that the older one gets, the more loss one will experience. Fortunately, on closer inspection, there is the opportunity for addition by subtraction, gain in the loss.

Despite appearances, loss allows for personal growth. Not only is loss inevitable, but it is also beneficial. The old needs to yield to make way for the new. We can all appreciate the practical examples of the losses of baby teeth and toys, but there are more important losses to discuss. In her book *Necessary Losses*, Judith Viorst reveals our psychological requirement to experience loss in order to progress developmentally.[1] Loss in a psychological sense must be considered for real objects (e.g., death of a family member) or for symbolic possessions such as images and beliefs (e.g., loss of a childhood fantasy of immortality). As young children, we must lose our exclusive relationships with our parents to become autonomous and to make room for other relationships. We must also surrender the freedom to liberally indulge our impulses and desires, in order to become moral, productive members of society. We must give up fantasies about finding flawless people and engaging in perfect, all-loving relationships so that we can enjoy genuinely intimate, human relationships. The relinquishing of images of ourselves is required for our growth; a fifteen-year-old male who begins to shave abandons his view of himself as a boy so that he can begin to feel and act more like a young man.

Personal development, once thought to be the exclusive province of the young, can occur well into old age. Psychoanalyst Erik Erikson was the first to teach us that human developmental challenges span the entire lifecycle.[2] Many residents at the nursing home have confided to me that they must admit that freedom from responsibilities and from the day-to-day grind of work and other obligations can be liberating. A ninety-eight-year-old resident, Edward, put it succinctly: "I'm glad to be out of the rat race. That's a young man's game." Erikson explained that with the kind of freedom that adults in their sixties have, they tend to gain interest in generativity, by which he meant the regard of an elder guiding and assisting the next generation. For example, a senior professional near the end of his career demonstrates this by taking an active interest in passing on knowledge and promoting the careers of his subordinates. In the nursing home, Litsa, a seventy-nine-year-old grandmother who was born in Greece, exhibited generativity some years prior when she helped her son parent his newborn and shared cooking tips with her daughter-in-law. In one fell swoop, she assured that her son and his family would eat well and that family traditions would be passed on. Litsa's simple acts of teaching her family about child rearing and cooking erected a bridge across continents and centuries, creating a continuum from far back in time forward in perpetuity. This behavior, usually possible as a result of the accumulation of wisdom and the availability of time found later in life, provides a way for an elder individual to feel an extension of herself that will last beyond her life—a positive legacy.

Admittedly, it can be more of a test to find any benefits in the losses of the elderly. The losses accrued with advancing age relate to loved ones, their social status and social roles, and their physical status. As Edward told me, "Everybody wants to live to be one hundred. Why?

Just about everybody you ever knew is dead." He had a point; his wife and two of his five children had predeceased him. It can take a toll on a person's self-esteem to retire from work and lose her earning capacity, as well as her youth, beauty, and sex appeal. Losses of good health, sensory acuity, mental skills, strength, independence, and autonomy are other unwelcome changes that can accompany the aging process. These serious losses, though, can provoke contemplation and reflection on one's life. When satisfactorily resolved, an elder will adopt an accepting attitude toward herself and life in general. The triumphs and failures, the good times and travails, are all seen as different threads in the fabric of life and are recognized as necessary parts of a larger whole. Achievement of ego integrity, which Erikson called the final developmental stage, is a process of coming to serenity and peace with the life lived and the inevitability of life's end. This evaluative process is more likely when time and space are created by removal from the rigors of life that dominate our time and minds at younger ages.

SWEET SORROW?

It can be decidedly more daunting to find any possible good in the sadness that accompanies loss. That the emotional torment associated with loss serves any positive functions is part of the marvel of our being. Troubling emotions are helpful in four major ways. As discussed in greater detail in chapter 17 ("Feelings: Our True Colors"), our experience of feelings is an indication that something important is happening to us. When the particular feeling is sadness, we are informed that we have experienced a loss of some kind. Our awareness of our sorrow motivates us to seek assistance and comfort from others. The misery also helps us to detach from the loss; dwelling on the lost person, image, or belief causes suffering, so that we are inclined to forsake it and to move on. Our obvious distress is also a signal to others and motivates them to comfort us. Finally, the experience of negative feelings in response to loss serves as part of a larger emotional repertoire that, ironically, allows for the experience of positive feelings. We can judge life events only by comparison. Joy, happiness, and other positive feelings all have meaning only in contrast to sadness, disappointment, and other negative feelings. Without agony there is no ecstasy: sweet sorrow indeed!

GRIEF OR DEPRESSION?

Grief is a normal reaction to loss, and depression is a mental-health condition that often requires professional attention. There is some overlap between the two, which accounts for the challenge of discerning between the two states of being. Nevertheless, in order to minimize unnecessary complications it is critical to identify depression if and when it exists. With both grief and depression there can be sadness, crying, and disturbances of sleep and appetite.

However, there are identifiable distinctions that allow for the proper identification of either state of mind. After an initial period of time (a time frame difficult to specify in any individual case, but one to three months would be reasonable in my experience), symptoms of grief begin to lessen. Depression, on the other hand, tends to be more enduring. Whereas bereaved individuals are able to be consoled, individuals experiencing depression tend to be inconsolable. Grief-stricken individuals usually maintain some variability and complexity of thought—they have some positive thoughts and feelings throughout the day and may only be down in spirits when thinking directly about the loss. Individuals with depression usually experience a narrowing of thought focused on their misery. They often experience attacks on the self; they report feelings of guilt, worthlessness, and hopelessness. In the extreme, they may even experience thoughts of suicide. In grief, self-esteem is usually preserved—the anguish is not about themselves but about the loss. Grief typically resolves with the help of family and friends; depression often requires treatment in order to achieve improvements.

The differences between grief and depression can be illustrated in the discussion of two cases. Jill, an eighty-two-year-old widowed resident at the nursing home, came to my attention because of concerns about her mood. Jill reported to me that she had recently received news of her sister's passing and that she was, naturally, upset. Jill was a proud and independent woman. She spoke about her years working in New York City, recalling her daily commute from a suburb in New Jersey, and told me of her many professional accomplishments. She had relocated from her home in the state of Washington following her marriage, in pursuit of a business opportunity for her husband, and left behind her parents and older sister. When her husband died prematurely in his fifties, Jill continued to live in New Jersey and to work in New York. Interestingly, although Jill maintained fond feelings for her sister, she had not seen her in over a half-century. The telephone calls that provided the means of connection in earlier years were replaced by the annual exchange of a holiday card in later years. Losing her sister had little bearing on her everyday life. Jill's sister did not provide material or financial support in any way. Yet the news of her sister's passing carried significant meaning for Jill. Her loss appeared more related to her sense of being a sister, a member of a family, than about the actual loss of her sister. She reported feeling all alone; without any family she was like "a dog left on the side of the road." She clearly felt abandoned and experienced sadness, anxiety, and difficulty sleeping through the night. Although she was upset, she was eager to discuss her thoughts and feelings, maintained relationships with other residents, and continued to function more or less as she always had at the nursing home. Within about two months, I discontinued treatment with Jill because her spirits appeared to be back to normal. This was a typical case of grief.

In sharp contrast was the case of Linda, a sixteen-year-old high-school sophomore, whom I saw in my private practice. She was brought to treatment by her parents because of their concern about notice-able changes in her mood and behavior since learning of her failure to earn a highly coveted position on a prestigious softball team. Linda reported difficulty sleeping as well as a loss of appetite. She experienced sadness, crying spells, anger, and a loss of interest in school and friends. She neglected personal hygiene. She also reported feeling humiliated, unable to face her friends, and a desire to die. Linda felt that she had experienced a blow from which she would never recover and that her future was ruined (she previously had entertained hope of receiving an athletic scholarship to college). She appeared angry much of the time and refused all reasonable offers of assistance from her coach, parents, and friends. Unlike Jill, who experienced her situation as more external, Linda experienced her loss as an indication of her ultimate worthlessness as a person; this is a key difference between grief (Jill) and depression (Linda). For approximately six weeks, Linda showed no signs of improvement. She was clearly depressed, and her treatment was lengthier than Jill's and more challenging, requiring referral to a psychiatrist for antidepressant medication.

In this chapter I have attempted to convey the insight that although sadness is the unpleasant and inevitable reaction to loss, the aversive feeling serves positive functions. Because Jill was motivated by her sorrow to seek the comfort and support of staff workers and residents at the nursing home, she recovered relatively quickly. Despite the fact that Linda also experienced sadness, she turned against herself and away from assistance, as is more typical of depression. Linda's recovery required more sustained and intensive treatment. The grief associated with loss is normal and healthy; the unhappiness and self-directed attacks associated with depression are abnormal and are more pernicious.

Lesson: The anguish associated with loss is necessary to help with separation from the lost person, image, or belief; to promote affiliation for comfort; and for emotion regulation.

Applying the Lesson to Your Life

- Recognize that, despite feeling awful, loss is not only unavoidable but also positive and growth-promoting.
- Allow yourself to feel the sadness of loss. The feelings will propel you to seek solace, to gain distance from the loss, and to maintain your emotional health.

- If you know someone experiencing loss and anguish, do what comes naturally—comfort her.
- Be alert to the signs and symptoms of depression. Depression is primarily a mood disorder. It is much more serious than less intense and more temporary responses to adversity and disappointment. Depressive states are identified by characteristic changes in behavior, mood, feelings, and thoughts. Often there are disturbances of sleep and appetite; excessive intake of alcohol may be observed in adolescents and adults. There may be crying, social isolation, and inactivity. Feelings of sadness, guilt, apathy, and loss of pleasure may be reported. An impairment of concentration, indecisiveness, a preoccupation with problems, self-loathing, and thoughts of suicide may exist. If signs and symptoms of depression are present, and severe enough to compromise social, academic, or work performance, or if there is any risk of self-harm, professional help should be sought.

CHAPTER 5

PHANTOM PAIN

I n neurology there is a peculiar phenomenon referred to as "phantom pain." The term relates to the experience of pain in a part of the body that is no longer physically present. For example, a person may have lost an arm in an automobile accident, but for the rest of her life, she not only "feels" the arm still being there but also perceives intense pain in the missing limb. Although phantom pain is not completely understood, scientists think that because the brain is accustomed to receiving these neurological messages, remnants of these messages and sensations remain in the brain long after the removal of the limb.[1] In the nursing home, I regularly see a different type of phantom pain: painful emotion related to *people* who are no longer there. Just as with a phantom limb, there are so many recorded links in the brain to a formerly present person that these representations persist in the brain of the survivor. An absent limb can still cause pain not because it is there, but because it is still represented in the brain. The same is true of an absent person.

Nursing-home residents often have outlived partners, lifelong friends, and other family members. Long-term relationships result in the storage of many memories in the brain. When a seventy-five-year-old woman loses a partner of fifty years, she retains an inestimable number of memories of their lives together, so many that virtually every experience may elicit an attached memory. This is where "the other half" is. When the other half is lost, nothing seems right.

Things that are paired in our memory are also linked via neuronal activity in the brain. Generally speaking, the strength of association of events in memory and in the brain is a function of repetition—more repetitions result in increased strength. If a resident has been with another person for decades while engaged in life's activities, that person's presence becomes an integral part of the memory traces of the survivor's experiences. In losing a longtime partner, seniors don't just lose that person. As so many elderly residents attest, almost every aspect of life is lost—nothing is the same without the partner. This is why so many nursing-home residents feel and look so lost. It is not just that a spouse is gone but that everything he was associated with is altered, incomplete—gone.

Robert, whose wife had passed away from cancer just two months prior to his admission to the nursing home, loudly lamented, "Why did you leave me, Ruth, why?" His anguish was obvious to anyone within earshot. At eighty-four years of age, and after sixty-one years together, his whole world changed with her passing. Robert told me that they did not have any children and that he came to the care center at the urging of his nephew, with whom he was close. Robert's nephew had observed that at home he was no longer taking proper care of himself: he was eating poorly, neglecting his personal hygiene, and declining mentally. Robert informed me that, in addition to missing his wife, nothing seemed the same without her—the bed was uncomfortable, food didn't taste the same, and TV shows that he had enjoyed with his wife seemed different and unappealing. In fact, he refused to sleep in his bed because he sensed Ruth's absence too sharply there; he reported that the sight of their kitchen table spoiled his appetite; and he was not even turning on his TV. The cup of coffee that was part of their daily morning ritual became a bitter reminder of her absence.

Robert's description of his experience of everything changing offered a revealing insight into the dynamics of loss. Sadness associated with the loss of his wife robbed previously enjoyed activities of pleasure. In addition to the emotional response, the cognitive aspect of loss was exposed. Identification of this latter facet provides a clue as to how to assist someone to recover from painful loss. (In chapter 4, "Loss: Subtraction and Addition," I address the emotional component of loss and recovery; here I want to concentrate attention more on cognitive processes associated with loss and coping with loss.) If part of the disturbing response derives from the strong mental association between the lost person and the activities, then one key to recovery is to construct some new associations. Put another way, if a person copes with the loss of a loved one by withdrawing from life, no new brain circuits are being built and he will be left with the gnawing sense of incompleteness. On the other hand, if a bereaved person continues to participate in activities, new associations will be formed that can partially compensate for the loss.

BUILD THEM AND YOU WILL RECOVER

Therefore, in addition to assisting him with the emotions of bereavement, I explained to Robert that it would speed his recovery if he re-engaged in his usual activities. I helped him to understand that it is well-nigh impossible to tolerate a void; healing from his loss must involve new experiences, actively building fresh, complete brain circuits. On a practical level, it meant that Robert should eat, clean and groom himself, attend activities, and socialize—even when his motivation to do so was low. To wait for the reverse, to feel better first before changing behavior as was his initial desire, would prolong his suffering and preclude his recovery. We cannot simply effect changes in our brains through the force of willpower. However, we can willfully change behavior, which alters the brain. Behavior change, which requires "rewiring" of the brain, can change the quality of experience. So it can be stated about the mental aspects of loss, *build them (create new brain circuits through action), and you will recover*. The haunting sense of the phantom is more acutely felt in the void. A previously gaping hole can be filled with new experiences.

Robert remained apathetic, with little appetite for food or life in general, until a chance meeting with another resident. At a Memorial Day picnic at the nursing home, Robert met Thomas. As luck would have it, both were World War II veterans and proud participants in the D-Day invasion. They became fast friends, and since Robert was able to walk with a cane, he frequently visited with Thomas. They discovered other shared interests (both were sports fans) and began to eat meals together in the dining room. This one relationship helped Robert to move forward in his recovery from the loss of Ruth and to regain interest in life.

Although there is more loss inherent in the aging process, loss is a natural part of life. From my perspective as a clinician, the power of strong associations is perhaps best illustrated in cases of substance abuse. Individuals attempting to recover from addictive disorders are advised to avoid people, places, and things associated with their drug use. In addition, it is recommended that they establish new, healthy habits to fill in the vacuum left by their abstinence. For example, an individual who was an alcohol abuser might be advised to go for a walk or to meditate as an initial activity of the day, rather than to consume an "eye opener" of alcohol or to do nothing. With persistence and repetition, the healthy alternative may become the new habit.

In our brains it appears to matter little whether someone is lost to us as in the case of death or something is given up in the pursuit of recovery from substance abuse. To the brain, a link is a link. The strength of the association can be diminished by engaging in new behaviors, establishing new habits, rather than doing nothing except to idly long for the lost person or object. Activity is preferable to passivity in recovering from loss of all kinds. It deserves mention that sometimes there exists a fear of completely forgetting a lost person, which is upsetting to a bereaved individual and which stands as a barrier to recuperation. When such a worry is reported to me, I reassure the individual that the goal is to reduce her mental preoccupation with the lost person, her withdrawal from life, her neglect of the self, and her intense misery; the desired outcome is not to wipe out all memories of the lost loved one (which could never be achieved anyway).

*Lesson: Longtime companions maintain a presence
in our brains when they go,
which renders our whole world different and incomplete.*

Applying the Lesson to Your Life

- Remember that there are different components to loss. There is the unavoidable sadness for which comfort should be sought. In addition, there is the cognitive component for which alternative measures are required.
- To promote recovery from loss, we must construct new brain circuits through behavior change and repetition. A new normal can eventually be established. Retirement from work sometimes confronts an individual with an unexpected test. If someone is too passive, behaving as if on a permanent vacation, he is at risk for an unhappy afterlife from work. I usually recommend the establishment of a new routine to help him constructively occupy his time and form a new sense of purpose.
- Although loss is difficult for people of any age to accept, we must be especially sensitive to the world-altering impact of loss for the elderly. They must literally begin to rebuild their lives and be assisted in generating new, positive experiences.

CHAPTER 6

BEST DAMN HEALTH PLAN

Control of healthcare costs has become a national obsession. With an aging population and dire fiscal concerns, heated debates at the highest levels of industry and government are widely publicized. The net effect of public squabbling is an undermining of our confidence. Do you trust that our representatives in government and our insurance-company executives will formulate solutions to the challenges of national healthcare that will be in our best interests? I do not. Even if we assume that all the major participants involved in shaping healthcare coverage and reimbursement schemes are acting in good faith, a system designed to meet the aggregate needs of a large nation could not reasonably be expected to be perfect, or even satisfactory, for every individual.

Even for those of us with health insurance and with good medical care, there is still no guarantee of sound health. National statistics paint an unmistakable picture of this caveat: many of the most deadly and debilitating conditions are, to some degree, related to how we conduct our lives. Relying on any outside agents—the government, a health-insurance company, or healthcare professionals—looks like risky business to me. The best healthcare plan is to take care of yourself. The most important person on your healthcare team, and the one you have most control of, is you.

The former belief—that vigor was largely attributable to good genes and good luck—has been replaced. Current research supports the theory that personal choices and habits can modify health outcomes. We have learned that certain lifestyle factors significantly affect health and longevity: smoking, inactivity, excessive drinking of alcohol, and overeating, for example, will damage health and shorten life. In contrast, other behaviors will enhance robustness and increase longevity: regular exercise, a good social support network of family and friends, meditation, and spiritual practice, to name a few examples.

THE BAD AND THE UGLY

It should be good news to all of us that we are not just sitting ducks waiting for our genes to deal us our physical-medical destinies. Surprisingly, the behavior that many people exhibit suggests that they are either unaware of their personal agency over their health, or that they reject it.

A review of statistics published by the Centers for Disease Control and Prevention (CDC) tells a sobering story. In 2010, the top ten leading causes of death in the United States were (in order, with actual number of deaths in parentheses): heart disease (597,689); cancer (574,743); chronic lower respiratory disease (including chronic obstructive pulmonary disease, COPD) (138,080); stroke (129,476); accidents (120,859); Alzheimer's disease (83,494); diabetes (69,071); nephritis and other kidney diseases (50,476); influenza and pneumonia (50,097); and suicide (38,364).[1] Five of the leading ten causes of death have clear and definite lifestyle components: heart disease, COPD, stroke, diabetes, and suicide. Two other conditions in which personal choice is involved, obesity and nicotine addiction, are variables with some bearing on these deadly diseases. Obesity is a major contributing factor in heart disease, stroke, and type 2 diabetes. (About one in three adults is obese.) And smoking is a significant cause of heart disease, certain types of cancer, and COPD.

Another element contributes to the risks for obesity, type 2 diabetes, hypertension, and depression, but few people ever consider it seriously: chronic sleep insufficiency. The CDC advises that a comprehensive program of health promotion and chronic disease prevention should include sleep hygiene.[2] In the short term, insufficient sleep can increase symptoms of anxiety and depression by reducing frustration tolerance and coping ability. Cognitive decrements may be observed, which include reduced alertness, diminished memory, and compromised information processing. Academic performance by school-age children and adolescents can be negatively affected by poor sleep. Recommended hours of sleep vary by age—eleven to twelve hours for children; nine to ten hours for teens; and seven to eight hours for adults.[3] Despite how critical it is for mental and emotional functioning in the short term, and for health in the long term, most people whom I see consider sleep unimportant. Children would rather play than sleep; adolescents and young adults prefer to socialize at night; and adults favor watching TV and surfing the Internet. Promoting healthy sleep is a staple of my work with elders in the nursing home. If residents are sleep deprived, they often attempt to sleep during the day, making them poor participants in their therapies and placing them out of sync with the nursing-home schedule and other residents.

Mortality statistics show us that by not smoking, maintaining weight within healthy limits, exercising, getting proper sleep, and treating depression, our national health could be significantly improved. But how do these numbers relate to the nursing home? To put it bluntly, people live with many of these conditions before they die from them. The mortality figures inevitably lead us to the conclusion that in this country we suffer excessively and unnecessarily from preventable diseases. For example, Regina was a fairly typical, medically complex nursing-home case. She was admitted to the nursing home for reconditioning following a prolonged hospital stay. A review of her chart showed that she was obese by medical standards and was suffering from congestive heart failure, a disorder in which heart functioning is inadequate to meet the needs of the body, which results in shortness of breath, fatigue, weakness, and swelling. Adding to Regina's list of medical problems was type 2 diabetes. She informed me that she always had been too casual about her blood-sugar management and she registered chronically high blood-sugar levels. Regina also had mild neuropathy in her feet, a complication caused by poor management of her diabetes.

Regina was referred for psychological evaluation because of treatment noncompliance and concerns about her mood. She was taking medication as prescribed, but she had not been cooperating with recommendations about diet and exercise and participation in occupational and physical therapies. Regina told me, "They want me to starve to death here. I have my family bring me what I like to eat." Around her room, I often noticed the remains of their food deliveries—cookies, potato chips, crackers, and other snack foods. She also complained, "They tell me I should move around more. Well, I can't do that until I feel better. They expect miracles." Regina cried about her health, discomfort, and disability. She also expressed anger that "they" were not doing more to help her.

Part of the problem for Regina was that to a significant degree, the damage already had been done. Still, her health did not fail overnight. Her weight gain, poor diabetes self-care, and failure to exercise sufficiently had predictable, cumulative consequences for her health. She could have altered the courses of these conditions at any point along the way. It appeared as though Regina's sense of ownership of her well-being had always been relatively weak. She seemed to expect medical professionals to make her better, a posture she had maintained for years. Once someone is as sick as Regina was, it can support or undermine efforts to change. When a person is suffering, she can potentially be more motivated to take corrective action. On the other hand, the same vexing symptoms can sometimes reduce motivation. The challenge with Regina was to use her discomfort in the service of enhancing her will to help herself.

Just how typical a case was Regina? In order to answer this question, I conducted an informal survey. From cases that I have treated in the nursing home over the past two years, I pulled one hundred randomly selected files and recorded the medical conditions listed for each patient; I selectively recorded only those conditions recognized as deadliest according to CDC statistics. To provide some context, I do not treat every resident in the 180-bed nursing home. Referrals are made for my services for residents presenting with cognitive, emotional, or behavioral problems only. Therefore, as a subsample of the total nursing-home population at the facility, the results may not be representative. Nevertheless, the results are characteristic of my case-load. The medical illnesses are listed in order of highest to lowest with the actual number of cases in parentheses: heart disease (41); COPD (22); cancer (17); dementia (12); and stroke (11). Please note that the numbers total more than one hundred because some residents were listed with more than one medical condition. A majority of the cases that I see in the nursing home present medically with heart disease or COPD. The results of my tabulation of illnesses of nursing-home cases tells the same general story as the national statistics: much of the disability and illness that we encounter is lifestyle related. Unfortunately, instances of lifestyle-induced illness, like Regina's case illustrates, are not the exception but the rule. Too many people are acting in ways that prove harmful to their health.

THE GOOD NEWS

In Regina's case, the lifestyle adjustments she needed to make were obvious: she needed to change her diet and exercise habits and accept responsibility for her behavior and health. A question worth considering: Are there general practices that we can employ to guide behavior that will lead to optimal health, longevity, and quality of life? Two impressive studies, using different methods, provide valuable answers to this question. Dan Buettner investigated several carefully chosen groups of people who exhibited superior longevity in order to identify the habits leading to their success.[4] George Vaillant has been the lead researcher in an ongoing, long-term research project in which participants have been followed for decades.[5] This longitudinal research method allows for a study of the relationship of behavior and health over time. Despite employing diverse research strategies, there is remarkable agreement in the findings of Buettner and Vaillant.

Buettner reports that about one quarter of how long we live is genetically determined; the other three quarters are a function of our way of life. What are the behaviors we can choose that confer longevity and well-being? To answer this question, Buettner identified five geographically distinct groups of people who live the healthiest, longest lives. These five Blue Zones, as he called them, were in the Italian island of Sardinia; the Japanese island of Okinawa; Loma Linda, California; Nicoya (Costa Rica); and the Greek island of Ikaria. His research yielded nine recommendations concerning physical activity, relationships, spiritual practice, and consumption.[6]

Buettner found that occupants of the Blue Zones engaged in regular physical activity, such as walking, gardening, and bike riding. For many individuals living in these areas, the exercise occurred naturally as part of their daily lives. Therefore, it happened effortlessly and was relatively easy to sustain over many years. For those of us whose daily work or chores do not include physical activity, effort should be made to get about thirty minutes of exercise at least five days a week. Low-intensity activities are preferred to more strenuous ones.

Recommendations for consumption apply to the amount of food that we eat, the kinds of foods we choose, and alcohol use. Buettner's advice is that eating should be guided by portion control and not by a subjective feeling of satisfaction; the latter approach to eating usually results in excessive intake. Concerning what we eat, a diet high in fruits and vegetables and low in meats and processed foods is associated with longevity. A daily drink of alcohol, especially red wine, is advised.

A daily allowance for leisure time was common among the residents of the Blue Zones. Taking breaks, resting, and engaging in recreational activities as part of stress management were deemed important.

Spirituality appeared beneficial for at least two reasons. Individuals in the Blue Zones tended to have a clear sense of purpose, a reason to get up each day, and something to look forward to. This personal mission allows for rising above the daily grind. In addition, participation in a spiritual community, of any religion, confers health benefits. It appears to be healthful because of stress relief, the promotion of positive behaviors, and social support.

Blue Zone occupants tended to center their lives on their families. Having meals together, socializing, and spending time on family vacations are ways to maintain these healthy connections.

Finally, health through association is suggested. Buettner recommends that it is a good practice to socialize with others who are engaging in healthy behaviors. Spending time with friends who share similar values about exercise, smoking, and alcohol consumption, for example, will be reinforcing of positive habits.

Vaillant has reported on the results of the Study of Adult Development. His findings are based on data collected from three groups of elderly men and women who have been followed for sixty to eighty years. The long-term nature of the study allows for the identification of factors associated with successful aging in the research subjects. Like the findings yielded by investigation of residents of Buettner's Blue Zones, Valliant offers recommendations about exercise, body weight, smoking behavior, alcohol consumption, and relationships. In addition, Vaillant discusses healthy coping skills. Summarizing Vaillant's results, successful aging is associated with being a nonsmoker; not abusing alcohol; maintaining a healthy weight; getting regular exercise; having a stable marriage; achieving more education; and employing mature coping skills.[7]

Education appears to be relevant to health outcomes because it tends to be associated with smoking status, weight, and alcohol use: individuals with higher education were less likely to smoke, to be overweight, or to drink alcohol excessively. Vaillant also opined that the correlation of education and successful aging may be explained by observing that the achievement of higher education and good self-care rely on the same skills relating to personal responsibility and efficacy as well as the adoption of a long-term outlook.

Effective coping skills are those that enable an individual to address the challenges of life in a practical way, while also maintaining tolerable levels of anxiety and guilt and favorable interpersonal relationships. Anita, a seventy-seven-year-old resident at the nursing home, had inferior coping behaviors. She was a widow with no children who claimed that she was tricked into coming to the nursing home by two younger female cousins with whom she used to feel close. Anita spoke to me about her intention to hire an attorney to sue her cousins and to move out of the nursing home and back into her apartment. Her apartment had been let go and her physical condition was such that it was unrealistic for her to be considering life in the community with virtually no support. Anita's cousins had broken off contact with her because they felt they could not tolerate her hostility toward them. She spent most of the day in her room, and in common areas of the nursing home she could be heard cursing and chasing off other residents.

By comparison, Sharon, an eighty-one-year-old resident, demonstrated the use of more mature and effective coping strategies. Even though she was unhappy when she first arrived at the care center, she never turned against her family, the nursing staff, or other residents. In sessions with me she would cry about the losses she experienced and the things she missed. Still, she attended activities and socialized with other residents. Instead of fighting a battle she could not win, Sharon surrendered and focused on making the best of the situation. This was more effective coping behavior.

Note the overlap of the findings of Buettner and Vaillant. Addressing the questions of successful aging, longevity, and quality of life, they arrived at similar conclusions using dissimilar methods. The commonality of findings gives confidence in their validity. However, correlations do not prove causality. A different type of evidence is necessary to substantiate a causal relationship between these behaviors and health outcomes.

FROM BLUE ZONES TO BLUE GENES

Adding to the impressive evidence of the health benefits associated with certain habits are the research findings of cardiologist Dean Ornish. He has summarized thirty years of his research, the results of which demonstrate that changes in diet, exercise, stress management, and social support can prevent, slow down, and even reverse the progression of medical conditions such as the ones we have been discussing above, including coronary heart disease, diabetes, hypertension, and obesity.[8] Perhaps most exciting, the more faithfully people adhered to the medically recommended behavior changes, the better the outcome—independent of age, disease severity, or family history. These results reveal a clear cause-and-effect relationship between behavior and health. Benefits were observed not only on clinical levels in terms of weight loss and symptom reduction, but there were changes on a genetic level also. Healthy behaviors resulted in increased activity of disease-preventing genes and decreased activity of disease-promoting genes. Findings such as these are extremely important because they reinforce the value of behavior change for combating disease and improving health. Having a genetic predisposition to heart disease, for example, is not a death sentence. Ornish's findings indicate that health is a matter not only of genetic inheritance but also of behavior that can influence which genes are active. Health-damaging genes are inconsequential if they are inactive. The growing field of epigenetics, the study of influences of gene expression, is focused on the premise that we can alter health by changing gene expression, even though we cannot change our genes.

Although hard scientific evidence supporting the health benefits of maintaining a certain lifestyle is only recently coming to light, much of this wisdom has been known for some time. Why is it so difficult to follow? Let's go back to Regina. The pain, disability, and unhappiness she experienced reduced her frustration tolerance and coping skills and made behavior change more difficult to achieve. But there was a more chronic emotional obstacle. When she even discussed lifestyle adjustments, she experienced tremendous guilt and regret for not doing it sooner. The recognition that behavior mattered led to the unavoidable conclusion that she was partly responsible for her predicament—an awareness historically she had decided to ignore. Regina had chosen not to be an active agent on her own behalf. As attractive as it should be, taking responsibility for one's destiny is not so appealing to many people. There is a level of accountability that many people prefer not to accept. It is simply easier to act as we please and expect the healthcare system to operate as a magical equalizer. For example, I have spoken to some youthful smokers who express no interest in stopping. They make statements such as, "I have faith that by the time it would matter to me, medicine will have a cure for whatever problems smoking creates." That is putting a lot of faith in healthcare and is not a plan I would recommend following.

Regina eventually turned the corner and became a participating member in her own recovery with some help from her family. I spoke with her daughter on the telephone about the importance of the family's support for Regina's healthy behaviors. She confessed that family members found it difficult to hear Regina express any distress and thought it harmless to bring in the food. Regina's daughter recognized that in this way they were unwittingly supporting negative behavior and agreed to stop. In sessions with Regina, I spoke with her about her critical role in her recovery: it was not "they" but *she* who needed to improve her health. She agreed to a verbal contract to attend her in-house rehabilitation therapies on a daily basis. This agreement helped increase her responsibility and accountability. In our discussions, I underscored the fact that she was capable of making changes in diet and exercise, and that it was not too late for improvements. This latter point is critical with elders who are already ill in some way. Being armed with research data such as those reported by Ornish provides for powerful intervention. The human body has impressive recuperative powers. Usually what is necessary for recovery is to stop injuring the body and to support conditions of health. Ornish's research demonstrated that even with advanced cardiac problems, benefits can be realized through proper changes in diet, exercise, social support, and stress management—and all of these elements were being provided to Regina. Because she had become an active participant in her treatment, she ultimately improved enough to go safely home.

Facts can be persuasive. I see this when working with smokers. Individuals who have smoked for years can question whether there is any point in troubling themselves to stop. With such patients I review the findings of the surgeon general's office, which convincingly demonstrate that smokers of any age and duration can benefit from stopping.[9] Even if they are experiencing a smoking-related illness, cessation can arrest its progress and allow for health improvements. Morbidity and mortality rates improve with cessation, so that the behavior change is worthwhile.

PUTTING IT ALL TOGETHER

The data are in and consistently support the point that our behavior is the primary determinant of our health and longevity. Certain habits will damage our health: smoking; drinking alcohol excessively; and eating poorly to the point of obesity. Consistent engagement in other behaviors promotes health and well-being: family activities; physical exercise; participation in spiritual/religious practices; socializing, especially with others who model healthy habits; managing stress effectively; drinking red wine moderately; eating a diet high in fruits and vegetables and low in meat and processed foods; sleeping sufficiently; and achieving higher education.

Let the politicians and big business grapple over the economics of health. The simple truth is that the better care you take of yourself, the less you will need to depend on the healthcare system.

Lesson: You can be an active architect of your own good health plan.

Applying the Lesson to Your Life

- Take ownership of your health.
- Devise your own personal healthcare plan. Start with the recognition that your behavior not only matters but also is the chief determinant of your health, longevity, and quality of life as you age.

- Be thankful that the information is readily available to guide healthy behavior and that no special skills or resources are necessary to be successful.
- Honestly evaluate yourself in terms of exercise, diet, stress management, sleep hygiene, tobacco and alcohol use, family and social relationships, religious and spiritual practice, and education.
- Find literature on any areas where you feel you need guidance to improve your personal health plan. Seek professional assistance in any areas you feel necessary. For example, if you determine that you would benefit by improving your stress-management skills and by quitting smoking, obtain information on these two topics. If you are unable to achieve the desired results on your own, seek the services of a mental-health professional or smoking-cessation program, respectively.
- If you notice that you lack desire or feel unable to assume responsibility for your health-related behavior, reach out to your support network for inspiration, guidance, and encouragement.

CHAPTER 7

NOBLESSE OBLIGE

In a country founded on the principle of equality, we do not like to think of our society in terms of one person having power over another. Of course, the reality is that we encounter inequalities in power all day, every day. We must begrudgingly admit to the often unequal distribution of power and authority that contributes to orderly, controlled, and productive behavior. Parents set rules for children, the store owner assigns prices to her goods, subordinates answer to superiors at work, corporals take orders from lieutenants, and so forth. However, to the degree that someone has the upper hand, she is expected not to abuse such a position of authority. The concept of noblesse oblige applies: literally, nobility obliges. The person in the superior position is under moral obligation to be kind and fair (that is, not to abuse her power). We are rightfully outraged by evidence of abuse of power: if an adult harms a child, a police officer oversteps his bounds, a boss rules by intimidation, or a large child bullies a small child, we recognize the wrong being perpetrated. Whenever we are in interaction with others, if we are in a superior position owing to rank, position, or personal attributes or advantages, we must behave with impeccable awareness in order to prevent unnecessary harm to others and perceptions of misuse of power—and to be worthy of our relative favor.

The potency inherent in certain roles has been a topic of interest to social psychologists in the United States for decades. Everybody who has taken psychology in high school, or an introductory psychology class in college, is likely familiar with the famous studies conducted by Stanley Milgram and Philip Zimbardo. A series of experiments was conducted by Milgram in order to investigate obedience to authority figures. In the classic study, subjects were recruited for an apparent learning experiment; they were supposedly participating in a study of the effects of punishment on learning.[1] The subjects were asked to deliver ostensibly harmful electric shocks to other subjects at the behest of the authority-figure university professor. No shocks were actually delivered, but the subjects under observation were unaware of this at the time; they thought they were shocking other experimental subjects. The results were as surprising as they were dismaying: a majority of subjects in the experiment behaved in accordance with the wishes of the experimenter even when it appeared that they were harming another individual, and even though there was no obvious reward for complying with the experimenter or punishment for failure to comply. In other words, the only motivating factor appeared to be the power of authority to promote obedience.

In the study led by Zimbardo, experimental subjects were recruited to participate in a simulated prison study.[2] The investigation was designed so as to determine the effects of role assignment (as either prison guard or prisoner) on behavior. The results of this study, alarming in their own right, again affirmed that there is power and influence attendant to the role of authority or superior, independent of individual personalities. The "prison guards" in the investigation became uncharacteristically harsh and severe in their behavior. Furthermore, "prisoners" exhibited attitudes described as passive, subservient, and occasionally rebellious that were out of character for those individuals. In other words, the role of prisoner carried its own potential for influence on attitude and behavior, demonstrating that social roles of all kinds can affect our attitudes and behavior.

Even the same person, behaving consistently, may be perceived differently by others after a change in status. For example, a young businesswoman named Paula sought psychotherapy services with me for symptoms of anxiety and depression. About a year prior to her seeking treatment, she had assumed the top position in a small business that was family-owned and family-operated. She was twenty-seven years old and had been working with the company since graduating college. She previously enjoyed her work and maintained good relationships with her co-workers; she socialized with several of them after work hours. The company employed about twenty people. Paula was smart, engaging, and conscientious. As an executive of the company, she was kind and giving. For example, she was providing benefits to her employees that many businesses would no longer offer, most notably a generous health-care package requiring no employee contribution.

Despite longstanding relationships with the company employees, Paula noticed that things had changed since she became the boss. Instead of including her in their conversations, the others would become quiet when she came into the lunchroom. She no longer felt like one of the girls. She accurately sensed that a barrier and tension existed where none had previously. She felt hurt and perplexed by the change in reception she received from the employees. When workers complained to her about aspects of their jobs, her decisions, or her conduct, she was upset. She also became aware of a growing anger and resentment she felt toward them. She was not only disturbed by their treatment of her but also by her own feelings and behavior. Paula began to tighten rules and contemplate benefits changes for the upcoming fiscal year. She fielded complaints that the position had "gone to her head" and that she was power-hungry. She was now unhappy with work, herself, and her employees.

The changes in her attitude and behavior, and those of her employees, were graphic illustrations of the influence of roles. Neither her workers nor she could have changed in character so quickly, but the power dynamics shifted when the professional relationships changed, altering the behavior, attitudes, and perceptions of all concerned. Paula's psychotherapeutic treatment centered on her gaining insight into the influence of the role changes and depersonalizing the behavior of the employees. Regarding her behavior, she learned to be more mindful of her motives and goals and to behave consistently with her values, independent of the behavior of her employees. When Paula began to take more conscious control of her behavior and kept herself more in line with her true values, she suffered less. The complaints and distancing behavior of her employees were seen as emanating from them; she felt the comfort of knowing that she was comporting herself in a manner above reproach. Classic social psychology research, and the experience of Paula, amply demonstrated how social roles can influence us, especially ones related to authority and power.

Power dynamics also may be present in social interactions because of disparities in personal variables, such as health status and strength. Nurses and aides caring for the often helpless nursing-home resident provide a very clear demonstration of this principle because younger, stronger, more capable staff members are caring for weak, disabled, relatively helpless residents. In effect, residents can feel as though they are contending with two sources of power, one deriving from the worker's position as a staff member, and the other from personal factors relating to a worker's physical superiority. Regarding the former, residents often make comments suggesting that the workers have all the power such as, "You make the rules here and what you say goes. What I want does not matter." I have noted that the larger the disparity between the person in charge and the other, the greater the need to be kind and gentle. Insufficient awareness of this principle is the cause of many complaints in the nursing home. Residents need to see ample evidence of their caretakers' benevolence and compassion in order to feel safe and secure.

Indeed, the tendency of residents to feel mistreated, bullied, and fearful may be more a reflection of the experience of the dynamics of power within the nursing home than of actual abuse. A fundamental ground rule is that the greater the power disparity, and the more powerless the recipient of care, the greater the potential for fear, anxiety, and a sense of victimization. Not that the staff members are harming residents by any reasonable standard of care, but the perception that *they could if they wanted to* generates troublesome feelings of fear and perceptions of abuse. The presence of this power dynamic requires the operation of exquisite sensitivity on the part of the caretaker in the nursing home. Imagine the following scenario: You are on an airplane and your steward is unfriendly, curt, hot-tempered, and even hostile to you. The attendant is a slightly built man in his late forties. It would be annoying to endure his obnoxious treatment of you, and you might consider complaining directly to him, or to someone else on the plane. What if the attendant were a six-foot-six behemoth in his late twenties? Wouldn't the same behavior be much more threatening because of the size and perceived power of the man in the second instance? You would likely be very aware that you were in a confined setting with this man and potentially angering him would not seem like a very good idea simply because of his potential to harm you if he so desired. Nursing-home residents are likely to perceive themselves as dealing with powerful brutes like the fictional flight attendant in the second example. Sometimes a resident's sense of vulnerability is so acute and the potential to experience fear so high that any act by a staff worker that causes discomfort for her may be interpreted as an intention to harm. For instance, Roseanne, one such individual whose mistrust is extreme, necessitates careful handling and repeated reassurance from staff workers.

Being physically brittle, with unreliable sensory systems, elders experience a heightened perception of invasion and assault relative to younger individuals. Roseanne is a frail eighty-three-year-old widow with no children. She is a short, small-framed woman weighing only ninety-three pounds. Aware of concerns of staff workers about her weight, she assured me that she was always tiny and any worries about her eating behavior were unfounded. Her sister confirmed this fact to me on the telephone. Roseanne frequently complains of the perceived rough handling she receives from staff. Her social worker and the nursing staff are aware of her concerns; she informed them directly, as did I. If any questions of maltreatment are raised by a resident, they must be investigated, but having ruled out any possible mishandling, her complaints appear to represent a different problem, one that is not uncommon in the nursing home. The problem relates more to Roseanne's feelings and perceptions than to objective misconduct on the part of staff workers.

Roseanne is a picture of defenselessness—you can almost look right through her skin to her internal anatomy. Since skin is the largest organ of the human body and interfaces very intimately with the environment, it provides essential protection of the body and sensory information from the environment. As we age, our skin thickness naturally

decreases, so much so that with some residents like Roseanne, it is virtually transparent. Blood vessels are visible in her exposed arms and legs.
The erosion of this natural defensive barrier can result in an increased
sense of vulnerability. When we refer to someone as thin-skinned, we
are saying that we think that they are touchy, overly sensitive, hyper-
reactive. The thinning of the skin and the consequent sensitivity to
touch stands as a suitable model for all of the sensory systems of the
elderly. As sensory systems degrade, the ability to regulate, organize,
and process incoming stimulation deteriorates, resulting in a subjective
sense of being assailed by stimulation. Imagine that you walked into a
dark room at night and it was suddenly and unexpectedly lit brightly
with lights, or that music was suddenly blasted; it would be offensive,
discombobulating, and you would likely have to recoil and cover your
eyes or ears in order to reduce the stimulation that was bombarding
you. You would have to recompose yourself. That kind of sensory over-
load may occur for elders at levels of stimulation that appear mild and
innocuous to the rest of us.

QUANTITY IS QUALITY

Regulating the flow of stimulation into our minds and bodies is vital
to health and well-being. When I was in grade school, and we were
all much less concerned about the everyday encounter with germs, we
routinely drank from garden hoses found lying in people's yards. It was
more convenient and time-efficient than going home in the middle of
play. A favorite trick played on one another was to suddenly turn up the
water flow while some unsuspecting playmate had his mouth wrapped
around the end of the hose, causing him to choke from the deluge of
water. Every bodily system has a comfortable rate of absorption—if it is
exceeded, it overpowers the system and a previously pleasant experience
can turn sour very quickly. The experience of enjoyment or aversion is
not simply a matter of what is being taken in but is also a function of
how much and how quickly. Water for a hot, sweaty grade-school boy

is delightful at one rate of flow from the hose and noxious at a higher rate. Quantity affects the quality of experience.

For Roseanne, almost any touch results in loud protest. I have been in her room while she is being groomed, and even when it appears to me that an aide is gently brushing her hair I have heard her shout, "What are you trying to do—tear out all of my hair?" I have even noticed that when I talk to Roseanne, I must speak very slowly; if not, she will become irritated and tell me that I talk too fast. If I pass by her in the hallway walking at a rapid pace, she will sometimes yell out, "Slow down. What's the hurry?" The rate at which she can process stimulation of any kind is slow and she is easily overcome, requiring a low-stimulating approach to keep from rattling her nerves. So if I am not careful around her, she can easily experience the interaction as harmful because I can unwittingly perpetrate an assault on her senses. As a professional, the onus is on me to tone down the stimulation in recognition of Roseanne's brittle nervous system. I also contend, however, that the same rule of conduct applies not only to other staff workers at the nursing home but also to anybody who interacts with Roseanne. The more capable individual should carry the bulk of the responsibility to regulate the interaction in a manner that is safe and comfortable to Roseanne, solely because he can: noblesse oblige.

In this chapter I have discussed the concept that the consequences of power dynamics are present in all areas of our lives. Whether one has been assigned power or authority at work, or possesses personal qualities or extraordinary resources that confer power (e.g., wealth, size, youth, health, strength, intelligence, beauty), it is best to be sensitive to the less well endowed.

*Lesson: Exhibit unmistakable beneficence
when in a superior position.*

Applying the Lesson to Your Life

- Be aware when you are in a superior position over another by virtue of work roles, political status, personal gifts, or other sources of power. Lording your specific gifts or advantages over others (even unintentionally) is unseemly and unattractive, if not immoral or illegal depending on the circumstances. For instance, the young should act with great gentleness toward the elderly, just as the physically strong and healthy should act toward those who are in a more fragile state.

- Recognize that with position and power comes greater responsibility; we are held to a higher standard of behavior. Resist the temptation to take unfair advantage of your good fortune.

- Also recognize the position of the other person. The more unequal your status, the greater the call for your sensitivity to another's feelings in order to reduce the potential for perceived misbehavior or maltreatment. If you find yourself in a relationship where you have much more authority, strength, and virility than your friend, you should take care to try to perceive the world from the perspective of your friend who is in a position of less power. What might appear as normal, acceptable behavior to you—say, speaking of your recent job promotion in an easygoing conversation—might be considered unmistakably ostentatious to your less-successful friend.

- Endeavor to behave consistently with high moral principles. If there are complaints about your conduct, you can be certain that you have acted appropriately and that any accusations issuing from another person are more likely related to his feelings of powerlessness and vulnerability, and not to your misbehavior.

CHAPTER 8

THINK SMALL FOR SUCCESS

Technology allows us to interact virtually with the entire world from within our homes. This morning before I began to write, from my home computer I looked at a live video feed from a beach at the Jersey Shore, searched for a book I wanted to buy from an online retailer, perused the national and international news headlines, and responded to some personal e-mail messages. With the computer, cable and satellite TV, and connection to various social media, we have twenty-four-hour access to worldwide information. This access creates an awareness that the world is one large community. The interrelatedness of all of our fates is much more apparent, and a global sensitivity seems an inevitable by-product of this awareness. Despite the obvious advantages of easy access to information, commerce, and people from far and wide, there can be a down side: since too much of what we see and hear about is unpleasant, it can lead some people to the conclusion that grand-scale changes must be made before personal happiness and serenity can be enjoyed.

Whereas we are bombarded with news from around the globe, remember that we also interact with the world on a very small scale. The microenvironment, the places we go and the people with whom we have direct contact, is where we most rub up against the world. The quality of these experiences and interactions significantly affect our sense of well-being. This is most apparent for the nursing-home resident. They remind us that to be happy we must also think small, very small. The rooms in the nursing home where I provide services are twelve feet by twenty-four feet and are semiprivate. What goes on in these modest little areas is surprisingly complex and largely determines the person's quality of life. For example, personalizing the living space with furniture and decorations from home can dramatically warm and improve the feeling of a resident's room.

PEOPLE IN GLASS HOUSES

Every living organism requires a satisfactory relationship with its environment. Humans are no exception. We are unique, however, in the degree to which we can choose and modify our environment. In agriculture, the benefits of intelligent environmental modification may be observed in the use of a glass house. A glass house, typically a greenhouse, is a structure with a carefully crafted environment designed for maximum health and development of plants. Precise control of sunlight, temperature, humidity, irrigation, and soil quality can promote the growth of plants even in the most inhospitable of climates. Just inches away, on the other side of the glass, the environment can be barren, hostile. By regulating factors in our personal environment, we can create our own human glass house, a protective surrounding to maximize our well-being and shield us from the harsher elements of life. Instead of controlling soil and humidity, ideal health for humans requires attention to aspects of the physical surrounding (e.g., order, cleanliness, beauty); social environment (e.g., quality of relationships, personal physical presentation, personal attitude and behavior); and internal environment (related to consumption of food and drink, and mental stimulation). *People in glass houses can actively modify their environment to their benefit.*

Let's first consider the physical environment. Nursing-home residents must condense the history of their entire lives within their rooms, which as a result offers an unusually revealing snapshot. When they move into a nursing home, residents are essentially tasked with deciding which elements of their lives to bring along with them into the facility. I have been invited into more than one thousand of these ersatz homes. When I enter, I am not there to inspect but rather to form an opinion in an impressionistic manner, as would anyone else. From my experience, I find that each room expresses the bidirectional relationship between a person and his environment. (Just as each person influences his environment, the environment has some effect on him.) I generally develop an impression of each resident from the physical environment, which includes both the person's room and the body of the individual living in the room. The moment I walk in, I experience a certain "vibe"—how do I feel when I enter the room? How does the room smell? Is it clean, orderly? If the room is dirty, cluttered, or has a bad smell, it will of course affect both the resident and the people who visit and/or provide care.

Then there is the "homey" quality: does the resident's room feel like a personal space or an institutional setting? Are there signs of engagement with life in the room: reading material, pictures, TV, telephone, radio/cd player, plants, furniture from home? In my practice I see the therapeutic value of personalizing space. For example, for children who are anxious about attending school it is often helpful for them to take something associated with home to school, such as a stuffed animal. Others may choose to take a picture of Mom, Dad, or a favorite relative to put in their desk, locker, or pocket. For college-age students, I routinely advise personalizing their dorm rooms as much as possible to minimize homesickness.

The physical appearance of the resident is more than skin deep. Billy Crystal, the comedian, used to jokingly say, "It's better to look good than to feel good!" I would actually take this a step further: Looking good *helps* you to feel good. Especially for someone who needs assistance in grooming and dressing, being clean and neatly dressed boosts self-esteem. I remember working with one family that questioned why their father had to be put through the physical discomfort of being cleaned, shaved, and dressed every day. My response addressed the obvious need to maintain good physical hygiene as well as good mental hygiene. Whereas I acknowledged the family's motivation to shield their father from unnecessary pain or discomfort, I felt concern that they were undervaluing the benefits of attention to personal appearance. In addition to feeling more attractive to oneself when well groomed, there is the additional social benefit—one is more attractive to others. If people are unkempt and malodorous, they evoke negative feelings of disgust and revulsion in others. Think of a child with dirt on his face, uncombed hair, and mucus running down, who also evokes negative reactions and social avoidance.

The microenvironment of the resident also includes the social and emotional climates of the individual's room. If the nursing-home room is nicely decorated, meticulously cleaned, and lovely to look at, and if the resident is handsomely dressed and well groomed, wonderful. However, if the resident feels lonely and abandoned, or experiences a lack of respect and concern from the people they have the most contact with, the resident will be very unhappy. The nursing home could have the best reputation in the world, but if the personal caretakers, roommate, or people most frequently encountered are disagreeable, the experience will be a bad one.

In my private practice I am often asked to assist parents in evaluating preschools for their children. I recommend that the parents evaluate the microenvironment of the school setting. Observe the specific classroom and teachers the child will be with: is it a positive, constructive environment that makes them feel good about leaving their child? The reputation of the school is only a very rough guide to how classroom experiences will affect a specific child. The school experience for a young child will be determined most significantly by one or two people in her room who are her teachers, aides, or primary support. That is the basis on which to determine the best educational setting for a child.

Think about the importance of the microenvironment in adult life. A boss at a job can make a huge difference in terms of job satisfaction and performance. Even in a highly desirable company, if an immediate superior is difficult to deal with, most people become demoralized and disgruntled. I have seen many instances where people remain in the same job, but because of an administrative change requiring them to report to a new boss, the job is experienced completely differently. The impact of change in one key person can profoundly influence our outlook. Many times we are forced to be in the company of others we would prefer to avoid, through work, social, or family obligation. This is why, when we have the choice, we must make a deliberate effort to associate with positive people when we can.

For this reason, family relationships are vital. Family members are typically the people with whom we feel the most comfort and trust. If family relationships are good, they serve as a buffer from the stress and strain of dealing with life. However, even with attentive family members who visit frequently, nursing-home residents spend most of their time in the company of other residents and staff members. Residents face the challenge of developing relationships in the facility that can provide emotional sustenance.

Management of our internal environment relates to consumption and what we are taking in from the outside. I am referring here not only to food and drink but also to mental stimulation. As a result of spending as much time as I do talking to people who grew up eight to ten decades ago, I have gained a very keen appreciation for a profound change in one fundamental task of life: seeking stimulation then, minimizing it now. For most current nursing-home residents, there was little assurance of plentiful food and drink when they were young. Many residents recall how in the past people had to work hard just to obtain the basic necessities of life. In the past it was also challenging—and often a luxury—just to have time or access to entertainment in one's life. Nowadays, people can easily eat food and drink beverages to excess. Mental stimulation and entertainment are also readily available. Today people suffer more from overconsumption: obesity, at epidemic proportions, compulsive playing of video games, addiction to computer pornography, and dependence on TV programming brimming with violence. Now, we must be mindful to turn down, turn away, and monitor what we consume, physically and mentally. Can there be any other outcome to a diet with an abundance of low-quality goods than an accumulation of junk in the trunk, belly, heart, veins, and mind?

In contrast to the trends in rising consumption, the frequency with which adults engage in physical exercise in this country has declined.

When current nursing-home residents were young, they were generally much more physically active. Lifestyles have gotten progressively more sedentary. With advancing age and failing health, activity naturally tends to decrease even more. Research has demonstrated very convincingly that increased activity is associated with good mental health as well as physical health.

When I first met Carmen, a seventy-two-year-old widowed mother of three children, she had her room arranged in an unusual manner: virtually everything she had brought to the facility was piled up in and around her bed. Although she explained the arrangement in terms of being able to easily access what she needed, the impression conveyed was that she somehow needed a protective barrier between herself and others. My initial thought when I walked into her room was not, "What a wonderfully efficient arrangement of things—she can get to everything so easily." Instead I wondered, "How am I going to get through the Great Wall of China she has fortified herself with—and how is she going to get out?" In fact, she rarely left her room and was not particularly receptive to people coming in to visit her. She was referred to me for evaluation by staff members who were concerned that Carmen was a social isolate; she often complained of loneliness, boredom, and a blue mood. She spent much of her time alone, watching TV, or listening to the radio. She showed an interest, however solitary, in watching the news and listening to politically oriented talk-radio shows. She often lamented the sorry state of the country, which seemed only to increase her depressed moods. Carmen left her room reluctantly, usually only at the urging of staff members, and when she did leave, she sat in the hallway in her wheelchair right outside her room. She complained about all the people with whom she came in contact in the hallway; she felt bothered by their conversation or their mere presence ("They are not my kind of people. The ones I like are all the way upstairs."). She showed no interest in attending activities offered in the facility and was physically inactive. Her dietary habits were poor; she was overweight and preferred to snack on junk food. Her mobility was impaired by an intractable condition, spinal stenosis, which had left her legs weak, painful, and unable to support her walking. Clearly, Carmen's micro-environment was far from one conducive to happiness. She had erected physical and psychological barriers to people seeing her, and to entering and leaving the room; piles of belongings generated discomfort and tension in anyone who visited with her. In addition, she mistreated her body through poor eating habits and little exercise. She failed to nourish her mind and instead occupied herself with negative TV and radio shows. Given her social isolation, it was no wonder she was blue.

But over the course of several months, Carmen made changes that contributed to her feeling better and improving her quality of life. A decisive moment in her treatment occurred when I was able to help her realize that *she* could improve her adjustment to the facility. It was a vital step for her to recognize that she could engineer her own happiness. Prior to this realization, she had passively complained and simply waited to feel better. Her diminished independence was accompanied by an increased sense of powerlessness. But effective action was a potent antidote to these feelings. Carmen removed the physical obstacles blocking her from exiting her room and preventing others from visiting her. Also, she allowed for more pleasant decoration of her room. She was encouraged to develop relationships with other residents with whom she enjoyed being, instead of relying on random encounters in the hallway. Carmen agreed to spend five minutes daily either reflecting on a gratitude list that she generated with me or recalling and savoring one positive life event that she had experienced. She also expanded the range of shows she watched and listened to, rather than focusing exclusively on current-events programming and all the attendant negativity. By explicitly and intentionally controlling what she focused her attention on, Carmen ensured that she would experience more positive emotion and receive the additional benefit of an increase in her sense of self-efficacy.

As Carmen's capacity to experience pleasure increased, she opted to watch some game shows on TV and to listen to more music on the radio. She also was convinced to eat healthier snacks, consisting of more fruit and fewer sweets. Finally, Carmen was encouraged to attend exercise activities several days per week. Through her efforts, she became more actively involved with the people and programs in the nursing home and her mood lifted significantly.

It is unnecessary to make major changes in the world in order to feel happy, safe, and comfortable. Just change a little slice of it. The changes in Carmen's life were relatively modest and very local. The problems of world hunger were not solved, crime and pestilence were not eradicated, and the economy was not fixed. Yet the changes Carmen made yielded big results for her. The original model for this concept occurs in homes every day with young children. Infants and small children know only what they directly experience. If things are copacetic there, the whole world is good.

Despite our global awareness, we typically interact with the world on a very personal and local level. What goes on at this essential level largely determines our degree of satisfaction and happiness. There is wisdom in the advice to "tend your own garden." I do not advise people to stick their heads in the sand and ignore everyone and everything else around them. Rather, I address the reality that in this huge world there is little that we can control; however, we should control or influence what we can. Build your glass house to maximize happiness and serenity.

Lesson: We can modify our environment to our benefit.

Applying the Lesson to Your Life

- No matter how small or how grand, make the effort to decorate and arrange your home, work, or school environments for maximum appeal. By decorating your office, for instance, with photographs of loved ones and a house plant, you can make yourself feel more at ease in the sometimes-stressful work environment. Photographs of loved ones and cherished memories can also serve to remind you of why you go to work—to support your family and to have the resources to make great memories with your loved ones.

- Spend as much time as you can with people you enjoy and who elevate you. We are forced by circumstances to endure a range of difficult people and personalities—but whenever possible, choose to be with people who are good to you and for you.
- Watch what you consume. If you make poor nutritional choices with food and drink, you pollute your body. If you take in only negative information or repetitively engage in mindless activity like video games, you pollute your mind. Diversify mental activity: read, write, listen to music, talk, meditate, and watch different types of movies and television shows. Just as it is beneficial to vary your food intake, so too with your mental intake.
- Take time to focus explicitly on positive aspects of your life by developing and regularly reviewing a gratitude list or making time to recall and savor favorable life events that you have experienced.
- Exercise regularly in whatever ways are enjoyable and safe. One needn't be a medal-winning triathlete to reap the positive benefits of exercise. Simply taking a walk around the block on your lunch break, parking your car in a far corner of a brightly lit grocery-store parking lot, or regularly "mall walking" during the cold winter months can not only boost your physical health but also elevate your mood.
- Set modest, achievable goals for changes in yourself and in your environment in order to assure success, and to increase self-efficacy, self-esteem, and mood. You don't need to create world peace to make your own world more peaceful.

CHAPTER 9

I TOUCH THEM ALL AND NEVER LIFT A FINGER

Invisible energy is ubiquitous. At this very moment, the room lights and the computer I am using, my cell phone, and the TV remote, operating on electricity, radio waves, and infrared light, respectively, are available at my fingertips. Perhaps less obvious is the fact that an extraordinarily potent form of energy is available at the tip of my tongue—words.

Who says words are often just hot air? Never underestimate the power of our words. Words have the power to harm or heal. The notion of the psyche in psychology suggests that the mind is the center of intellectual and emotional functioning, and our soul or spiritual essence. It turns out that the language of the psyche is, well, language. A conversion takes place in the mind whereby abstract information is transformed into physical (electrical and chemical) form and transmitted throughout our own body. Through the use of words, we can touch each other's minds, bodies, and souls.

I do not need to be a physicist with expensive equipment to know that there are energies at work. Commonsense observations confirm that when I touch the light switch, or the remote and cell phone buttons, certain effects will follow. The same is true of words. In the nursing home I am able to use this invisible touch to comfort and support people through conversation. When I say to a resident, "I admire what a good mother you have been to your family," I see the positive effects of my words in terms of posture, tone of voice, attitude, and feelings. Words act as a means of influence of the mind and body through the conveyance of information. That one person can affect another by words is a fascinating manifestation of the mind-body connection.

WORDS AS MEDICINE

What place does psychotherapy have in a medical-rehabilitative facility? How can a healing profession be based solely on talking? Don't these patients need real, tangible physical interventions and pharmaceutical products? These questions go to the heart of psychotherapy. Before I address them more directly, let me describe how residents arrive at the care center where I work. They do not usually gain direct admission to the care facility from their homes. The nursing home is typically the second stop; they are sent here from a hospital for rehabilitation or for long-term placement. By the time a resident has arrived at the nursing facility, he has already endured illness, injury, or medical procedures that necessitated the hospital stay, and all the ancillary challenges that make it so difficult a time. For example, a resident will usually have to cope with the obvious pain and discomfort of medical maladies. In addition, he is dealing with the separation from home; missing his family and friends; living with strangers; experiencing a loss of control of his schedule; eating institutional food; and so forth. Essentially, new residents arrive in the nursing home feeling broken and bewildered. Body, mind, and soul are shaken to the core. The physicians, nurses, and rehabilitation specialists are dedicated to the repair of the body; mind and soul, constituents of the psyche, are my main concern and that of other mental-health professionals in the nursing home (i.e., the social workers and psychiatrist).

The short answer to the questions posed above about the value of psychotherapy in the nursing home is that mind, body, and soul are all interconnected in one human being. Even in a medical-rehabilitative facility it would be a serious mistake to address only the physical-medical requirements of an individual to the exclusion of his mental-health needs. Talking is a deceptively powerful and complex form of self-expression and social interaction. Some people come to the false conclusion that because talking is common, it is inert or inconsequential. Some may ask, "Everybody talks—how is that therapy?" I might respond that many pharmaceutical therapies are derived by isolating and concentrating active ingredients found in common foods. Likewise, certain factors have been identified that, when separated out, focused, and skillfully used by a therapist, may act as mechanisms of healing, elevating ordinary conversation to therapeutic interaction. Irvin Yalom, a psychiatrist, provided a comprehensive discussion of the beneficial elements of therapy that affords some insight into how talking can be salutary.[1] Yalom identifies the following therapeutic factors: the instillation of hope (which I address in my discussion of morale in the chapter titled, "Humpty Dumpty or Bionic Man?"); universality; education; and catharsis. To his list I would add the recovery of personal value (self-esteem) and promotion of self-efficacy.

The installation of hope and morale are of the highest priority in my work in the nursing home. Residents must feel some hope and possess some fighting spirit in order to benefit from the care being offered. Often, physical therapies increase pain and discomfort in the short term, so that there is a natural tendency for residents to want to avoid them. Residents will meet these challenges successfully only when they feel there is gain to be achieved from the pain.

Based on patient reports to me in the nursing home, an implicit assumption that we all seem to maintain is that everyone else is healthy and fully functional. This secret notion is revealed the moment an individual suffers ill health or disability: he experiences a sense of discontinuity from the rest of humanity. Patients tell me that they feel unique and as if nobody can understand or relate to how they feel. Addressing this, I establish the normalcy or universality of what they are going through. This can be accomplished by discussing a self-evident fact: the building is full of others with similar experiences—no resident is unique in his suffering. It is also beneficial for a resident to know that he is having the proper emotional reaction to the circumstances—virtually all the residents experience emotional distress.

Direct educational interventions that I find helpful derive straightforwardly from many years of experience in the nursing-home setting. I am referring to the setting of appropriate expectations for recovery. I inform patients in the first meeting that they will not resume former levels of comfort and functioning nearly as quickly or as easily as they think they ought to. Everyone I meet thinks that they should recover as they did when they were twenty-five years old. When they do not, they fear something is wrong with them or with their care. I find that anticipating this reaction with them helps prevent unnecessary doubts and consternation.

The other expectation I like to address right up front relates to their having to wait for services. Expecting concierge-level service similar to that which they might receive in a top hotel is only going to result in undue anger and frustration. I advise the resident that waiting for service is a common complaint and recommend that she engage in coping strategies, including practicing acceptance of this fact and finding ways to pass the time while waiting—before it becomes a problem.

Residents ordinarily feel a surplus of emotions and are in need of an outlet. Many times residents report to me that even if they have supportive family members, they are uncomfortable sharing their feelings with them for fear of upsetting them. In addition, staff workers are too busy addressing specific issues to have time for extensive discussions with residents. Emotions are generated by experiences that are of great significance to us, and since our health and well-being are of paramount importance, when they are threatened, strong emotions are evoked. Having time solely devoted to talking to a therapist provides an essential emotional outlet for residents and can lead to catharsis, the venting of strong emotion.

As a result of feeling shaken up and beaten down, a resident experiences low self-esteem. Part of the rebuilding of a resident's sense of personal worth comes from my spending time with her, giving her attention, listening to her, and making the effort to help her. Making regular visits to a resident, remembering the content of previous conversations, and offering assistance are generally experienced as caring concern and can help to restore her sense of worth.

Being rendered dependent and in need of assistance from others provides ample opportunity for the development of feelings of helplessness, which can greatly undermine a resident's motivation and participation in the various therapies. Residents who experience uncomfortably high levels of emotions, such as sadness or anxiety, frequently feel unable to manage them. Few experiences are more disturbing than to feel that we cannot control our own feelings. Indeed, people often report feeling as if they are losing their minds when overpowered by emotion. On the other hand, it is empowering to gain mastery over our feelings. Although it is true that we are witnesses of our feelings, we are not helpless victims of them. We do not tell ourselves what to feel; we observe how we feel. Once we are aware, however, we can make efforts to cope with and to regulate our feelings. Empowering residents with the knowledge that we have proven methods to modify sadness and anxiety, and helping them to manage these unpleasant feelings more effectively, helps establish a pervasive belief in one's effectiveness, one's self-efficacy.

So where do words figure into this? All the psychotherapeutic interventions that I have discussed above happen through the exchange of words between people. The use of words can affect healing; words also provide the foundation for intimacy. In a general way, we can surmise how another person is feeling by her attitude and behavior, but not with the specificity and certainty that accrues from the spoken word. When the nursing-home resident Vanessa sobbed while telling me about the pain she was experiencing in her right knee, her fear of permanent disability, and the incapacity to engage in previously cherished activities, I was certain that I knew the intensity of her suffering and the reasons for her agony. I also knew that there were high degrees of trust and intimacy when she shared her concerns with me. When someone shares such sensitive personal information, there can be no doubt about how she feels and what she needs. Thoughts are completely private subjective events until they are expressed. I always make it a point to acknowledge the trust that is shown in me and the honor I feel that a resident would share such deeply personal information with me. It is rarely easy to be so revealing of oneself, but it is especially difficult in a nursing-home setting where exposure is high and privacy minimal. A resident has greater control of divulging her thoughts and feelings than she does exhibiting her body. In the case of Vanessa, once she informed me of the sources of her emotional anguish, we directly addressed her feelings in therapy.

Not only does putting words to feelings allow for the speaker to be helped by another, but impressive research has demonstrated that there are psychological and health benefits to the verbal expression of thoughts and feelings—even without an audience present. James Pennebaker found in his research that the act of expressing thoughts and feelings about upsetting experiences, in either written or spoken form, has beneficial effects on the actor.[2] For example, in one of his studies with college students, he asked one group of subjects to write their thoughts and feelings about their most traumatic or most upsetting life experience for fifteen minutes on four consecutive days. After a four-month period, the subjects reported improved moods and physical health compared to three other groups of subjects who either wrote only about the cold facts of their trauma; simply vented their feelings about the trauma; or wrote about neutral topics. In other words, in order to receive benefit from the writing, combining the facts of the trauma with the accompanying thoughts and feelings was critical. A detached recitation of the facts or sounding off with emotion without reference to the experience provided no benefit. Putting emotional experiences into words transforms how we think and feel about ourselves and reduces stress in our bodies, which promotes health and wellness. The benefits appear to stem from relieving the mind of the work of inhibiting the expression of distressing thoughts and feelings, and from promoting understanding and insight. In order to express our thoughts, we "speak" to an implicit audience, requiring us to organize our thoughts. Developing a clear story about important life events imposes structure, order, and sense. In short, by rendering complex and upsetting life experiences into words, we gain perspective, separation, and objectivity. Once expressed, the experience is an object in the world, not just a thought in our minds. An expressed thought is external to us, less threatening, and easier to examine and to understand.

The case of Craig nicely demonstrates this healing power of words. Craig, a seventy-seven-year-old married father of two children, was sent to the care center for reconditioning after a recent hospital stay. Craig is a polio survivor who suffers some of the ill effects of post-polio syndrome, including pain and weakness. His wife, Hilde, is home and receiving chemotherapy treatment for cancer. The couple's two children are providing assistance to Hilde at her home. Needless to say, between his health challenges and Hilde's, Craig experiences tremendous stress. Craig is well educated, holds a master's degree in English, and is a retired educator; he taught in both a private high school and at a local college. He is smart, is articulate, and likes to talk. Interestingly, he tends to direct conversation to early childhood experiences rather than to current concerns. As a result of the polio infection, he had a disfigured, atrophied right leg that made him the object of teasing by peers in his youth. Craig expressed much sadness and shame and informed me that he never discussed these horrific experiences or his feelings about them with anyone, including his parents (now deceased) and his wife.

Because Craig kept these painful experiences to himself, he never allowed for healing to occur. Despite over a half-century having passed, when he discussed these memories he expressed undiminished emotion. The simple passage of time does not heal trauma. He described that he still felt like a "freak" and an embarrassment and spoke of hating his body and appearance—and the polio. It occurred to me while speaking with Craig that I was listening to a writer who had composed only a small portion of his life story. He talked as if his personal narrative had stopped in adolescence, yet he had successfully acquired a graduate education, had a laudable career in education, and continued to enjoy a good marriage and family life. This was not a story worthy of scorn and derision. No, Craig's story was one of overcoming, of triumph. Discussion with him about the need to revise and update his life story proved helpful to him.

On a spiritual level, I engaged Craig in discussion about the previously unexplored silver linings in his childhood experiences. That he should hate the polio, and the social rejection and torment he experienced, was natural. Who would he have been, however, without them? Would he have been the same nice man? Would he have met his wife and fathered his children? Who knows? All we can know is that he turned out really well. In therapy sessions I frequently discuss the life lessons we receive that we would never ask for but which help us to grow in certain ways that may not be so apparent at the time. Feeling the pain of social rejection, Craig focused on academic studies and religious practice with excellent results.

Craig was helped by talking. Through the first-time telling of his long-hidden negative life experiences, he purged painful feelings, gained a different perspective on these experiences, came to a new understanding of himself and his life story, and suffered less.

If a person can influence the mind and mood of another through words and meaning, can't this also explain how one's own mind can affect one's own body? The mind, intangible thing that it is, can influence the tangible body via meaning. Words received or conceived in the mind are bits of information that are assigned meaning; the information is then transmitted throughout the body via electrical and chemical systems of internal communication. For example, if you received a call from your doctor that laboratory tests indicated that you might have a serious illness, you would react strongly. Your health would not have changed one bit in the instant that you heard the news, but you would feel very differently because of the meaning of the call. The mind generates meaning ("My life is over; this is horrible") and the body responds accordingly. Take a positive example: you read the newspaper and realize that you won the lottery. You likely experience tremendous emotional and physical changes, although you have not yet received a dime. The mind interprets the information ("I'm rich; this is fantastic") and the body responds in a manner consistent with this positive internal message. Words become potent forms of energy in the body through the physical, chemical, and electrical changes that generate positive or negative feelings (depending on the nature of the information).

Using words can be beneficial or deleterious. We affect not only people's thoughts with words but also their hearts, souls, and every cell of their bodies. We likewise influence our own bodies by what we tell ourselves. A clinical observation I have made is that we react to the words we say to ourselves in our minds just as if someone else were saying them to us. Be careful what you say to yourself: You are listening!

WORDS GONE WILD

As noted above, verbalization of thoughts and feelings can be beneficial, especially with the assistance of a trained psychotherapist. There may be times, however, when thoughts can be problematic in and of themselves. Obsessional thinking, consisting of rigid, repetitive thoughts, frequently haunts people more than it helps them. Rigid thinking is unproductive and never leads to a satisfying solution or conclusion; in fact, it is experienced as intrusive, unwanted, and unpleasant. Craig engaged in some repetitive thinking. He reported that for most of his life, whenever he was upset, he would focus on thoughts such as, "I was doomed from the beginning. Even when people were nice to my face, I know they were wondering what was wrong with me." It usually does no good to try to stop thinking obsessional, repetitive thoughts—indeed, attempting to prevent or ignore them frequently exacerbates the problem. We may have little control over thoughts that spontaneously occur to us, but once they appear to us, we have much more control over them. In line with this reasoning, Craig was advised that whenever the thoughts presented to him, he should accept them and say to himself, "Here are those negative thoughts again. I realize that they are part of a negative obsession and I don't need to pay any more attention to them." Or, "That is one way I used to think about myself. Not anymore. I prefer to focus on my victories." In effect, I was not advising Craig to stop the negative thinking. He could not. I directed him to add to the thoughts and not let them be the final words. He was fighting fire with fire—using words to promote healing rather than to perpetuate suffering.

Lesson: Words are potent forms of energy that you can wield wisely to promote good for yourself and others.

Applying the Lesson to Your Life

- Recognize the power of the spoken word. Words can harm or heal. Take special care to use this power constructively on yourself and others.

- Important life events, positive or negative, evoke strong feelings. Verbalizing our thoughts and feelings on a regular basis is a good general practice on the order of engaging in regular exercise and observing good nutritional habits. Putting our thoughts into words may be beneficial, whether written or spoken to another person or into a recording device. Sharing our thoughts with a confidant provides additional benefits of promoting intimacy and availing ourselves of the helpful assistance of another.

- If necessary, see a trained psychotherapist. Although there are no hard-and-fast rules to tell you when you should seek the assistance of a psychotherapist, you might want to consider pursuing treatment if you find yourself frequently distraught and you are unable to resolve your distress on your own or with the help of family members or friends. The reasons people commonly pursue professional services include relationship problems, the experience of persistently high anxiety, unshakable sadness and depression, and alcohol or drug abuse. Eating disorders with disturbances of body image, hyperactivity, and certain unusual experiences (for example, hallucinations—seeing or hearing things that are not present) are some other reasons people see psychotherapists.

CHAPTER 10

THE ULTIMATE RENEWABLE RESOURCE: LOVE

Is the capacity for love, compassion, and caring for others finite? We all have memories of a crotchety schoolteacher who worked long after he lost his ability to care for his students. Do the burdens of human service necessarily result in exhaustion of caretakers so that they either have limited careers or become emotionally debilitated? Early in my career I wondered if there was a limited supply of these feelings that could be depleted. This is a major issue for anyone providing care to people personally or professionally. In meeting hundreds of nursing-home residents over the years and seeing the behavior of so many other professional caretakers, the answer to this question becomes clear: there is no limit to the depths of these reserves or the number of people one can love or care about. However, there are certain basic conditions that I believe must exist in order to maintain the supply of compassion.

SHE AIN'T HEAVY. SHE'S MY GRANDMOTHER.

The primary factor that promotes loving care in the nursing home is that the caretaker must get to know the resident personally. The typically overworked nursing-home caretaker, performing in any capacity, may tend to experience a new resident as just another mouth to feed, pill to dispense, or report to write—in other words, more work. However, her view changes when a more informal, friendly relationship is formed. Personal knowledge is likely to engender empathy and connection.

Everyone has a story to tell. The intimacy achieved in the sharing of a life story is more important than the facts and details themselves. Once a resident becomes known in this manner, she ceases to be just a "case"—she is humanized and the relationship more personal. In order to illustrate this process, I will briefly describe the initial stage of treatment of Betty Ann. I received the referral for an evaluation in the usual manner, a note consisting of minimal detail: "A ninety-one-year-old woman admitted to the long-term care unit who scored high on the depression assessment measure and who is isolating in her room." This bare-bones description provided all that was necessary to justify an assessment of Betty Ann, but it was not the least bit personal. As is customary, I reviewed her nursing-home chart before interviewing her and recorded the relevant demographic and medical history. Betty Ann was transferred to the nursing home from a nearby hospital. An emergency-room visit and hospital stay were necessitated by a fall that resulted in a broken bone in her back. She was a widow with six children and was living alone in her home. There was no mention of mental-health problems or treatment history in her chart.

Although her file contained important clinical information, I still felt no personal connection. Why would I? Even private details about a resident tend to be perceived as cold facts until they are attached to the person through direct interaction. When I met Betty Ann, she was genial, willing and able to talk. After just three sessions with her, I had a clear picture of who she was and where she came from. She was born in 1906 in her home on a farm in Iowa, one of seven children. With one younger sister and five older brothers (or as she referred to her brothers, "farmhands"), she was part of a prized family in that area of the country at that time. As all family members did, she had jobs growing up—feeding the chickens, collecting eggs, and keeping the dogs out of the henhouse. I learned that once dogs tasted fresh eggs, they became obsessed to the extent that they would sometimes have to be euthanized. Betty Ann was a high-school graduate and had considered attending nursing school but opted instead for marriage at eighteen. She and her husband bought and ran a general store for several years, until the business failed during the Great Depression. In search of economic opportunity, the couple moved east to New Jersey, where her husband found a factory job. They bought a house where they raised their children; she was still living in the family residence until she moved into the nursing home. Her husband had passed away some twenty years prior to my meeting her.

Betty Ann enjoyed telling stories that she knew were characteristic of a time long passed. For example, she described Christmas memories consisting of feasts attended by the whole family and highlighted by the ritual lighting of the Christmas tree. The Christmas-tree lighting lasted several minutes only and was celebrated once each year on Christmas Eve. Candles with open flames were affixed to the branches of the tree and extinguished quickly for fear of fire. A typical Christmas present during her childhood was a single piece of candy or fresh fruit. She gleefully told me about Sunday church services, attended in Sunday-best clothing, with transportation by horse and buggy. There were stories of ten-cent movie-theater admission fares, her first sighting of an airplane in the sky, and her initial automobile ride.

Naturally, Betty Ann was unhappy about leaving a house that had been her home for over fifty years. She tearfully discussed other losses of objects and memories attached to the home. After several weeks of meeting with her, she seemed to be adjusting satisfactorily to her new residence. Betty Ann was eating well, and her sleep was improving after a couple of weeks of long nights. The pain she was experiencing in her back and leg was waning, which allowed for increased mobility in her wheelchair. Her mood was elevated and she was coming out of her room frequently to participate in activities.

Is this a clinical case or your family history as told by your grandmother? You get my point. Listening to Betty Ann's life story could only result in my interest, respect, and compassion for her. Please note that there was nothing spectacular about her life story; the information has meaning only to those people in her life, which now includes me. A hundred stories told in this manner would result in a hundred connections. It is foolproof. When engaged with a resident in such a manner, the human element is magnified and the burden or work aspects recede.

My interaction with Betty Ann was driven as much by positive emotion as by requirements of the job. Emotional engagement can make a significant difference in the quality of care and the degree of duress a caretaker experiences.

It is not, by the way, necessary for residents to know about the personal lives of their caretakers in order for residents to develop personal feelings for them or to benefit from the relationships; they learn all they need to know in their interaction. Let me explain. Think about a three-year-old child. The primary basis of his loving relationships with his parents is how they behave when with him in a variety of contexts that are shared. Once a mother leaves the home and is no longer in direct contact with her child, he has no other information on which to base his feelings toward her. What I mean to say is that the feelings a young child has toward his mother (and other caretakers) turn solely on the quality of their interaction with one another. Likewise, if a nursing-home aide is gracious and sensitive in her care of a resident, it would matter little to the resident how her caretaker behaved when she was out of the resident's room, at home, or with friends.

The one-sided disclosure by a resident is not a problem; rather, it is desirable. Professional relationships in the nursing home exist for the benefit of residents. As a workplace, the nursing home is a setting that can encourage the blurring of professional boundaries. Caretakers often render services in residents' rooms and have frequent informal encounters in hallways and other common areas in the building. A worker can feel as though there is no barrier between herself and the residents. Much of a caretaker's work is visible and public. A worker's maintaining control of personal information is especially important for keeping proper distance and boundaries and maintaining a professional relationship.

CARETAKER, HEAL THYSELF

Another major factor that affects a caretaker's ability to give positive, loving care to residents is the general condition of his own life. Caretakers who suffer from physical or mental problems, or who have insufficient supplies of love and support, will find the demands of the work difficult to tolerate. Ministering to very sick, disabled, chronically and terminally ill elders is inherently challenging. The high incidence of family-caregiver burnout is well documented. Perhaps surprisingly, the experience of a professional rendering care to an elderly nursing-home resident may be similar to that of a family caregiver.[1] Despite the many rewards of the work, providing human services to people who are fragile, in distress, and often unhappy can exact a toll on the most seasoned professional. At times, it may seem to a worker as though there is a one-way flow of concern and compassion from himself to the residents, and a unidirectional return of negativity from them, which results in tension and distress for the worker.

Be that as it may, the responsibility to adequately meet these challenges rests squarely on nursing-home professionals. Residents and their families have every right to expect their caretakers to be "fit for duty." Caregiver burnout occurs when an individual feels depleted physically, emotionally, and mentally, to the point that she begins to suffer personally and her attitude about offering assistance becomes negative. Burnout is, essentially, a response to chronic stress. In the nursing home it is not only a workplace issue but also a personal health concern. Professional caretakers are held to a very high standard of behavior because they are working with an extremely vulnerable population. Anything that might negatively affect a worker's ability to compassionately perform services is a cause for concern. Additionally, when experiencing burnout, a worker's health and well-being are at stake. Workers need to regulate stress capably in order to maintain their demeanor and performance at work, and their wellness.

Psychologist Richard Lazarus has written extensively about stress and coping.[2] Lazarus conceives of stress as an individual's response to a situation he judges as both potentially harmful and beyond his ability to handle. Note that in this conception, stress is not something found "out there." There is no universal cause of stress because each individual reacts differently to life events. For example, in my private practice, I have seen widely divergent responses to divorce. For Robert, a thirty-eight-year-old sales account executive and father of two boys, the dissolution of his marriage was experienced as a crushing blow. Despite their joint efforts to save their marriage, Robert and his wife came to the conclusion that the relationship was unsalvageable. In individual therapy, Robert expressed sadness, embarrassment, and intense feelings of rejection and failure.

To forty-four-year-old Michael, on the other hand, divorce was akin to Independence Day—a reason to rejoice. Rather than focusing on regrets, much of his time in therapy was spent in positive anticipation of good things to come for him. Michael felt unappreciated in his marriage, and he welcomed his wife's pursuit of divorce. He figured that his life only could improve thereafter.

From the above information we must conclude that stress and distress are in the mind of the beholder. There is an interaction of the person and the situation that determines the quality of the experience; it is not determined solely by circumstances or the person. Even apparently positive occurrences can evoke a range of responses among people. For example, when twenty-six-year-old Lee was admitted to law school, a lifelong dream of his, he became crippled with anxiety and self-doubt. In contrast, Marina's promotion to a high-profile executive position in a financial institution represented a coveted opportunity for her to showcase her skills; she was excited and eagerly accepted her new challenge. One person's stress may be another person's pleasure.

I occasionally conduct staff education and training sessions at the nursing home. One of the topics I discuss is stress management. I like to emphasize two points—the toxic effects of stress on the body and mind and the coping strategies workers can employ to their benefit. The experience of chronic stress is a contributing factor to virtually every human malady. It may cause or worsen symptoms of medical conditions, including heart disease, irritable bowel syndrome (IBS), chronic obstructive pulmonary disease (COPD), and hypertension; the experience of pain can be exacerbated, and the activity of the immune system can be suppressed. Sustained mental pressure can also result in anxiety, depression, apathy, irritability, and excessive worry.

Behavioral problems may emerge (representing misguided attempts at coping), including excessive alcohol consumption, cigarette smoking, and overeating. In order to handle challenging situations, we engage in coping maneuvers, what Lazarus refers to as cognitive and behavioral efforts to manage either the stress-inducing situation (problem-focused coping), or the alarming internal reaction to the situation (emotion-focused coping). Activities aimed at changing disturbing circumstances in the nursing home might involve a worker's petitioning administration to reduce her workload; this would represent problem-focused coping. Most of the stress-mitigating methods that I discuss with workers, however, are of the emotion-focused kind. Behavioral coping strategies that workers can employ to reduce internal distress consist of ventilating feelings, seeking social support, engaging in physical exercise, and practicing relaxation exercises. The stress-fighting, and health-promoting, benefits of expressing thoughts and feelings, and of receiving social support, are amply discussed throughout this book. Physical exercise probably does not receive the proper acknowledgment it is due. Regular exercise has demonstrated efficacy in reducing depression and inducing well-being and self-esteem.[3] I routinely recommend physical exercise to my private patients as well. It is interesting to note that whereas people initially tend to underestimate the benefits of physical activity, improvements are frequently observed with relatively modest regimens of maybe three-to-five days per week, for twenty or more minutes each workout.

Nursing-home staff members are generally less familiar with cognitive coping strategies, which include reframing, compartmentalization, selective attention, positive comparison, and positive self-talk. All these mental interventions involve an individual taking active control of his thought processes. Recognizing that this is possible and desirable is the first step.

Reframing a stressful situation, a cognitive coping strategy, refers to finding a different context within which to understand an otherwise vexing situation. For example, having to deal with a verbally hostile resident can be seen as an opportunity to practice the spiritual principle of turning the other cheek or the chance to practice depersonalizing negative comments.

Compartmentalization describes a process whereby work and home life are kept mentally separate. Often, especially if an employee is upset, work problems are brought home, where they negatively affect personal feelings and relationships. Workers are advised to change clothes and imagine changing roles, so that work stays with the uniform and is distinct from home. Separation of home and work is necessary in the opposite direction as well: it is inappropriate and unprofessional to bring problems from home to the job. Once in the workplace, residents should not be able to discern whether the caretaker had a great night's sleep or whether he was up all night with a sick child.

Selective attention refers to the practice of ignoring negative situations. If there is conflict with a coworker or a troubling relationship with a resident, a worker would be wise stay away from them as much as possible. Sometimes, but not always, avoiding a situation is actually an effective coping strategy.

Positive comparison is a coping strategy that workers can employ to accentuate the advantages of the current job. For example, a worker can state to herself, "My short commute allows me to have more family time; I lost almost two hours a day traveling to my last job."

Positive self-talk relates to the internal conversation a worker allows in his mind. Although we cannot stop negative thoughts from entering our minds, we can control the amount of time we dwell on such thoughts. I usually recommend to workers to acknowledge a negative thought and to supplant it with a positive coping statement. For example, during a particularly difficult day, a worker might think, "I don't know how I am going to get through this day." Rather than dwell on this thought, it would be better to focus on a thought like, "I've had tough days before and managed to get through them," or "This, too, shall pass."

LIFE MANAGEMENT

But stress management is not just about handling challenges and our emotional reactions to them; it is also about life management. Staff workers are encouraged to consider the general qualities of their lives. The more satisfying a life someone is leading, the better he will feel and the deeper his reserves to cope with stress will be. Recommendations for maintaining overall satisfaction and wellness include making time for interests and hobbies; employing relaxation exercises and mediation; and partaking in religious and spiritual practices. I also advise caretakers to think about time-management skills (set priorities, schedule reasonably); organizing home space well; and managing personal chemical consumption (watching caffeine, alcohol, sugar, and nicotine intake).

The final factor relevant to the emotional supply of a caretaker relates to whether or not her caring efforts are well received. No matter how genuine the intentions and how ample the energy to provide the services, if her caring behaviors are rejected or complained about by a resident, it can potentially block the caretaker's compassionate feelings. Unfortunately, because a significant proportion of residents in the nursing home are incapable of providing this kind of feedback, the onus falls on the caretaker to use her coping resources for sustenance.

In this chapter I endeavor to help readers understand factors that support the development and maintenance of positive relationships. In order to act with love and compassion, whether in the nursing home, nursery, or any other work or personal environment, we need to get personal with the people we are interacting with. We need a supply of loving concern to replenish us, and we need to have our efforts be well received. The capacity for love, compassion, and caring feelings is unlimited in the same way as any other biologically determined system. We do not wonder if the capacities to blink or produce stomach acid are finite; we rightly assume that if we irritate the eye or stimulate the stomach with food, we will blink or produce acid. Likewise, if stimulated properly by social circumstances, we will respond positively, lovingly.

*Lesson: The capacity to give loving care is unlimited,
under the proper conditions.*

Applying the Lesson to Your Life

- Be aware that caretaking in any capacity—parent, teacher, nurse's aide, personal trainer, or psychologist, involves a suspension of personal needs.
- To enhance your compassionate feelings toward another person— be it a neighbor, a coworker, a fellow student, or a patient—learn her life story from her.
- Understand that a chronic emotional imbalance, where output of love and compassion exceeds intake, can result in the experience of stress and harm to you. Recognize that the ability to act as a loving, compassionate person is unlimited provided you maintain supplies of love and enjoyment in your life.
- Be a good caretaker of yourself. Learn and practice stress-mitigating coping strategies.
- Exercise an ounce of prevention. It is best that you think about stress and life management before the onset of fatigue and burnout.
- If you are feeling chronically distressed and burned out, seek assistance. You may recognize burnout as a sense of exhaustion accompanied by a negative attitude toward the person or persons you are caring for. Affected caregivers often complain of problems sleeping, feeling easily overwhelmed and upset, and experiencing tension and distress; they are irritable, neglect themselves, and avoid people and activities that they previously enjoyed. Things you can do when experiencing any of these troubles include talking to a confidant and seeking practical assistance for your burdens; if you are caring for a family member, make certain to share the responsibilities with other caretakers. You might also remember not to neglect yourself—see friends, go shopping or to the movies, exercise, and practice other stress-management and coping skills. Additional relief and guidance can be found in professional support groups and with mental-health professionals.

CHAPTER 11

THE MOST IMPORTANT DECISIONS YOU WILL EVER MAKE: FORGIVENESS, ACCEPTANCE, AND ATTITUDE

We have a lifelong tendency to view ourselves as reactors to the world rather than actors on the world. As a result, we tend to feel victimized when we are injured or upset. Whereas the experience of victimhood sounds unpleasant, it can become a surprisingly alluring trap. Despite the ostensible benefits of entitlement to sympathy and freedom from blame, however, viewing ourselves as victims involves a fatal surrender of power. When we place blame and responsibility for our well-being outside of ourselves, there is little we can do to alter disagreeable situations, maintain favorable ones, or regulate our internal emotional environments.

Life comes at us fast and hard. If we are not careful, it can seem as if our feelings and personal welfare are determined exclusively by external events. In this mind-set, if fortune favors us and good things are happening, we are happy. But what if bad things are occurring? Are we doomed? I hope not, because bad things are always happening. If we can feel good only when everything in our lives is perfect and acceptable in the rest of the world, we will be unable to be happy for a single day.

Imagine the challenge of the typical nursing-home resident. People come to live in a nursing home by necessity only. Usually this means that they are unable to live safely in the community because of diminished mental or physical capacity and that they either lack a sufficient support system or require excessive services they are unable to access at home. If spirit and mood are determined only by life's circumstances, then every single nursing-home resident should tend toward a state of utter despair.

How do we account for the fortunate circumstance that not all residents are hopelessly, miserably depressed? By the obvious answer that it is their minds help determine their responses to the world; they are not reflexive beings who lack the ability to control perceptions or reactions. I have found that there are several critical attributes that affect a person's ability to adjust to the challenges in the nursing home: forgiveness, acceptance, and attitude. When residents are furious with whomever they feel is responsible for putting them in the nursing home, they demonstrate a failure to forgive. If residents persist in fighting tooth and nail and reject the reality of their disability and needs for assistance, they show a lack of acceptance. Acting antagonistically toward staff workers as if confronting their enemies, they adopt negative attitudes. The failure to forgive, to arrive at a position of acceptance, and to choose a positive attitude all result in a state of bitterness, unhappiness, powerlessness, and low motivation, which squanders opportunities for pleasure and growth. By choosing to forgive, to accept, and to assume a positive attitude, residents can become empowered, able to focus on the here and now, and able to derive benefit from people and resources available to them. It is not external circumstances alone that determine the quality of life experience in the nursing home—clearly, state of mind does matter.

FORGIVENESS

Forgiveness is the positive act of taking responsibility for your feelings and reclaiming control of your well-being by releasing another person from blame for perceived or actual harm to you. Retaining grievances, planning retribution, and demanding apologies or restitution generate stress and unhappiness. With regards to feelings, once you have been injured or offended, *the emotions you experience are yours*. They are expressed in *your* body and register in *your* mind. Only *you*, and *you* alone, can do anything constructive with your feelings. If *you* feel sad, angry, embarrassed, or frightened, *you* must take steps to modify these negative feelings.

Releasing an offending person from blame is a way of establishing personal agency for your recovery from a hurtful experience. When your contentment depends on the behavior of another, you are at her mercy. What if she never behaves as you desire? You can never be whole again? That is granting too much power to another person. I often remind patients that since most people can hardly control themselves, forget trying to force someone else to behave according to your wishes.

The detrimental effects of failing to forgive were evident with the nursing-home resident Brooke. During one conversation with me, she was brimming with rage: "That doctor, my brother, and my son, teamed up against me. The three of them are no good. I'm going to sue that quack and I'm never going to talk to my family again. I'll get them all back for putting me in here." Even when obviously necessary, a nursing-home admission is never an occasion for celebration. It takes time to adjust to life away from home and inside an unfamiliar institution. The fact remains, nonetheless, that some individuals make the transition more quickly and easily than others. In my experience, most residents satisfactorily adapt in the first one to two months. But Brooke's statements that she was making to me about her family and doctor, and the vehemence with which she spoke, occurred approximately six weeks into her stay and did not appear to be waning in intensity. Undoubtedly, her preoccupation with her perceived wrongdoers, desire for revenge, and bitter anger locked her into a state of misery.

The research of psychologist Fred Luskin demonstrates the value of the practice of forgiveness.[1] Individuals who forgive receive physical, emotional, psychological, and social benefits. They experience fewer health problems and less stress; improved moods; increased self-confidence and optimism; and better relationships.

If the act of forgiving is advantageous, why does it seem so hard to do? Many times, there is fear of some kind that acts as an obstacle, such as thinking that forgiving makes you weak, minimizes the harm done to you, is a tacit endorsement of the behavior of the offending person, or releases the offender from all responsibility or consequences of his behavior. The latter fear, of an offender getting off without paying for his misdeeds, is alarmingly compelling. As irresistible as it may seem to seek justice, you are directing your attention to the wrong person.

Luskin describes the keys to forgiveness as depersonalizing the offense, taking responsibility for your feelings, and becoming an author telling your own story of successful recovery. In practice, the trick is in motivating the offended individual to act on her own behalf. I have found that it can be helpful to emphasize that the act of forgiving is for you and your recovery, it has nothing to do with the other party.

ACCEPTANCE

Acceptance refers to a peaceful admission of an unpleasant fact of life: a quiet surrender to an unalterable negative situation. Fighting requires energy and attention of which we do not possess inexhaustible supplies. To waste precious mental resources on unwinnable skirmishes is unwise and unnecessarily stressful. In addition, concentration on negative situations precludes enjoyment of other things. You may wonder why anyone would engage in futile endeavors, especially when the process is taxing and absorbs time and energy that could be used for more fruitful pursuits. The reason is obvious: the individual has conceived of surrender to a painful truth as a capitulation rather than as something positive. Brooke was simultaneously operating on several battlefronts. In addition to the conflict with her family members and doctor, she was fighting recognition of the need to be in the nursing home. To her, it represented an unacceptable submission to a falsehood—she saw no need to be there and was not about to knuckle under. The problem was that the conditions in which she was living were proof of her diminished capacity. By her son's account, she was living in deplorable circumstances prior to her nursing-home admission.

Widowed and alone, Brooke had fallen and broken her hip. Her son reported that she had a history of untreated depression and was incorrigible; she angrily refused his overtures to assist her. Her home was cluttered and dirty, and her son worried about Brooke being malnourished and unsafe there. When I questioned Brooke about his concerns, she replied, "I was fine at home. I have been independent my whole life. People should just butt out of my life." Her objection to being in the nursing home had nothing to do with the facility and everything to do with her unwillingness to accept her incapacity. This was a conflict neither with her family nor with the nursing home. It was an internal clash with an unpleasant truth.

A denial of reality is apparent in Brooke's comments. Denial gets a bad name because of the role this defense mechanism plays in addiction to alcohol and drugs. Like all psychological defenses, however, denial serves positive functions. It can protect an individual from overwhelming, intolerable emotions. On a short-term basis this can be beneficial, allowing time for a person to come to terms with a truth that is initially difficult to assimilate. When denial is employed as a long-term coping strategy, though, it can be deleterious. If after discovering a lump under her breast, a woman were to wait a week to gather herself before calling her doctor, that would not be a problem. On the other hand, if she chose to ignore the lump indefinitely in order to keep her anxiety at bay, it would be unacceptably risky. A frontal assault on denial with naked facts is not recommended unless a person is placing herself in danger by a failure to act. For example, if Brooke had refused to go to the hospital after falling, then safety considerations would have called for a confrontation. Since she was already in a safe environment in the nursing home, there was no need to challenge her distorted assessment of her capabilities. Denial was protecting her from the disturbing admission of personal decline, and I thought it best to defer challenging her for fear of precipitating a larger emotional crisis. Besides, her son had attempted to convince her of her inability to live independently and it had led to an escalation of mutual hostilities and alienation.

ATTITUDE

Attitude may be described as one's determination of something or someone as either positive or negative, good or bad. This simple judgment has a profound influence on a person's mood, motivation, and behavior. Much of the time it appears to us as though our attitude is dictated by circumstances. We might think, "I have a positive attitude today because I received the praise I desired from my boss" or "I have a bad attitude because the credit-card bill arrived today and I don't have the money to pay it." What those thoughts fail to take into account is that choice is involved.

One of the most powerful and convincing discussions of the role of choice in determining attitude was presented by psychiatrist Viktor Frankl. Observing fellow prisoners in a Nazi concentration camp in World War II, he noted that even under the most atrocious conditions in human history, responses of inmates were not uniform; individual differences were revealed, indicating that the attitude a person adopts cannot be completely determined by external circumstances. Frankl concluded that even as a captive, an individual retains his freedom to choose his attitude.[2] He recognized that some prisoners succumbed to the brutality of the environment and behaved selfishly and cruelly. Others, however, held on to their humanity, addressing fellow prisoners with kindness and thoughtfulness. If concentration-camp prisoners can choose a positive attitude, what excuse can any of us claim for not doing the same?

Brooke's attitude toward the nursing home, its staff members, and other residents constituted her third battlefront. She initially decided that she was imprisoned against her will, rendering everyone and everything in the facility bad. She complained ceaselessly about her meals, bed, roommate, TV service, doctor, and staff workers. To summarize her perspective, everybody she encountered was stupid, lazy, or annoying. By her own description, Alcatraz would have been an upgrade. This is how important attitude is: it colors perception and inclines us to certain feelings and behaviors. Because Brooke decided that the facility was negative, even kind acts were interpreted through this dark prism. One morning, for example, while we were talking in her room, an aide came in to offer her a snack. After the aide left, Brooke complained, "They never leave you alone here. See how they always bug you?"

Brooke's case exemplifies several important points about psychological injury and recovery. Whenever an individual feels hurt or offended, he usually feels and expresses intense emotions. In this state of mind, he is irrational; his mind is dominated by feelings, not by reason. Any attempt to persuade him in this condition of acute arousal will be ineffective at best and may create an elevation of emotion at worst. He needs emotional discharge; he must be calmed before he can be engaged in reasoned, logical discussion. Brooke's agitation and uncontrolled emotions initially required soothing interventions—assistance ventilating her feelings and support with sympathetic comments.

In addition to restoring emotional balance and reason, it is necessary to address the misguided focus on the perceived offender. Although it is natural to direct attention to a person or a fact of reality that is causing you harm or distress, at some point it is counterproductive. Preoccupation with the offender and his behavior, or a hard-to-accept truth, ensures powerlessness and forestalls forward movement. This external focus also encourages assumption of a bad attitude; typical thoughts include, "How could I feel anything but bad about what's been done to me? Can anyone blame me for having a bad attitude?" Brooke was preoccupied with punishing her doctor and family; she fought the idea that she was declining and in need of assistance; and she treated the nursing home as if it were a prison. Once she settled down emotionally, she was able to think about alternative explanations for what was happening in her life. She could appreciate that her doctor and loved ones were motivated by a desire to help her. After initially banishing them, she allowed her brother and son to visit, much to her benefit. She acknowledged that she was no longer able to care for herself and that she needed help. She consented to taking psychotropic medication to help improve her mood. And she became open to possibilities for fun and enjoyment in the nursing home. Focusing on herself, what she wanted, and opportunities for satisfaction in the nursing home resulted in a superior adjustment for Brooke.

There are many aspects of life out of your control, but inevitably there are also critical choices you can make to improve your situation—whether within a nursing home, or in other challenging situations. Regardless of circumstance, choosing forgiveness, acceptance, and a positive attitude leads to self-empowerment and happiness.

Lesson: Good news: you can choose happiness.

Applying the Lesson to Your Life

- Be cognizant of the fact that life is hard and that you will inevitably encounter hurt and pain.
- Expect to experience emotional upset and distress from your challenges.
- Remember that, no matter what happens, you can retain personal power and control of your well-being by focusing on yourself rather than on those you consider to be personal offenders. For example, imagine that you are parallel parked on the side of the road. You are in a parking spot legally, and you've wisely left enough room between your car and others and between your car and the curb to allow for careful maneuvering. As you sit in your car and gather your belongings before exiting, you are suddenly, violently, jerked to the side—another driver has impacted your car and has sped off without stopping to see if you and your vehicle are alright! There is no way for you to determine who caused the car accident since it was a hit-and-run. Should you stand there, cursing the unknown driver? Or, better, should you make sure that you are uninjured, inspect your vehicle for damage, start making the necessary phone calls, and try to calm yourself down? Clearly only the latter decisions will ultimately resolve your predicament. You have a right to your anger for the

negative situation, but if you forgive the other driver, accept that your car is in need of repair due to no fault of your own, and decide to move forward and control what you can, you will be much better off than the person who would stand in the road and shake his fists at an unknown wrongdoer. You must resist the temptation to allow your unhappiness to linger for days or weeks, because by doing so you would inadvertently ruin your own mood. Although shock and outrage would be natural at the time of the incident, thereafter only you can act to improve your spirits by accepting that you were an innocent victim, forgiving the careless driver, and determining to feel better by adopting a positive attitude again.

- Choose a healing path by forgiving offenders, accepting difficult truths, and adopting a positive attitude about yourself and your life.

CHAPTER 12

PUMP THE BRAKES

The pleasure principle, the human tendency to seek pleasure and to avoid pain, was initially described by psychoanalyst Sigmund Freud. It is still considered a fundamental motivational factor by psychologists today. For example, the emotion researcher Paul Ekman describes our emotion system as a primary organizing and motivational entity that guides us to act in order to maximize positive feelings and to minimize negative ones.[1] In the nursing home, the influence of this powerful dynamic can been seen on a daily basis. While sick or injured and separated from home and loved ones, a person may act impulsively in seeking immediate relief without sufficient consideration of the intermediate to long-term implications of behaviors or decisions. For example, since physical therapy after a hip replacement might cause temporary pain, a patient might avoid attending physical-therapy sessions. While this avoids pain in the short term, her long-term healing process is compromised as a result. As essential as feelings and impulses are for driving behavior, they are not all important. Stated simply: our minds are bigger than our feelings and desires. We are gifted with impressive faculties that allow us to anticipate the future and to employ critical-thinking skills. The exercise of good judgment and sound decision making requires the simultaneous weighing of much information, including our present feelings and desires, our long-term goals, our abilities to execute our plans, and the probable outcomes of our efforts, to name some variables. In fact, sometimes we must act against our feelings in order to achieve important goals.

The predicament that William found himself in at the nursing home exemplifies the presence and sway of the pleasure principle. William was in the subacute, short-stay unit of the nursing home for rehabilitation following surgery on his right leg. It had been a bitter, snowy winter in New Jersey. Unfortunately for William, he slipped on some ice and shattered his femur. The injury necessitated emergency surgery and extensive rehabilitation. He arrived at the nursing home unable to bear weight on the repaired leg, and he was badly deconditioned after being laid up in the hospital. He was weak and experiencing serious pain.

William planned to return home after his rehabilitation. He was eighty-two years old and lived with his wife of fifty-five years, Edith. Well educated and holding a master's degree, William was a retired school superintendent and still sharp of mind. He was also highly emotional during our initial interviews, frequently verbally agitated, and even yelling at times. William reported a desperate desire to go home. Edith, he informed me, had been diagnosed with mild dementia, and he was worried about her. She was being cared for by a part-time private aide whom the couple had been using for some time. In addition, their two daughters, both of whom lived near to the couple, were also providing assistance. Although he reported confidence that Edith was being satisfactorily cared for, William was used to being present and involved and had an admirable desire to hurry home to her. Prior to his injury, William was impressively independent. He was driving his car, shopping, and managing his home (e.g., paying the bills and handling the finances). The couple received assistance with cooking, laundry, and lawn care. William was worried about the cost of the increased hours for the aide, the burden on his daughters, the paying of his bills, and his wife missing his presence in the home.

I am always pleased to see that a resident in the short-term care unit has a robust desire to go home. It indicates the presence of passion that can work in the service of recovery. I worry when I see the opposite: apathy and amotivation (an absence of motivation). In William's case, however, the drive to return home was excessive and threatening to prematurely end his rehabilitation. The emotional upheaval he felt was evident in his obvious distress, crying, and agitation; his discomposure also contributed to disturbances in sleep and appetite, weight loss, irritability, and an inadequate commitment to his physical therapies. In fact, William had refused to participate in any treatment on several occasions while also demanding to be sent home against the advice of his surgeon, attending physician, and nursing-home staff.

It is extremely unpleasant when our feelings reach a fever pitch—we experience an aversive sense of being overwhelmed and an almost-irresistible urge to act to seek immediate relief, with little or no regard for the consequences. In my experience, the highest priority in such a crisis is to quell the internal maelstrom, not necessarily to take action on problems. Restoring emotional equilibrium allows for more reasonable conversation and more effective problem solving. When we are over-wrought, our judgment is adversely affected. William demonstrated this in his responses to several of my questions. When I asked him if he could foresee any potential risks in his leaving the nursing home immediately, he replied, "None." In response to my wondering how he thought he might function at home on one leg, he stated, "I'll worry about that when I get there." When I asked why he thought that his doctors and nursing-home personnel thought he should not go home so quickly, he remarked, "They all want to keep me here for the money." William's answers reflected the shallow, shortsighted, inflexible thought process that is characteristic of someone being driven by emotion.

Emotions are known to affect our thoughts, motivation, and be-havior. We usually want to maintain our feeling intensity somewhere in the mid-range between apathy on one extreme and emotional flooding on the other. Being aroused too little or too much does not allow for full depth or breadth of intellectual processing, or attention to all the infor-mation we should consider in order to exercise solid judgment. William needed to "pump the brakes," slow down, and regain his emotional balance. His mind was racing too quickly, and his goal was too narrow and shortsighted—to go home no matter what the consequences. Although he experienced a mixture of feelings, the predominant and most persistent was anxiety. Essentially a fear response, William's anxiety was behind his subjective discomfort, agitation, perception of mistrust and of hostile intentions by the staff, and defensive belligerence. Happily, William's daughters both agreed that his coming home would be a bad decision, and they were able to convince him to remain at the care center. He retained full trust in his daughter's good intentions and was heartened by their assurances of Edith's well-being and of their competent handling of his and Edith's affairs. William had also been evaluated by the psychiatrist and was receiving psychotropic medication, which also contributed to his being able to calm down, engage in more reasonable discussion, and be more compliant with treatment recommendations.

The crisis threatening to force William out of the nursing home was quelled. With considerable attention from the full complement of service professionals and his family, William was able to resist the temptation to act in pursuit of fast relief from his guilt and anxiety. He came to recognize the necessity of tolerating psychic pain in order to allow for a more complete physical recovery. For instance, when William began to participate more earnestly in his physical therapies, he experienced increased pain and discomfort. His body was telling him to stay off the leg, and his doctors, nursing-home staff, and daughters were telling him to persevere through the pain. He began to report the experience of waves of anxiety prior to rehabilitation sessions, which were again threatening to undercut his motivation. The psychotherapeutic interventions I employed were the same ones used to deal with the fear emanating from the psychic pain—assisting William to maintain focus on the bigger goal: to acknowledge the fear as a natural response to pain but to resist capitulation to the automatic tendency to avoid the pain-causing situation. I repeatedly reinforced the advice that our goals must be established with more in mind than our current feelings.

The tendency to action when we are acutely upset is a strong one. There is good reason why it is standard in mental-health treatment to recommend that new patients wait six to twelve months after they initiate treatment before making major decisions, such as seeking a divorce, making a job or career change, or relocating. It may be best to make significant changes in one's life, but it is unadvisable to make potentially life-altering decisions under the influence of intense emotion. An exception to this general rule would be if a person is in immediate danger. For example, if a woman comes to a therapist because she's being abused by her spouse, it might be unacceptably risky for her to wait six to twelve months before escaping the dangerous abuser.

Joseph, a young adult who recently came to my office for an initial consultation, demonstrates the wisdom of waiting even when feelings press for action. Having just completed his junior year at college, he was in dire straits. His first two years of college went acceptably well. During the most-recently completed semester, his girlfriend of two years broke up with him. He started to drink alcohol and to smoke marijuana excessively, failed two courses, and was in conflict with his parents (with whom he was living). He was experiencing panic episodes and having difficulty sleeping. The solutions Joseph was considering involved making radical changes to his life. He felt guilty about wasting his parent's money and too upset to go back to college in the fall, so he was thinking about quitting. In response to his now-poor relationship with his parents, he reported his intention to move out to live with some friends in an off-campus apartment near the college he had attended. He figured that he could get a job to support himself. Joseph considered his alcohol and marijuana use unproblematic. Rather, he felt that the substances were assisting him to cope with his crisis.

Discussion of other details of Joseph's case is beyond the scope of this chapter, but suffice it so say that my initial recommendation to Joseph was the same one I made to William: Pump the brakes. Changing certain aspects of his life might prove best, but it was unknowable at the time. Joseph needed to regain control of his emotions first, then engage in more deliberate, systematic processes of evaluation and decision-making.

This chapter reinforces the principle that when you are feeling your lowest, that is usually the worst time to make major life decisions. Even though it is ill advised, it is easy to understand the desire to make profound changes when distressed. In effect, William and Joseph were expressing, "I am very upset with my life, so quickly changing everything that appears to be disturbing me has got to bring me the fastest relief from my misery. Nothing else matters at this point." Since all of us frequently feel upset and derailed from our goals, the first aim should be to regain our sense of emotional equanimity. In a crisis it is important to seek support and resist the urge to take immediate action.

Lesson: Resist the temptation to act in haste: your intellectual faculties and judgment are at their worst in a crisis.

Applying the Lesson to Your Life

- In a crisis or in any situation that arouses intense emotions, recognize that the tendency is to act hastily.
- Resist the urge to take immediate action.
- Understand that options for action will be weighted differently depending on which feelings you are experiencing and their intensity. For example, screaming at your son who persistently wakes you in the middle of the night might seem like a good idea when you are angry about the interruptions of sleep, but when you are calmer, and feeling more loving and concerned about him, more constructive responses can be considered, like developing an incentive program for his remaining in bed all night or assisting him to feel safer with a nightlight.
- When at our most emotional, we are in the worst condition to make major decisions. The priority should be placed on reacquiring emotional control before taking action or making decisions. For instance, if your employer asks you to take on more responsibility at work when you are already overwhelmed, you might be afraid of taking on the new duties. Your immediate, fear-based response might be to quit and deal with the consequences later—mortgage and car payments be damned. But if you pump the brakes and recognize that you're experiencing an emotional reaction rather than thinking through a viable career option, you might see that there are better alternatives available

to you. Uprooting your whole life to the detriment of your financial well-being might not be the best response, which you would recognize once you calmed down and thought through the situation logically.

- Seek support to calm down and assistance from others in making decisions if you are unable to regulate your emotions satisfactorily. You might recognize that your emotions are getting the better of you by subjective sensations like feeling keyed up, ill at ease, or overwhelmed. Or, since when we are overly emotional we are irrational, you may require a friend to advise you of the state you are in before recognizing the need to calm yourself.

CHAPTER 13

FINDING MY RELIGION

Boredom is a complaint I rarely hear in either my personal or professional life; feeling overwhelmed, on the other hand, is an experience I hear about daily. Our lives today are fast paced and hectic—too much information to take in, too many things to do, and too little time to do them is the typical American lament. One facet of the silver linings of aging is that by the time someone is in his later years, there is not as much "out there" left to do as there used to be. And the older one gets, the more evident this becomes. With many people and possessions gone, abilities diminished, senses and faculties dulling, health fading, and fewer day-to-day responsibilities, there is a natural tendency to look inward. Or maybe, to be more accurate, to look upward. Indeed, it would be difficult to overestimate the value of spirituality (through religious practice or more informally) in the maintenance of well-being of residents and staff at the nursing home.

The nursing home I work in has no religious affiliation, but this does not preclude the presence or practice of spirituality. One gets the distinct impression from residents that, "now that all of these other things are out of the way, I can have a more direct relationship with God." Impressive and surprising, the attitude I witness most commonly does not involve worship or prayer to petition for a magical transformation to bring back youth and health. Rather, the attitude expressed involves love, gratitude, and receiving comfort, purpose, and meaning for loss and suffering. The experience of loss in the material world seems to clear more space for a spiritual focus. The spiritual perspective is good not only to help neutralize what is difficult but also to help achieve constructive goals. A positive focus on spirituality provides a strong tonic for relieving suffering, serves to counteract negativity, and helps ease loneliness. Residents who otherwise share little in common often join one another in religious services offered at the facility. Even for residents who pray or engage in spiritual practice alone, the sense of the presence of God or another higher power provides much-needed company.

The advantages of religious practice in particular for providing meaning and comfort were most obvious with Tina. Widowed with three sons (all of whom lived out of state), she was eighty-nine years old when I met her. Tina had lived alone in her home for many years after her husband died. Debilitation resulting from congestive heart failure, chronic obstructive pulmonary disease, and obesity had necessitated her coming to the nursing home. Tina told me that she had had the option to live with one of her sons and his family but had chosen to remain close to home and to the Catholic church in which she had been a member for approximately sixty years.

When Tina was still living in her home and functioning independently, the church was the hub of her social life. She had been involved in numerous church committees over the years and had developed many friendships through her service. Consistent with the role of homemaker in her era, Tina never worked. Most of her time had been devoted to child rearing and domestic responsibilities, which left little time to socialize. After her children left home, the church provided opportunities for service and social activity in addition to the practice of her faith. She had attended daily services in the morning and spent good portions of the day volunteering her time and assistance. The church family that she developed over the years had helped to support her through the loss of her husband and continued to be a positive factor in her life for years thereafter.

In the nursing home, Tina required assistance getting out of bed, and even when in her wheelchair she was immobile for all intents and purposes. With a heart condition, impaired breathing, and excess weight, she did not have the strength to propel herself in the wheelchair. She was a social isolate, except for visits from friends from the community whom she had come to know through the church. Her mind was still nimble, and her vision adequate, which allowed Tina to enjoy her favorite activity—reading. She preferred to read the Bible, prayer books, and other Christian-themed literature. She was not particularly friendly to other residents and to my knowledge had not developed any close relationships within the walls of the nursing home. Tina disliked most of the activities offered at the facility and rarely attended any except for Sunday religious services and weekly meetings to pray the Rosary. Tina was not a particularly happy person. She was often uncomfortable and greatly reliant on staff for assistance, and her life was more or less confined to her room.

I believe that the most critical factor separating life and death for Tina was her religious faith and practice. I think that she felt little other reason to go on. When I spoke to her, she would spend five to ten minutes complaining about her physical discomfort and sundry negative aspects of institution life, and another thirty minutes talking about her reading. Both of us were practicing Catholics, although separated in age by thirty-five years, and from very different backgrounds, we found we had much in common. Through the Catholic religion we shared a vocabulary, knowledge base, and life experience. When Tina referred to the Holy Rosary or to the beatitudes, I knew exactly what she meant. When she talked about her joy of the Christmas service, I related.

Tina's body was no longer a source of pleasure. More often than not she was experiencing some sort of discomfort. In addition, she was physically unable to participate in most activities. Yet her mental existence was alive and well. Tina's religious practices consisted of reading, discussing what she read, and attending services and prayer meetings. Through these activities she maintained her mental acuity, got some physical exertion, engaged in social interaction, and reinforced her motivation to live. Even with her strong faith and religion as the center of her life, she was unhappy. It would be most accurate to say that she was accepting of her current life, not that she was enjoying it. She said to me many times, "I am ready to go any time the Good Lord wants me. Until then, it is His will, not mine. He must have some purpose for me to stay here, so I just keep praying." Without such a spiritual perspective, her life would have been intolerable.

It is not just residents in the nursing home who benefit from religious, spiritual, or personal-development practices. For staff members, mindful adherence to spiritual principles or higher values can spell the difference between performing thankless duties in a dark, depressing setting and being uplifted by providing compassionate care to the disabled, sick, and needy. The same challenging work can be viewed totally differently when spiritual principles or higher values are identified. It is inevitably stressful to work with people who are fragile, in distress, or terminally ill, and who are often unhappy, demanding and complaining because of their predicaments. Professional and ethical concerns reinforce the need for workers to deal with difficult aspects of their jobs in a responsible and caring manner. At the same time, they must take steps to maintain their morale in this challenging work environment. In addition to the importance of receiving support from other workers, family, and friends, recognition of spiritual aspects of the work is very beneficial. For example, staff workers may consider how providing care to others relates to inspirational spiritual practices as exemplified by St. Francis and Mother Teresa, and advocated presently by self-help groups such as Alcoholics Anonymous. Or they may reflect about being thankful for the opportunity to learn patience, to have a meaningful job, or to be productive and able to provide financially for oneself or one's family.

For example, Darlene has worked as an aide at the nursing home for twelve years. She is divorced and is the custodial parent of two middle-school-aged children. Darlene is in her midforties and lives with her mother. She works hard—in addition to her full-time employment at the care center, she also does some private-duty work. Despite the serious pressures and responsibilities she shoulders, Darlene is a delightful person. She is a joy to be around. Smiling, happy, never complaining, her spirit is positive and she is an attractive person. Residents request her to be their caregiver—the highest compliment in the nursing home. To my observation, she has never had a bad day. She could not be that professional or that good an actress to hide it so well if she did. She is not a jokester or silly, yet she spreads joy. Darlene is a very spiritual woman. She does not tell me this directly. However, I hear her talking with coworkers about the church-related activities she attends and her spontaneous comments, such as "I am blessed," "Today is a present," and "I'm healthy and have a job—that's all I need," are dead giveaways.

Darlene's demeanor and behavior illustrate how spirit and attitude are separate from setting and circumstances. Her life does not appear to be one of leisure and ease, yet she is a font of positive energy. Behaving in accordance with spiritual principles such as compassion, forgiveness, tolerance, service to others, patience, and responsibility is intrinsically rewarding. We all know people who appear to have everything but who are spiritually and morally bankrupt and miserable. If we are fortunate, we know many people like Darlene who are rich in spirit. Although formal religions have historically been the main sources of spiritual information and training, the principles have been popularized and stand separate from any particular religion. Alcoholics Anonymous and other twelve-step programs, as well as service organizations such as Habitat for Humanity are spiritually, but not religiously based, for example.

DROP TO YOUR KNEES

It is perhaps an unflattering admission that we must be humbled in some way in order to grant spiritual practice its proper place in our lives. What some consider to be a constituent of our psyche alongside intellect and emotion, the soul often appears to be lowest in priority and attention. I believe we would all do well to pay attention to our spiritual needs before hitting some sort of bottom. What could ever be detrimental about meditating, contemplating and appreciating the good in ourselves and others, praying, practicing gratitude, providing service for others, attending a religious service, or admiring nature? It would be better to drop to our knees humbly and willingly before being forced to them.

Not only might such practice prevent our falling down in some way, but it can be enriching even when things are going well. Maintaining a positive mind-set will attract good things to an individual. A negative attitude and focus will only attract bad things. Psychological studies support the notion that there are mental benefits to accentuating the positive. People tend to take favorable aspects of life for granted and ruminate on the disagreeable. Reversing this tendency and savoring the good appears not only to elevate spirits but also to provide a reserve to counterbalance and attenuate the impact of negative events when they occur.[1]

SEEK AND YOU WILL FIND

It does not require special training or background to develop your spirituality. When you are of the mind to, it is possible to find spiritual messages in virtually every occurrence. For example, last winter in northern New Jersey was an unusually cold, harsh season. Because of heavy damage to the roads, potholes were everywhere. At night, when visibility is reduced, it was almost impossible to spot holes in black pavement. One night, while coming home from work, I found an especially deep pothole with my front passenger-side tire, and it quickly went flat. It was after 10:00 p.m., dark and cold outside, and I was tired and hungry. I was not happy. However, after angrily cursing the predicament I found myself in, I called for roadside assistance. While waiting for my rescue, I was able to identify several positive messages that I could take from the experience. This difficult situation could have been a reminder to slow down and be more careful. I was not speeding, but because of the road conditions I would have been wise to drive well below the speed limit. Perhaps this was a wake-up call to be more alert and present when driving on a familiar route rather than driving on automatic pilot—I needed heightened awareness to combat a subtle complacency that may have been unknowingly dangerous. This incident may have prevented a worse accident by forcing me to be more alert and cautious.

I was also aware of gratitude I was feeling. I had a working, charged cell phone that allowed me to get help. I was thankful for roadside assistance—I did not have to change the tire in the dark, freezing, cold. I was also grateful that it was late at night; when I needed to move quickly off the road, I did not have to be concerned with striking another vehicle. By moving one step away from the displeasing facts and focusing on a larger, spiritual context, my experience was transformed. I attempt to find the spiritual context for most situations in life and frequently advise others to do the same. I seek success and happiness in the material world, but it would be a bleak and scary existence if there were no more to life than that. I promote spiritual considerations as a *complement* to more material pursuits, not a replacement.

Lesson: Material loss clears the way for spiritual gain (but why wait?).

Applying the Lesson to Your Life

- Consider that the emotion-balancing, serenity-enhancing benefits of spiritual practice can, and should, be enjoyed well before old age, and before pain or loss prompts us. For instance, I routinely advise patients to positively start each day by reflecting on a gratitude list, or engaging in meditation, rather than begin with negativity from the TV, radio, or newspaper.
- Spiritual guidance can be sought through religious institutions or in nonreligious sources. Much of the self-help, new age, and humanist literature is spiritually based and is easy to find.

CHAPTER 14

A BODY ON LOAN

So often, we are content to accept things as they appear unless jarred from complacency by extreme circumstances. The fusion of mind and body is so complete that they appear to operate as one, and for all practical purposes are. Few of us even consider the mind-body relationship before there is some disturbance. Observing countless men and women engaging in rehabilitative exercises in the nursing home has left me with the impression that physical disability provides just the kind of situation that causes an individual to consider the possibility that his will is not the sole, or even main, influence on his body. Acknowledging this separation of mind and body, perhaps for the first time, can be humbling and disturbing.

I cannot claim to have resolved one of the most challenging questions in philosophy and life: How does an immaterial spirit that appears to reside in the brain animate and control the material body? Assuming the existence of the spirit or soul, is it really separate from the body, or is this only a false sense we have, a brain trick, as some neurologists might suggest? What I can say about this with certainty is based on what I observe in the nursing home. It appears as though residents experience the mind and body, psyche and soma, as separate, often with horror and dismay. Whether the separation is real or illusory is for the philosophers to debate. Through observation and discussion with elder residents I have come to view the body from their perspective as the mind's registrar of perception and pleasure, executor of will, material embodiment; and a gift from the creator.

In the chapter "Best Damn Health Plan," I discuss behavioral practices that promote long-term health and wellness. In this chapter I am approaching personal caretaking from a different perspective, one that might be considered moral or philosophical. I am loathe to veer too far afield from traditional psychology as I am neither a philosopher nor a theologian. Nevertheless, if we accept that the mind is the nexus of intelligence, emotion, and what many call the soul, we cannot escape some discussion of this kind. Moreover, I am confining the discussion of mind and body to those matters suggested by observation and direct interaction with residents. There is an alternative way to view ourselves other than either healthy or sick; usually, long before health is a serious concern we each have a relationship with our body that we can benefit from thinking about. My ultimate goal is simple: to foster a loving attitude toward our bodies and to promote superb personal caretaking.

When I walked into his room, Albert was crying. Already familiar and comfortable with each other from prior sessions, he jumped right into conversation with me: "I can't believe my goddamned hand and foot won't do what they are supposed to do! Goddamn it to hell!" Anger alternated with sadness. The sense of betrayal Albert felt was palpable and understandable. Hands and feet, and every other body part, are supposed to do just as we will them to do.

Does anyone ever consider otherwise? Only those ill-fated individuals who are forcibly informed by illness or injury that the body may not always be at their command, or others who know such individuals personally or professionally. Usually we tend to blithely assume that our bodies are always able to execute our will. Albert never expected to find himself in this position and was none too happy to be there. A retired plumber, at seventy-four years old he was very active and independent before the stroke. He was driving his car, shopping, and playing golf the three seasons of the year weather allowed for it in New Jersey. Albert and his wife of forty-six years, JoAnne, enjoyed doing yard work, going for walks and hikes, and visiting with their children and grandchildren.

Although formally retired, Albert maintained his license to practice and would do an occasional plumbing job. He made his living with his hands and the sporadic work he performed was more for the satisfaction of knowing he had retained his knowledge and skills, and that others still valued his services, than it was for income. In prior conversations with me, Albert expressed pride in the size and scale of his business. He had been self-employed, with four trucks and several plumbers working for him. In addition to providing residential services, he did work in office buildings and apartment complexes. Albert was a hard worker and was pleased with his professional accomplishments and financial success. He was able to provide a nice home for his family and to put three children through college—all this accomplished with his capable hands, strong back, and determined attitude.

Presently, Albert could not stand without assistance or use his left hand competently. The stroke he experienced had left him with a condition called left-sided hemiparesis; he experienced weakness on the left side of his body. Albert retained movement and feeling in the affected areas, but, in addition to reduced strength and control of the compromised limbs, he was prone to fatigue. Albert reported feeling tired most of the time and exhausted following sessions in physical and occupational therapies. He applied maximum effort to his rehabilitation—he was driven to retrieve his skills and life. That his body was not complying with his desire was maddening for him. As much as he tried, Albert could not speed up the recovery process by brute force or willpower. Mind and body had come uncoupled. It had become clear to him that he was no longer the absolute master of his own body, which was a mortifying realization.

If Albert was no longer completely in charge of his body and its recovery, who or what was? Nature was his partner. His spirit was willing, but his flesh was damaged. Albert still possessed some control over the process—he was certain to continue to engage in behaviors that promoted healing, such as getting sufficient rest, eating properly, participating in his therapies, and maintaining his spirits—but the remainder was in the hands of nature. Once your body is damaged, you are not the boss anymore. We must reluctantly concede that we neither design nor create our bodies. We are occupiers of our bodies.

Whose body is it, then? My experiences in the nursing home have led to the somewhat-surprising possibility that we may exist in a *body on loan*. It is humbling to think of our bodies as belonging to God, to nature, or to the universal source, rather than solely to us; however challenging this view may be to our personal sense of narcissism, it can be helpful as a motivator for taking good care of ourselves. Virtually every person I have seen in the nursing home expresses some surprise that he is seriously sick or disabled. I am frequently asked, "How could this happen to me?" The sobering truth is, How could it not? Of the several billion humans on the planet, and countless other animals, each and every one will get sick and die.

This separate relationship between mind and body is exposed through the experience of children learning about what their bodies can do, as well as anyone relearning skills if lost due to illness or injury. For example, small children are fascinated by looking at their hands and learning that they can move their fingers by intention, and grasp objects, and eventually develop additional motor skills in order to stand, walk, kick, and perform other volitional actions. In physical therapy and occupational therapy, men and women in the nursing home struggle to reestablish the link between mind and body that has been disturbed. It has been so long since we learned of the intimate relationship between mind and body that we forget they are apart. Instead of the fascination and euphoria of the youngster, the older person experiences negative emotions of frustration, disappointment, sadness, and outrage that the body does not respond as commanded and fears that it may never again.

THE BODY AS REGISTRAR OF PERCEPTION AND PLEASURE

The human body may be viewed as the mind's connection to the material world and receiver of carnal pleasures. We have been furnished with sensory systems dedicated to taking in stimulation from the environment. This provides innumerable opportunities for enjoyment. There is music for our ears, tender touch, visual beauty, delectable food and drink, and delightful scent. When the body is healthy it can act as a well-tuned instrument of pleasure. When compromised, sources of joy are lost.

Now consider the predicament that Douglas finds himself in. He had been a chronic smoker and was diagnosed with chronic obstructive pulmonary disease (COPD) several years prior to my meeting him in the nursing home. Douglas speaks in a breathless whisper that is effortful for him to utter and for me to hear. On one particular morning I came into his room while his aide was grooming him and assisting him to get into his wheelchair. If you have never seen anyone with COPD, the best description I can offer is that they appear like a fish out of water—gasping for air, uncomfortable, and anxious. It was 9:15 a.m. and Douglas was talking about needing to take a nap; all he had done was wake up, eat breakfast, and get dressed and groomed, and he was wiped out. We had to end the session early this day because his breathing was particularly difficult and neither one of us felt comfortable continuing. On other days, Douglas is able to breathe and communicate more effectively, but there appear to be more bad days than good.

How much enjoyment do you think that he experiences right now? Practically none. With his diminished capacity to breathe, Douglas describes eating as more like work than fun. I am not singling out Douglas, or other smokers. The same point can be made with any disabling disease—when the body is damaged, it provides for less enjoyment of life.

Our bodies ground us in the natural world. They are part of nature and will return to nature one day. The human body is the instrument that registers all of our carnal pleasures. To maximize enjoyment and happiness, we should endeavor to be in top form. Instead of focusing on his meal, the music playing in his room, or visitors, Douglas is consumed by a struggle to breathe and eat; there is little opportunity for enjoyment.

THE BODY AS EXECUTOR OF WILL

We not only take in from the world but act on it, too. The body is a vehicle for action. Activities provide for satisfaction and are another source of pleasure in life. This fleshen machine will perform best when well maintained. The more we can utilize our bodies, the more we are able to enjoy.

Vivian always reaches out for a reassuring touch of hands when I come into her room to talk. Her sight is impaired by macular degeneration and, like most people with low vision, she is anxious and wary. Although she recognizes my voice, she desires the comfort of physical contact. On this particular visit, the TV was on and she was listening to a popular morning cooking show: "This girl doesn't know what she's doing. I don't know how she got her own TV show." Her comment served as a segue into a discussion of her love of cooking and of her missing it: "When my husband was alive and my kids were home, I cooked every night. Even after the kids moved out, I cooked for my husband and myself, and everybody would come over for a big Sunday dinner. We didn't go out like they do today. Why spend all that money when I could make it better at home?" Vivian expressed pride in her skills: "And I could bake, too. Now they just run out to the supermarket when they need a cake; I think it's junk anyway." Like many people with a passion for cooking, she probably had indulged in her own creations a little too often: she was diagnosed with obesity, hypertension, and high cholesterol, all known risk factors for macular degeneration.

Cooking is not all that Vivian misses. Playing cards, shopping at the mall, and going to bingo were favorite pastimes. But the activity she misses the most is doing needlepoint: "I made a needlepoint quilt for every one of my grandkids when they were born. If there was one thing I wish I could still do, it would be needlepoint. Why did God have to take that from me? I could give everything else up."

It is unknowable if Vivian's obesity caused or contributed in any way to her visual decline, but the fact remains that her impairment resulted in a great reduction of the sources of joy in her life. A healthy body permits activity; an unhealthy one limits it.

BODY AS PHYSICAL MANIFESTATION
OF YOUR PSYCHE

Your body may be conceived as a physical expression of your mind. You are a walking, talking, living, breathing representation of your spirit or essence. In the most obvious and straightforward way, every person shows who he is through his physique, posture, movement, tone of voice, and grooming. What message does your physical presentation send to the world? Do you project self-love, self-esteem, and self-respect? We obviously express ourselves with words, but we also communicate with our bodies. It is accepted as fact that toxic mental states, such as chronic stress, can be expressed in the body as physical ailments. Doesn't it stand to reason that other states of mind will be expressed physically as well? Have you ever made an honest appraisal of what message you are sending to the world through your physical appearance? If you are comfortable with that message, do nothing. If not, consider changing both the inner attitude and the outward expression of it.

THE BODY AS A GIFT

The human body is an awesome vehicle in which to carry our psyche around in this world, but, like any other machine, it requires proper maintenance. Imagine that you were given a beautiful car on your seventeenth birthday. If you beat the heck out of the vehicle, it will not perform its best. It will break down. The result is less pleasure and more frustration, inconvenience, and cost to you. In addition, if this automobile is in disrepair, how does it look to others? What does it say about you? What's the message to the giver of the gift if you turn this wonderful present into garbage? Unlike a car that can be replaced, we get one body per lifetime, making its maintenance even more critical. The religious notion that it is sinful to abuse or destroy the body derives from this idea: it is not really ours to mistreat. It is a gift from the creator and should be treated as such. Considering this point of view, regardless of whether or not you are religious, do you view your body as a precious gift? Does your behavior reflect appreciation and gratitude for this gift?

That we cannot foresee or prevent all bodily harm does not release us from the responsibility to try. We are accustomed to thinking of ourselves as stewards of the earth. In this chapter I suggest that we are caretakers also of our own bodies. There is a plethora of information available on nutrition, movement, and stress management that can be utilized in order to maintain our pleasure machine at its peak (see chapter 6, "Best Damn Health Plan"). The best way to show love to your body and to project a self-adoring attitude to others is through good personal caretaking.

Lesson: Despite the close interaction, mind and body are separate entities; a loving attitude toward the body is the basis of good personal caretaking and well-being.

Applying the Lesson to Your Life

- Recognize that when your body is injured by disease or accident, you surrender control over it and over your life.
- Accept the premise that mind and body are separate entities. Adopt a loving attitude toward your body.
- Think of all of the sensual pleasures you relish. Bring to mind all of the activities you enjoy. Let the desire to continue to partake of these pleasures and activities serve as positive motivation to maintain your body in peak working order. Say your passion is viewing art. Now imagine that because you ignored your doctor's advice to take better care of your diabetes, you suffered visual impairment—this source of enjoyment would be lost. Or suppose you are an enthusiast of outdoor activity and you take advantage of every opportunity to walk, hike, garden, and swim. Think about how awful it would feel to be unable to participate in your favorite interests because of chronic smoking resulting

in disabling respiratory and cardiac conditions. A healthy body is one key to a satisfying life. To enjoy life you must respect and care for your body.

- Consider the message you are conveying with your body and appearance. If it is different than you desire, change it. If, while taking an objective look at the message your appearance conveys, you realize that your poorly groomed hair, ill-fitting clothing, and expanding waistline don't match up with the person you really know you are, consider putting a little more effort into the image you project. Taking better care of your diet, sitting less often and becoming more active, tossing your much-loved sweats in favor of more flattering outfits, and getting a haircut can do more than just make you look more attractive to others. Taking care of your body can work wonders also for your self-esteem and general outlook on life as well. Projecting an image of self-respect will be positively perceived by others, which encourages their high opinion of you. Your body is a gift, and taking care of it can be a gift to yourself as well.

- As a good caretaker, show love to yourself by learning and employing healthy habits.

CHAPTER 15

THE GHOST IN THE BROKEN MACHINE

W hat makes Grandmom Grandmom? If she has a hip replaced with a synthetic one, is she still Grandmom? What if she has chronic obstructive pulmonary disease (COPD)? Or is paralyzed on the left side of her body? Or if she goes blind? If she's afflicted with Parkinson's disease? She is still Grandmom. What if Grandmom has excellent vital signs, is in good general health, but is always confused, fails to recognize family members, is incontinent, needs assistance eating, and is completely apathetic and lacking in purpose and self-determination? It is not so obvious that this is still Grandmom. What are we connected to—her body or her spirit/mind, when usually the two appear as one? What, in fact, determines the essence of the person? Dementing disorders force us to consider such odd and unsettling questions.

In the nursing home, I have seen people suffer permanent injury rendering limbs inoperative, lose significant body parts, and receive prosthetic replacements. They are still recognizable to others despite profound changes in body and functioning. The body is machinelike in this way and is able to tolerate dysfunction and replacement parts without losing its essential nature. Actor Christopher Reeve provided a classic example of how the personality can endure despite almost total loss of use of the body when the horrific accident he suffered rendered him essentially a "talking head." His mind and personality were strong up until his premature death. He could not act in any way except to talk, but in TV interviews he was easily recognizable and retained his identity.

When disorders such as Alzheimer's disease, or other types of dementia, attack the brain, though, the person may be familiar physically but not be the person who was once known. The mind is unique, irreplaceable. When it is lost, the personality is gone and the essence of the individual is missing; although the face and body of Grandmom remain unchanged, there is a void. That the eyes are the window to the soul is evident in cases of advanced dementia: the unfocused, faraway look tells us all we need to know. It is not unusual for family members to visit unquestioningly nursing-home residents who are gravely physically ill, with end-stage cancer, for example, and hardly responsive. In brief periods of alertness, the resident can acknowledge the presence of loved ones, perhaps only with a glance, facial expression, or wordless touch; this is all it takes to maintain a personal connection. When the mind is damaged, however, it can be a very different story. With dementia, the ghost has all but abandoned the machine; it appears as if there is sufficient spirit to animate the body but not enough to operate the brain. In cases of dementia, questions arise that people rarely consider until confronted with such a situation. For example, when do I mourn? If my grandmother is physically present, but her mind absent, is she still here? Should I keep visiting once she fails to recognize me? Does it matter? What will people think of me if I stop coming? What will I think of myself?

There are no definite or easy answers, as the case of Norman, a seventy-eight-year-old retired attorney who came to the nursing home to improve his strength and conditioning, illustrates. He was weakened by a cardiac condition and a urinary tract infection (UTI). On admission to the nursing home, Norman exhibited confusion, irritability, and emotional instability that raised concerns about his mental status. Although the exact reasons appear unknown, perhaps because of fever, dehydration, or general stress on the body, UTIs in the elderly are notorious for disturbances of mentation. Usually, if properly identified and treated, the mind clears as the infection resolves. Unfortunately for Norman, this was not the case; successful treatment of the infection with an antibiotic medication did not yield expected improvements in his mental status. What became apparent was that he was showing signs and symptoms of dementia. He has never left the nursing home. I worked directly with Norman for about a year, starting shortly after his admission. It has been three years since I discontinued treatment with him. His story points to the tragic decline of a mind and loss of identity that accompany destruction of the brain from a dementing disorder.

When I first met Norman, his physical presentation was impressive. He was nicely dressed in a button-down shirt and blue jeans, had thick, white, nicely groomed hair, and appeared young for his age. Friendly and fully cooperative with the diagnostic interview, he exhibited no difficulty with comprehension or verbal articulation. His vocabulary reflected his superior intellect and high educational achievement, and he exhibited a sense of humor as indicated by a comment he spontaneously offered, "Anyone who thinks talk is cheap, has never spoken to a shrink or a lawyer!" His responses to direct questions, however, were at times excessively long, unfocused, and rambling. For example, a simple background question about his place of birth, which for most interviewees elicits a short response (a typical answer consists of the name of the city or hospital), evoked a several-minute monologue about his hometown and how it had changed over the years. Throughout the interview, when I attempted to redirect Norman to maintain relevancy, he spoke over me until he completed his thoughts, an indication of cognitive difficulty.

Norman also was disoriented with respect to the date and his whereabouts. He reported thinking that he was in a hospital and that it was "around Thanksgiving." A week prior to the interview, we had celebrated Independence Day at the nursing home, so he seemed to have retained the sense that a holiday had recently passed, but not which one. When asked why he thought he was in the facility, he stated "I was hoping you would tell me." Other signs of cognitive impairment were evident: his performance on memory screening items was poor, indicating problems on both short-term and long-term recall. His concentration was also faulty, as he was unable to spell a common word backward, despite his obvious intelligence. Norman's insight was nil; he had no clue why he was in the nursing home and for what he was receiving care. His judgment was poor, as noted by his statement, "I just need my wife to come get me and take me home. I'll be fine there." He maintained self-care skills—he shaved and groomed himself, and he was continent, requiring assistance only to get out of bed.

Norman had no prior history of mental-health problems or treatment. In speaking with his wife, Miriam, I learned that there were reasons to question his mental functioning as far back as eighteen months prior to his nursing-home admission. Miriam reported that she had noticed changes in Norman but had attributed them to, at various times, his cardiac problems, medications, getting old, and emotional distress about limitations imposed by his cardiac condition. A common experience of elders at home, they usually are confronting complex situations with contributions from illness, medicine, and psychological reactions, so that it is very difficult to discern which condition is causing which symptoms. With both Norman and Miriam retired and living together in their house, she was the best informant. Memory lapses that she observed included Norman's forgetting multiple items on a shopping list and bringing home things not on the list—something this very capable man had never previously done. Paying bills, managing the retirement accounts and investments, and responding to telephone messages became bothersome to Norman, necessitating Miriam's assumption of these duties. Although he was previously gregarious, Norman began to express less interest in socializing. Despite always being strong-minded and opinionated, he seemed to be crossing the line of appropriateness at home, becoming more argumentative and more easily angered. His judgment was suffering too, as Norman fired several landscaping companies, yelled at wait staff in restaurants, and argued with an electrician in their home. In retrospect, Miriam realized that many of these behaviors could be viewed as early signs of dementia.

My treatment of Norman centered on two issues: his adjustment to long-term placement in the nursing home and his coming to terms with his declining mental skills. Retired since age sixty-two, he and Miriam had been constant companions for the previous sixteen years. They spent the bulk of their time together, engaged in the typical activities of homeowners—cooking, cleaning, shopping, gardening, and maintaining the house and property. Both enjoyed leisure activities, such as golfing, going to the gym several days a week, dining out, and going to the movies. They loved to travel, domestically and abroad, although it had been several years since their last big trip to Europe. Norman missed these activities, but he missed sharing them with Miriam more. He explained to me that after two failed marriages, "I finally got it right. I found my soul mate." He yearned for her presence and frequently told me of this. Her daily visits were the highlight of his day and were what made the whole situation tolerable to him.

Interestingly, in spite of the fact that he experienced problems with his memory and his control of his emotions and behavior, Norman was keenly aware of what was happening to his mind and frequently mentioned it in our discussions. During our conversations, he was frustrated by failures to recall certain words or by losing his train of thought. He stated, "I used to be very intelligent," an indication that he now felt otherwise. Instead, he knew enough to be frustrated and embarrassed. And he worried about what was to come. He admitted, "I know where this all ends. In my law practice, I had to deal with these issues, helping people protect their assets before they became incompetent." In order to maintain his spirits and to counteract his tendency to mentally project into the future, the primary interventions consisted of encouraging Norman to savor positive memories and to narrow his focus to the present. Regarding the latter, I often said to him, "I don't really know what might happen in a year or two, but let's talk about what you can do *today* to be happy."

In the year that I worked with him, Norman showed a considerable decline in mental functioning, ultimately necessitating my discontinuation of his treatment. The most apparent changes were in memory and emotion regulation. Near the end of his treatment, Norman was no longer able to recall the content of our previous discussions. Moreover, he could not remember when my last visit was. Although he recognized me, he could not recall exactly who I was. He would describe me in vague terms, such as "the guy who comes to see me" or "that person who asks a lot of questions." He frequently complained of his wife's absence and perceived abandonment of him, even though she continued to make daily visits. His ability to understand events was compromised. During one session, for example, he reported that he had experienced a particularly rough night. When invited to elaborate, he explained, "I was in the ocean swimming and I never changed my trunks. I got into the bed and was soaked all night." In reality, his diaper was wet, and sensing this he fabricated a fantastic story to account for it.

Norman had become much more excitable and easily upset. While telling me about his long, wet night he was speaking loudly and hitting his hand on his table. He also expressed mistrust of everyone, including his wife, whom he suspected of "fooling around with other men" while he was away. Nursing staff informed me of a decline in Norman's ability to perform activities of daily living (ADLs)—he required assistance with personal hygiene and toileting, although he was still able to feed himself competently and safely. He was reportedly more argumentative and difficult to care for. Volition and interest in things and activities diminished—Norman stopped attending activities, reading, and watching TV.

No longer a patient under my care, I see Norman only on chance encounters in the building. Most of the time, he is sitting passively while awaiting transportation to the in-house program for residents with dementia. My greeting might evoke an orienting response, but his eyes are now vacant and there is no evidence that he recognizes me. He does not respond verbally but may offer a faint, reflexive smile. Volition, communication, and personality appear to be gone. A testament to her devotion, I am informed that Miriam still dutifully visits.

There are several elements of Norman's sad tale that deserve emphasis. In casual conversation, we refer to the fragility of life. What about the brittleness of mind? The sanctity and uniqueness of spirit? Norman's physical health remains remarkably robust. His personality, his characteristic way of being, is what gave him his identity, more so than his physique. His case, and others like it, remind us that our minds are our invisible fingerprints. Each and every one of us deserves recognition of our specialness.

I would also like to point out that this is not only Norman's story. Miriam's loyalty to her husband is heartwarming and impressive. Do her visits make a difference for Norman? Earlier in his stay, there was no doubt. Now, who can say? I am certain that at this stage of Norman's life, Miriam's visits do not significantly alter the course of the illness. Does her regular presence register with Norman on some level? Maybe. Visiting is definitely a way for Miriam to express her fidelity to Norman, and for that reason alone, it is good.

A final comment on Norman's case relates to the nursing home. Some people may take them for granted, others may even wish they never existed, but nursing homes provide a very important service. When I see the care that Norman continues to receive, I cannot help but feel thankful that a place exists where humane treatment is given for an individual experiencing the worst-case scenario of having his mind ravaged by dementia.

ANATOMY OF A MIND

Just as the anatomy of the human body is an assemblage of flesh and bones, the structure of the mind is a collection of psychological functions commonly referred to as faculties. With advancing age there are inevitable declines in physical and mental abilities. No one would expect a typical seventy-year-old male to possess the physical strength or endurance of a thirty-year-old. A similar lowering of expectations applies to mental abilities as well. When skill degradation surpasses an expectable level, however, dysfunction or disease are suspected. Progressive, incurable, and a leading cause of death in the United States, dementing disorders are the scourge of mental functioning. There are several different types of dementia, but Alzheimer's disease and vascular dementia (brain damage resulting from stroke) account for the majority of cases. Given the degree of disability and functional impairment that ensue from these conditions, it is surprising that almost nine out of ten afflicted individuals are cared for at home by family members.[1] This may be a reflection of the fact that many individuals go undiagnosed by healthcare providers, primarily because concerns are not always reported to professionals by individuals with the disorders or by their family members. Since aging is the highest risk factor for the development of dementia, and Americans are enjoying increasing longevity, the prevalence of dementing disorders is expected to dramatically rise. It is estimated that approximately fourteen million individuals will be living with Alzheimer's disease by the year 2050.[2] Each and every one of us will be touched personally by these conditions in one way or another.

Although neuroimaging equipment may be used, the most common method for determining a diagnosis of dementia is from a clinical interview with the person in question, and ideally, with a family member as well. When I conduct a mental-status examination, I follow the model of neurologists Richard Strub and William Black.[3] Questions are employed that allow for a comprehensive assessment of the patient's level of consciousness, attention, language, memory, visual-spatial ability, and higher cognitive skills, such as personal fund of acquired knowledge, calculation, judgment, and concept formation. In order to meet the diagnostic criteria for a dementing disorder, an individual must demonstrate memory problems and other cognitive deficits that represent a decline in functioning and also result in impairment of work and social behavior. An all-inclusive mental-status examination is lengthy, is expensive, and must be conducted by a trained professional. For all practical purposes, individuals need only to know enough to seek professional assistance if they are worried about themselves or a loved one.

Some people might rightly question whether, if dementing disorders are incurable, seeing a medical or mental-health professional is even necessary. The answer is that the quality of life of the affected individual and his caretakers can be improved measurably with treatment. For example, medications can be prescribed that will slow the rate at which deterioration progresses. Medications that are currently available do not restore lost skills, so the earlier a medicine is introduced, the better. In addition, early identification of dementia allows for financial and care planning while the affected individual can still participate in decision making. Also, some conditions that present like dementia, such as depression and delirium, may be reversible with proper intervention. Furthermore, many people with dementia also exhibit behavioral and psychological symptoms that greatly complicate their care and increase caregiver burden. Problematic behaviors such as agitation and aggression, which create safety issues, and symptoms of anxiety, depression, hallucinations, and delusions can all be treated with traditional mental-health interventions.

Obviously, nonprofessionals cannot be expected to conduct clinical interviews in their homes. Realistically, they should look for changes in everyday behavior. Some dementia rating scales rely primarily on observations and reports relating to performance of ADLs by family members or close friends. For example, the Dementia Severity Rating Scale[4] elicits caretaker ratings on eleven dimensions: memory, orientation, judgment, social interaction/community affairs, home activities/responsibilities, personal care, speech/language, recognition, feeding, incontinence, and motility/walking. Norman's wife first noted problems with his memory of the shopping list. Later came recognition of his inability to manage home responsibilities and his impaired social interaction. By the time I met Norman, advanced problems with memory and orientation were evident. At present, he shows problems in all eleven dimensions.

There can be little doubt that if Norman had sought an evaluation at the first hint of cognitive problems and initiated treatment sooner, there would have been an improved outcome. Despite his having an observing and caring partner, the signs were not identified as early manifestations of dementia. Because dementia progresses in a slow, insidious manner, rather than quickly and dramatically, it can be difficult for family members to properly recognize the clues for what they are. Subtle, continuous changes can be hardly noticeable when you interact daily with someone. Weight loss serves as a suitable example of this problem. If your spouse were losing weight at a modest rate of two pounds per month, you might not notice for quite some time. After six months or so of dieting, someone who had not seen your spouse in a long time would easily spot the change in her body weight, though.

I recently conducted an evaluation of a female resident, Donnella, at the nursing home. A nurse requested that I perform the assessment because she was concerned about a possible decline in Donnella's cognitive functioning. I was familiar with Donnella because I had treated her when she was first admitted to the nursing home, approximately two years prior. Within minutes of talking with her, it was apparent that Donnella's cognitive functioning was much worse than when I last saw her. That it was not so evident to staff members underscores the point that everyday interaction with someone can obscure the obvious. For this reason, even the slightest sign of cognitive dysfunction should be sufficient grounds to seek professional attention.

In this chapter, readers are reminded of the uniqueness of the mind and of the need to take special care of it. Maintaining good health of the body helps to accomplish this goal (see chapter 6, "Best Damn Health Plan"). Also, specific brain exercises can help maintain and enhance intellectual faculties (see chapter 21, "Mental Exercise Is Brain Surgery")]. Dementing disorders present a growing challenge. At this time, these disorders are incurable and progressive, but early detection, intervention, and planning can result in improvements in the quality of lives of all those affected.

Lesson: Your body is generic, with exchangeable parts; your mind is unique and irreplaceable.

Applying the Lesson to Your Life

- Take care of your body and intellectual faculties. Good physical and mental health is no lifetime guarantee of mental fitness but acts as a protective factor.
- Be aware of the early signs and symptoms of dementing disorders. One of the classic signs of dementia is a decline in short-term memory as evidenced by such experiences as losing valuables (e.g., your car keys, eye glasses, or purse) or forgetting the bath-

water is running until you see water cascading over the tub. Disorientation may be observed so that you might not know the day of the week or the full date. Other potential warning signs relate to communication skills: you may notice that you experience difficulty following conversations, expressing yourself, or naming common objects such as a watch or a pen. You might also experience significant changes in mood or personality, becoming more erratic, unpredictable, and emotional than usual. Sometimes with early-stage dementing disorders, you might lose interest in previously enjoyed people and activities, become passive and reclusive, and possibly even neglect practices of basic hygiene and grooming. Feeling lost in familiar settings, such as failing to recognize you are shopping in your local grocery store, and difficulty completing routine tasks, like banking or paying your bills, would be other reasons for concern.

- Do not attempt to diagnose a dementing disorder by yourself. If you observe anything of concern, seek professional help. Most medical and mental-health professionals are trained to screen for these conditions and can refer you for more specialized tests or services, if necessary. Screening tools used by professionals consist of a few questions and only take minutes to complete, so there is virtually no down side to getting help.

CHAPTER 16

EVERYBODY WANTS
TO BE LOVED;
NOBODY WANTS
TO BE LOVEABLE

I have very bad news. I even hate to say it aloud, but: Your crap stinks! Yours, mine, and everybody else's. For this reason, nobody likes to deal with this reality. Our parents attended to us as infants and children out of love and obligation; love seems to neutralize the natural repulsion about excrement. As many people lose bowel control in their later years, it falls to their caretakers to handle this problem as a responsibility of their job. If we are smart, we should endeavor to bring loving, compassionate feelings back into the equation when we are the recipient of any caretaking, especially the dirty work.

There is a common dynamic I observe in the nursing home: residents feel some mixture of embarrassment, guilt, and anger about needing to receive personal services, especially when it involves more intimate and basic care such as being fed, having a diaper changed, or being bathed. As a consequence, they are exquisitely sensitive to the attitudes and behavior of the caretaker providing the service. If a caretaker conveys any feeling other than joy, residents often feel hurt, offended, and upset. Let's put aside the notion that caretakers are paid professionals who should exercise the highest caution and sensitivity and focus on the behavior of the recipient of the care. The bottom line is that it is in the better interests of the elderly person to be loveable when receiving assistance. Early in development, babies instinctively show a positive reaction to being cared for, which provides natural reinforcement to the caretaker. Babies with colic are so difficult to deal with in part because their incessant crying leads caretakers to feel hopeless, ineffective, unappreciated, and angry. Even my experience with my dog, Teddy, demonstrates the importance of this principle. In terms of work, our relationship is completely one-sided. He's never done a darn thing for me! Yet, I walk him—rain, snow, or shine. I feed him, clean him, and pay for his food, toys, and healthcare. Teddy has never cut the grass, picked up a dish, answered the phone, or paid a single bill. And I love him like crazy! How is this arrangement tolerable? Because he is unconflicted about his dependency, always happy to see me or be with me—he is infinitely loveable.

I realize that people may object to my suggestion that they can learn something about human relations from a dog. However, I believe my observation is apt: the more loveable, grateful, and positive a person is with a caretaker, the better the caretaker will feel, and the better the care received, period. We need to be a good receiver of care in order to improve our care.

Joyce, a native of Virginia, seemed to understand and practice this principle naturally. Widowed with no children, and eighty-four years of age, she was the personification of Southern charm. Joyce was genial and greeted everybody with a smile and some term of endearment such as "Darlin'," "Sugar," or "Dear." Despite the pleasantries, Joyce offered as many complaints to me as many other residents in the nursing home. She regularly voiced her discontent over meals, TV service, various social activities, and her roommate. Although she was frail, unable to function independently, and unhappy, she was easy to spend time with. Even after an upsetting session where she might angrily protest, or weep, she would pleasantly inquire about when I was planning to return, and offer a fond farewell, such as, "You take good care. You can come any time."

How could you not enjoy providing service to Joyce? Let me point out that the content of her sessions was similar in character to that of most other residents in the nursing home: an abundance of complaints and corresponding negative emotions. Time with her was not "happy hour." I was always greeted with delight, however, and sent away with warmth and gratitude—there was a "wagging tail" on both ends of the meeting that made it pleasing to care for her. In my experience, most workers in the nursing home desire to provide good services and relish being seen as, and feeling like, compassionate caregivers. When their services are well received, it is very satisfying and the work seems effortless to them. If met with antagonism, the work can feel laborious and unpleasant.

LIKEABILITY: NATURE OR NURTURE?

Is social allure an inborn trait or is it a product of parenting? Perhaps most important to ask is whether social skills can be learned and likeability increased? These questions are often posed with cases involving children enduring social rejection or neglect. In my experience, children who encounter social problems perceive themselves as lacking in intrinsic appeal, suggesting a permanent, immutable lack of likeability. Their parents often harbor the same gloomy thoughts. Fortunately, social skills can be taught and social appeal enhanced. Children experiencing social problems may engage in certain unattractive behaviors, such as angry outbursts or invasion of personal space, or fail to display attractive behaviors, such as smiling or offering compliments. When changes are made in behavior, the responses of others often change as well. Ultimately, other people respond to your behavior and if you respond in attractive ways, you will entice others and engender good will.

There are some unfortunate individuals who do not possess either adequate self-awareness or self-control to behave in an engaging or pleasing manner. For example, an elder with moderate to severe dementia cannot be expected to participate in any social interaction skillfully enough to ensure a positive connection the way Joyce does. In such instances where inability precludes deft social behavior, the onus is completely on the caretaker to manage the interaction. If the elder is at home, family members have to accept the limitations of their loved one and treat her accordingly. If in the nursing home, professional staff have to do the same. When professionals are involved in the care of a mentally incapacitated elder, family members can act as proxies. If the elder is incapable of acting so as to induce good feelings in their caretakers, then family members can. When I suggest this tactic, most family members understand and agree with me. In my experience, verbal thanks, written notes, and treats (e.g., donuts or other goodies) go a long way toward maintaining warm feelings in the caretaker-elder relationship. Of course, some family members of nursing-home residents have challenged the recommendation on the grounds that they should not have to do anything extra for paid professional staff. When such sentiments are expressed, I inform family members that they are correct that they do not have to do anything for staff workers but that it is advised because such offers are a great way to bring out the best in human nature. Can that ever be bad when the gestures need only be modest tokens?

In general, people seem to have forgotten this very basic tenet of human relations. The golden rule is as applicable today as ever. Projecting happiness, gratitude, and respect will bring these positive expressions right back around to us.

*Lesson: A good attitude and positive behaviors
will encourage excellent care from others.*

Applying the Lesson to Your Life

- Make it easy for people to be with you. The purpose of your meeting is inconsequential. What matters most is that you express happiness, kindness, respect, and affection. When your behavior and attitude reflect these positive qualities, you are more likely to get them back from those with whom you interact.
- Understand that being lovable is under your control; it is not determined by your circumstances or your genes. Even people

who require assistance, necessitating work for someone else, can behave in ways that are very appealing to a caretaker, which makes the interaction less cumbersome or awkward for both involved. Whereas some lucky individuals may be naturally more loveable by temperament or upbringing, we can all learn and enact these principles.

CHAPTER 17

FEELINGS: OUR TRUE COLORS

Many displays of emotion occur in the nursing home, so many, that if there were sand on the floor, a visitor might think he were on a grade-school playground. A recent encounter illustrates a typical expression of feelings in this setting. I was walking toward the first-floor nurse's station, which sits at the intersection of four wings, like the center of a compass, with four equal-length corridors extending out in each direction at ninety-degree angles. Residents often congregate at the end of hallways near the nurse's station—there is always at least one staff member available (and usually more during the morning shift when I am there), and residents quickly learn that they can easily gain assistance there, if needed. As I neared the area, I heard an exchange between two female residents and one male resident. The women were sitting in their wheelchairs talking to each other, and the male resident was approaching from their rear, intent on coming to the nurse's station. The women were situated in such a way as to partially block the hallway. The man: "Why don't you two get the hell out of the way? Can't you see people need to get by?" The women: "You are so rude. Why don't you just go around? We were here first." The man: "Who do you think you are—you don't own this place. Just move, you're blocking everybody." Spotting me, one of the women called out, "Dr. Dodgen, he's bothering us." The man snarled, "Now you're bringing him into this? Just shut your mouth and get out of the way."

Does an exchange between residents, such as the one above, reveal the nonsensical chatter of addled minds, meaning they should be tolerated or ignored by caregivers, or is there more import in these statements, which means that they deserve serious attention? If so, what is their meaning?

As a society, we place too little value on feelings and often fail to decode them. For example, in school we are taught academic skills in preparation for higher education, personal development, and the workforce. We are also instructed in other useful classes about nutrition, exercise, and the dangers of smoking and other potential substances of abuse. However, there is typically little or no education provided about feelings or relationships. In fact, there is often resistance to addressing such "personal" subjects in a school setting despite their relevance for our functioning as happy and competent human beings.

The central premise of Daniel Goleman's bestselling book *Emotional Intelligence: Why It Can Matter More Than IQ* is that emotional maturity is a neglected but critical ingredient of academic, professional, and social success.[1] As a psychotherapist, I see evidence of this neglect all the time. People don't usually give much attention to feelings unless they are troubled by them. Human experience consists essentially of thought, images, behavior, and feelings. Whereas all realms of experience are important, feelings may be the most crucial component. People frequently seek mental-health services because of emotional disturbances (e.g., sadness, anxiety) or for assistance with problematic behaviors stemming from troubling feelings (e.g., excessive alcohol consumption as an attempt to quell anxiety or to avoid confronting other problems in daily living). People often fail to realize that feelings serve important functions, including communication (to self and others) and motivation. Being skilled in acknowledging and understanding feelings is necessary for personal health and positive relationships.

Nature equips us with feelings for good reason. We are born preverbal and only begin to develop language skills in the second to third years of life. We learn about the world through the traditional five senses, yet feelings act as a sixth sense.[2] Information is not processed merely as cold, hard facts; we have feelings about what we perceive. Feelings comprise our only form of communication and basis for relating to the world before we can speak. Good caretakers are skilled in the language of emotions, and this guides their interaction with children. Feelings and their expression are universal and can be considered a common language.

Just as significant emotional communication precedes speech early in development, emotional expression becomes more prominent as sensory processing and communication skills deteriorate in the elderly. How much do feelings matter for a person in his eighties with medical problems, sensory trouble, and so on? Aren't there many more important things to be concerned about than their feelings? Right? Wrong. Certainly to be an effective caretaker, one needs to understand how the other person is feeling. Since an elderly person may not be effective at verbally communicating feelings, the caretaker must develop skills and insights in order to figure out a person's needs or concerns.

Review the following brief scenarios. As you read each one, attempt to identify the emotion being expressed by each individual and how you arrived at your conclusion.

- Edgar smiled while telling me of the reduction of pain and discomfort he was feeling. He was sleeping better and able to participate more fully in his physical therapies. As he sat in a relaxed manner on his bed, he also described a recent surprise visit from his daughter and her family.
- Speaking rapidly and loudly, Lynne stated, "She's always in that damn bathroom." With a scowl, she continued, "If she wants her own bathroom, she should get a single room. I'd like to yank her right out of there."
- With tears welling in his eyes and a quivering voice, Sean concluded, "I've lost everything—my house, my car, my money, and my health. All gone."
- In response to my question about her refusal to attend a physical-therapy appointment earlier in the morning, Marina leaned toward me, with eyes wide open and beads of sweat on her forehead: "They think I can do better than I can. I don't want to fall and I'm not going back there until I feel steady on my feet."

What feelings were being expressed by Edgar, Lynne, Sean, and Marina? You would be correct if you thought happiness, anger, sadness, and fear, respectively. What are the clues that helped you determine which emotion was being expressed? Facial expression is the most obvious source of information. Edgar's smile revealed enjoyment, just as Lynne's scowl, Sean's tears, and Marina's sweaty, wide-eyed expression signaled their feelings. Speech also provides key information about the emotional state of an individual; the rapidity and volume with which someone speaks, and the content of what is said, are useful evidence, too. Regarding the latter, specific themes are known to evoke characteristic feelings. Enjoyment indicates relief from a negative state (e.g., pain, hunger, or loneliness). For Edgar, the reduction of physical pain and discomfort from sleep deprivation, and relief of loneliness from a family visit, yielded happiness. Anger is evoked by frustration; Lynne's anger was stimulated by being denied access to her bathroom. Sadness, as expressed by Sean, informed us that a loss theme was active for him. Finally, the anxiety Marina expressed indicated the experience of fear, a concern about possible physical or emotional harm.

I purposely made the above vignettes brief to demonstrate how much we can learn about an individual simply by paying attention to his emotional state. We can quickly determine what he is feeling, what is important to him, and how best to respond. Referring to our residents, Edgar expressed happiness. Since in his case there was no problem, need anything be done? Actually, there was. His happiness communicated that he was in a positive state of mind. A general rule I observe is that it is equally necessary to respond to positive as to negative emotions. It was good to let Edgar know his message was received and to underscore his positive experience. For example, with Edgar, I stated, "That must feel so good to experience less pain," and, "Tell me more about the nice visit from your daughter." I gave these positive feeling states deliberate attention so that they would be more likely to remain in the forefront of Edgar's mind—this helps to maintain mood, morale, and motivation for more constructive behavior. It is generally helpful to accentuate the positive.

To deal with Lynne's frustration-induced anger, I initially allowed her a few minutes to blow off steam. It was evident to me that she could only talk, and not listen, while so upset. When I sensed the time was right, I offered a statement to convey my understanding of her sentiments, "It is frustrating to have to wait to do something like going to the bathroom. I understand how that could make you furious." Benefitting from venting her feelings and receiving emotional support, she calmed considerably. Recomposed, she was able to engage in a more practical problem-solving discussion. I offered her two alternatives, one was to wait with me until she could get into her bathroom and the other was to find her aide, who could take her to another bathroom; she chose the second option.

I want to point out how critical the tone and nature of my response were to helping Lynne. Can you imagine her reaction if I had offered a critical or unsympathetic reply, such as, "You are not the only person in here—you'll have to wait like everybody else." It obviously would have infuriated her. Since emotions function as communication, one of the most effective ways to interact with someone who is intensely emotional is to respond in a way to indicate you received the message—not to challenge her feelings or attempt to persuade her to feel another way.

Sean, the third resident, was distraught, as he reflected on the many losses he was experiencing. The primary function of sadness and crying is to call on caretakers for comfort. Compassionate witnessing, the presence of an understanding and concerned other, was the salve that I provided Sean. He required the reapplication of this emotional support numerous times until his grief subsided.

Marina was extremely fearful of falling. Moreover, she was upset with physical-therapy staff workers whom she perceived as insensitive to her worries. With Marina's consent, I spoke with her physical therapist, who was able to communicate his understanding of her concern and to work with her so that she felt safer and more secure.

From the vignettes, we see that when an individual is experiencing intense emotions, he is in a discharge mode; he is intent on expression and unable to attend well to what is being said to him. When emotional, the tendency is to seek relief, not take in. This is why therapists usually encourage individuals to talk first, before attempting to solve problems. They might also attempt to validate the feelings of an upset individual, but they would not try to alter or stop the expression of feeling. Emotions are automatic reactions; we are witnesses of our feelings. If we told ourselves what to feel, wouldn't we all just command ourselves to be happy all of the time? (The results, of course, would be disastrous, as we would be dangerously out of touch with the world. Substance abusers learn this painful lesson when they artificially induce happiness while their lives crumble around them.) The key to coping with a person's upset is to soothe feelings, restore balance, and then engage in practical problem solving.

I encounter many people in the nursing home and in my private practice who are unskilled in the ability to recognize their feelings. For example, Cynthia, a thirty-seven-year-old mother of three children, once commented, "I don't understand why I'm crying—it bothers me." She was sad and crying because her mother had died only five weeks earlier and she was not done grieving. She was unable to make the obvious connection. A failure to recognize their own emotions results in a very unsettling experience for people. They often complain of feeling possessed by an alien force, or crazy, because their feelings do not make sense to them. Sometimes a simple connection of the dots can be a powerful intervention, as was the case with Cynthia.

COLORS OF THE RAINBOW

How many different emotions do we experience? I could probably name fifty off the top of my head. Are they too numerous to label, as they appear to be? How do we recognize them in ourselves and others? Although there is scholarly debate, researchers agree enough to generate a list of primary emotions that serve as the basis of all emotional experiences. Silvan Tomkins, the widely acknowledged father of emotion research and theory, and one of his disciples, Paul Ekman, himself a highly acclaimed researcher and theoretician, have generated a list of primary emotions.[3] Tomkins and Ekman consider emotions innate, distinct, biologically programmed responses. As such, they are unlearned and universal—unlike language, for example. Ekman's cross-cultural research convincingly demonstrates the universality of emotional expression. In a typical experiment, Ekman asked subjects from different countries, including industrialized nations such as the United States and Japan, and undeveloped countries such as Papua New Guinea, to identify emotions being portrayed in facial pictures. All subjects performed with a high degree of accuracy, despite the widely divergent backgrounds of the subjects. Feelings tell us that something relevant to our well-being is happening. Every single human experiences the same feelings and expresses them in the same way. It should be noted, however, that circumstances may promote or inhibit the free expression of emotions. For example, in the workplace, people are generally more likely to attempt to suppress or disguise their feelings. Also, some individuals are more guarded than others and are less likely to openly reveal their feelings.

Tomkins describes emotions in terms of ranges of intensity. For example, he identifies anger–rage as a distinct emotion family, with the less intense anger on the left and more intense rage on the right. A representative list includes: the neutral emotion of surprise–startle; the positive emotions of interest–excitement and enjoyment–joy; and negative emotions of anger–rage, fear–terror, distress–anguish, and disgust–contempt. Tomkins posits that our emotions provide color and meaning to life and are the basis of a fundamental motivational scheme—to express all feelings and manage our lives to maximize the experience of positive feelings and minimize the negative. Below is a description of seven primary emotions, characteristic circumstances that evoke them, the function of each emotion, and associated facial expressions. Although physiological responses, such as heart rate and blood pressure, correlate with feeling states, because they are not easily detected they are not included in this discussion. In order to improve your feeling-recognition skills, it may be helpful to make faces in the mirror, watch actors portraying emotions, or obtain Ekman's book *Emotions Revealed: Recognizing Faces and Feelings to Improve Communication and Emotional Life*.[4]

Surprise–Startle. This emotion is designed to grab our attention, clear our minds, and orient us to a sudden, unexpected occurrence. Such a response allows for rapid evaluation for the determination of meaning and relevance. A loud scream from a resident's room, for example, will demand priority and immediate investigation from nursing-home staff workers. Or if you are walking down the street and hear a loud bang, you would need to be on the alert for potential danger until you identified the source. The feeling of surprise is expressed by wide-open eyes, open mouth, and raised eyebrows.

Interest–Excitement. The emotion of interest, characterized by a focused gaze and lowered eyebrows, supports concentration and thinking, and makes learning pleasurable and profitable.

Enjoyment–Joy. A smile is the unmistakable facial expression of enjoyment. This emotion is stimulated by relief from negative states such as hunger, physical pain, sexual tension, boredom, and loneliness. The function of this emotion is to reinforce and promote positive behavior, such as eating and socializing.

Anger–Rage. Anger is induced by two different circumstances, interference/obstruction/frustration, and physical or psychological attack. The function of anger in the first case is to forcefully remove obstacles; in the second to defend oneself. We recognize the expression of this emotion in a red face, a loud voice, and wide-open eyes. Dealing with an angry resident poses a special challenge for caretakers and demands the utmost in professionalism. Because anger is a natural response to anger, staff workers must be mindful to control their automatic reactions, as it would be most inappropriate to direct anger back at a resident. Once stimulated, we have no control over what we feel. We have considerable control, however, of how we express feelings. Caretakers must be sufficiently disciplined to maintain the privacy of their own feelings.

Fear–Terror. Characterized by a pale face, sweating, and wide-open eyes, fear is a reaction to the perceived threat of harm. The well-known fight-or-flight response is evoked by fear.

Distress–Anguish. Stimulated by the experience of loss, distress is evidenced by crying, a red face, and upward arching of the inner eyebrows. As discussed fully in another chapter (see "Loss: Subtraction and Addition"), the primary functions of this emotion are to motivate an individual to seek support and encourage others to provide comfort to the distressed individual.

Disgust–Contempt. Recognized by a raised upper lip and open mouth, disgust is experienced when we encounter something we consider offensive (e.g., foul-smelling food, an obnoxious person). The feeling is designed to motivate us to reject or move away from a repugnant stimulus.

From the foregoing discussion, it is abundantly clear that we are designed to feel, and do so continuously. What we feel is rarely a problem; how we handle our emotions is usually where the challenge lies. I often advise, "*Feel* like a barbarian, but *act* like a gentleman." Be aware of your feelings, but behave strategically, deliberately. In most situations, neither extreme of attempting to deny your feelings, or giving unfettered expression of them, is advisable. Emotions occur automatically, and often out of awareness, so it is helpful to develop ways to identify them. Recognition of feelings comes from knowing characteristic circumstances that evoke them (e.g., loss yields sadness); nonverbal behaviors (e.g., changes in facial expression and voice); and cognitive changes (e.g., content of thought).

Lesson: An understanding and skillful management of feelings are necessary for health, effective behavior, and good relationships.

Applying the Lesson to Your Life

- Memorize the list of primary emotions that I presented above. There is one neutral emotion, surprise–startle; two positive emotions, interest–excitement and enjoyment–joy; and four negative emotions, anger–rage, fear–terror, distress–anguish, and disgust–contempt.

- Monitor yourself regularly to identify how you are feeling. Express your feelings when and where appropriate. On a daily basis, act to maximize positive and minimize negative feelings. If you recognize that you're feeling sad, allow yourself to express that sadness in an appropriate place—with loved ones or alone, whatever feels most natural to you. Once you've expressed your sadness, you may find that you are better able to cope with the emotions such that they interfere less with your normal, daily functioning.

- Pay attention to the emotions expressed by others. Assist them to emote by encouraging them to share their feelings with you, and discussing the circumstances responsible for evoking their reaction. Let their feelings be your guide to effective interaction. For example, if a friend is sad, provide comfort; if happy, celebrate with him.

CHAPTER 18

CIRCLE OF LIFE

The circularity of life is perhaps most obvious in the similarities between young children and older adults. As the truism expresses, "We come into this world naked, toothless, and bald, and go out the same way." Highlighting the similarities of people at the end points of the life continuum, one finds that the person-environment relationship follows a predictable arc: we require heavy interpersonal support initially, which can be relaxed when we develop and mature and which must again be reapplied when we demonstrate diminishing physical abilities and mental competence.

Owing primarily to advances in public health, nutrition, and medicine, Americans are living longer and our population is aging. One corollary of a burgeoning elder population is that the number of nursing-home residents will continue to grow. Current estimates identify approximately 1.5 million nursing-home residents in the United States.[1] This number represents 1.5 million families, affecting many times more people. Because of the increasing prevalence of elders seeking placement in residential programs, many of us will have experiences with loved ones in nursing homes or other senior-care facilities (e.g., assisted-living facilities). Dealing with the elderly in residential facilities is not a challenge just for healthcare professionals or a small group of unfortunate families anymore: it will be a part of virtually all of our futures. Possessing insights and a conceptual framework to understand certain challenges attendant to the aging process can be helpful in reducing emotional upheaval and the consternation of family members and others who come into contact with our elders in care facilities; and it can promote compassion and enhance caretaking of this vulnerable population.

In my work in the nursing home, I have seen too many instances of family members of residents experiencing chagrin and responding with impatience and ridicule to their loved ones because of a failure to understand what they are observing. I have found it helpful for family, as well as staff members at times, when I relate some of the behavior of residents to that of small children in order to establish a more realistic mind-set and expectations. Generally speaking, the younger the child and the older the adult, the more alike they appear. Below is a discussion of commonalities to which I have become sensitive through my work at the nursing home.

Helplessness and dependency. Young children need a caretaker in order to survive. Their mental and motor skills are immature and undeveloped, so they cannot act or respond effectively. They are incapable of satisfying their most basic needs to be kept warm, clean, and fed, and to treat themselves if ill. Their dependence on their caretakers is complete; without the caretaker, the child would suffer and perish. The situation is the same with elder adults who have lost cognitive and motor skills due to illness, injury, or age-related deterioration. They, too, must rely on caretakers for survival. Patients often become frustrated and unhappy because they must rely on caretakers to meet their needs, and, unlike infants, adults can recognize the inefficiency inherent in having their needs met by another person.

Focus on the body and internal states. The human sensory systems are the means by which we learn about and make contact with the world outside of our bodies. Since both infants and older adults are not well connected to the outside world because of under-developed or deteriorated sensory systems, respectively, there is a preoccupation with bodily states. If impressions from the outside world register dimly in the mind, the inside world will be the focus. Small pains and discomforts become exaggerated, and complaining becomes a natural outgrowth of this, both to communicate what infants and elders are experiencing and to make some contact from the environment (the caretaker).

Our minds are designed to perceive and analyze stimulation coming from inside our bodies and from the external world. Normally, stimulation coming from the body is minimal and we pay little attention to our body. Common experiences resulting in an increased awareness of our body include feeling hunger or feeling extremely hot. Less commonly, we may become aware of an ankle after experiencing pain from falling; otherwise, we almost never pay any attention to our ankles. In the elder nursing-home population, residents often have ailments that cause pain and discomfort, drawing unusual attention to their bodies; when these ailments are combined with fading impressions from the world around them, nursing-home patients can become negatively focused, almost obsessed with their complaints. An antidote to this negative self-absorption is trying to keep residents "in the world." That is, since the mind cannot focus on the internal and external information at the same time, it is best to occupy the mind with activity and interactions with others in order to maintain an external focus. Indeed, it can helpful to redirect attention away from negative self-absorption whether the person in question is a child, an adolescent, or an adult.

Emotions have primacy over intellect. As children develop, their mental faculties grow and improve. With better mental skills, children become more effective at controlling behavior and regulating emotional reactions with thoughts and reason. The emotions of very young children have much more influence over their behavior than do the emotions of older children and adults. As a result, children are progressively improving in self-control. Asking a baby not to cry would prove fruitless; such small children are driven by feeling. However, a school-age child may feel like crying but not do so if he thinks it might be inappropriate or poorly received by his peers or by the teacher. Adults often have strong emotions but do not act on them. At work, for example, one may be very upset but show no outward sign of it. As adults advance in age, intellectual skills fade just as physical skills do. As these skills wane, so does self-control and the ability to respond appropriately. This is why older adults can be more easily upset, unreasonable, and "babylike." It is not unusual to see residents in the nursing home behaving like children in cliques, threatening one another (or staff), making outrageous demands, and using other emotion-driven behavior.

Detachment from the environment and from responsibility. Being totally dependent, immobile, and with weak sensory systems, small children are hardly aware of the world around them. The little awareness they possess is focused on the meeting of their basic needs for survival and comfort by the immediate environment. With age and maturation, their awareness of their surroundings grows from familiarity with caretakers, to siblings, extended family, schoolmates and friends, and so on. In other words, the zone of awareness goes from just the home to ever larger circles outside of the home. The process is the opposite for the aging adult. From the larger world their environment shrinks to the nursing home, their family, and their room. With this process comes disorientation. Even residents with relatively well-maintained mental faculties still have difficulty identifying the day of the week, the month or the year, as this information is less relevant for functioning in their shrinking worlds.

Fragility and sensitivity to change. In order to cope effectively with challenges, we need certain critical-thinking skills and the ability to act to solve problems. Since young children have meager coping skills, they cannot adapt well to changes in their environments. Significant changes in temperature, diet, light, and sound will be very disturbing to them, so their caretakers are required to manage these and other conditions. As adults advance in age and experience an erosion of mental and physical skills, they become increasingly sensitive to changes and are easily disturbed as well. For example, a minor change in the daily schedule at the nursing home will often result in confusion and emotional upset among residents.

Limited communication skills. In order for a caretaker to meet the needs of a child, the child must be able to communicate her needs. Very early in development, the communication is crude and generalized (i.e., crying) and requires an interested caretaker to go through the usual checklist of possibilities to determine what the child needs. As a child grows older and becomes verbal, she can be much more precise in communicating her needs, and this makes for much more efficient caretaking. As adults age, communication can be compromised by impaired hearing, problems with speech (e.g., poor articulation due to a stroke), or mental impairment affecting thought. The combination of dependency on a caretaker and poor communication skills is especially unfortunate and often results in mutual frustration of caretaker and child or nursing-home resident.

Surplus of negative emotions. One of our most important but least discussed functions as parents is to assist children to manage negative emotions. Children have a surplus of negative feelings generated by dealing with the large and complex world. Anxiety, embarrassment, anger, jealousy, envy, disappointment, and sadness are experienced in dealing with different life circumstances, and satisfactory development depends on the adequate handling of these emotions and the situations that evoke them. Most parents recognize that even the happiest, most well-adjusted child experiences all these emotions. To think that a happy child should not experience negative emotions is to misunderstand children, and life, completely. It is not the existence of these feelings that is problematic but how they are mishandled.

Again, as it is with children, so it is with elder adults. Older adults experience many negative feelings and need assistance with their effective management. Imagine the kinds of feelings generated by feeling ill; being dependent on others; being separated from your home, family, and friends; being cared for by strangers; and living with strangers. Anyone not expecting strong negative feelings under these circumstances is in for a very rude awakening. This is probably where I see the most common and biggest mistake made by families dealing with the placement of family members in the nursing home. Children or others responsible for the placement of the elder adult in the nursing home often attempt to deny or suppress the negative reactions of the person being placed there, and this creates a much worse situation.

Levels of competence differ. Children acquire skills and capabilities along a loosely defined timeline. One child may begin to talk at fourteen months, another at twenty-four months. As long as the developmental milestones are achieved by certain ages, there is nothing to be concerned about. There is natural variation in human development. Pushing a child, or worse, criticizing a child for her speed of acquisition does not accelerate the process and often generates problems.

Similarly, adults *lose* skills at different rates. One adult may function totally independently and normally at seventy-five years of age while another may be completely dependent and seriously incapacitated at age sixty-five. Neither the child nor the impaired adult has much choice in the matter, and pushing them usually only makes things worse.

Women are most often the caretakers. Although gender roles have changed from several decades ago, women are still typically the primary caretakers of children and elderly parents. I mention this point as an alert to all daughters. Through my work at the nursing home, I have seen daughters be the lead contact person for their resident parent even when there were multiple male siblings. If this is not a role you would want, it is advisable to have a meeting with your siblings to do some planning before your parents require family assistance.

With so many similarities between elders and infants, why does it seem much more difficult to care for elderly parents than for children?

I believe that there are several factors that contribute to the difficulty of adult children caring for elderly parents (relative to caring for their young children). When parents care for their children, they are relatively young themselves. When they care for their elderly parents, they are relatively old themselves. There is also a stage-of-life issue: at the time when they need to provide assistance to their elderly parents, they are feeling more like coasting than taking on more responsibility and work. The role reversal is also difficult to accept. Our parents are supposed to care for us and not the reverse. In caring for them when aged or infirmed or both, we are aware of their future passing—and of our own mortality.

One general point I wish to convey with this discussion is that people possess different skill levels and competencies. In order to improve the chances of an individual's success, we should tailor the environment to suit his specific needs. Human development is an amazing process that can be described as the internalization of elements of the material and social environments to build physical and mental structures. A supportive environment is necessary to provide food and emotional nutrients that a person can absorb and use to promote personal growth. In addition to our obvious needs for water, air, and nourishment, we require the presence of caretakers to ensure supplies of the psychological necessities. Just as nutrients for the body are consumed and employed by infants to build and operate their bodies, psychological functions must be learned from caretakers to achieve emotional, intellectual, and behavioral maturation. As we master skills and gain competence to function independently, the need for outside assistance shrinks. When there is regression in independent functioning for any reason, the appropriate level of assistance must be provided in order to compensate for the loss of life skills.

It can be helpful to have a system to gauge a person's functional skills in order to determine whether there is a need for assistance. In my practice I employ a developmental inventory to provide some objective assessment of the developmental achievement of young children.[2] The scale provides guidelines against which to compare a child in order to measure his progress on such skill dimensions as fine motor skills (e.g., writing, buttoning, and picking things up), gross motor skills (e.g., walking, running, jumping), self-care skills (e.g., feeding and dressing), receptive and expressive language skills (e.g., following verbal instructions and speaking in sentences, respectively), and social skills (e.g., making eye contact). I employ the scale for children who are six years of age and younger and have suspected developmental problems; this provides a more objective and definitive way of identifying deficient areas and guiding interventions.

I have found that the developmental scale can be useful, too, in the nursing home to assist family and staff members to adjust expectations and to ensure that the proper level of assistance is provided. For example, James was a married seventy-three-year-old, stroke-impaired resident who was often cantankerous with everyone—family and staff members alike. The stroke that James suffered was on the right side of his brain, with obvious functional impairments from paralysis of the left side of his body. Because his speech was unaffected, he appeared more competent than he actually was. Cognitive and emotional changes from the stroke were less apparent but no less real; they included emotional outbursts, a limited attention span, and social problems resulting from his mercurial ways. According to his family members, this behavior was out of character for him. It was clear to me that James was being perceived by his family as willfully difficult and childish, rather than mentally impaired. It was helpful to point out to his family members that despite his verbal competence and apparent normality, James was functioning on emotional, behavioral, and social levels like a preschool child. For example, since he was unable to stand or walk without assistance, his gross motor skills were equivalent to those of about a one-year-old child. His requirements for assistance during dressing and undressing and washing his face placed his self-help skills in the range of a typical two-to-three-year-old. And his poor ability to maintain attention and tendency to blame others for his temper outbursts were similar to the social behavior of a three-to-four-year-old child.

Recognizing James's levels of functioning helped family and staff members to adjust their expectations, experience less emotional upset, and provide proper assistance to him.

Lesson: The young and the elderly have much in common, which generates insights into caretaking.

Applying the Lesson to Your Life

- As a family member and/or caretaker of an elder, consider making the extra effort to be aware of the strengths, weaknesses, and competencies of the one you are caring for. Although it may be uncomfortable and upsetting to loosely measure a parent's behavior by the standards of young children, it can be useful for setting appropriate expectations. Especially for elders residing in care facilities, family members should seek the advice and support of professionals who are caring for the resident.
- In order to ensure happiness and success, make certain to adjust your ministrations to the specific abilities, needs, and desires of the one whose well-being you are in charge of. The world tends to provide for our needs in a coarse, one-size-fits-all manner; customizing support helps to optimize the fit and to improve the chances of good outcomes, reducing stress for family members, caretakers, and recipients of the care.

CHAPTER 19

TURN OFF, UNPLUG, DROP OUT

"This isn't so bad here. Simple life. Outside world is of little or no concern. Nice bed, TV, and meals provided." The first time I noticed myself having these thoughts, I wondered if I were losing my mind: I was admiring the life of a nursing-home resident! On the face of it, a very active, able-bodied man has no business being envious of nursing-home life. Further reflection allowed me to recognize that I was reacting to two factors that are particularly salient in the nursing-home setting: seclusion and simplicity. As an institution with residents, some temporary and others permanent, the nursing home is a self-contained world; a resident could literally come here and never have to leave for years, if ever. In addition, it is an uncomplicated environment compared to many other settings that we encounter in life outside of the nursing-home walls. Set up this way for the comfort of the elders living here, the nursing home has made me aware of the advantages of integrating measured doses of seclusion and simplicity into anyone's life.

Regarding the insular nature of the nursing home, I do not mean to suggest that it is literally cut off from civilization—it is nicely situated in a suburban setting fully accessible by roads, and it provides the conveniences of modern life, including TV and telephone services, among other amenities. It is the residents who are detached from aspects of the world, and spending time with them really is a process of entering into their narrowed domains. This observation was driven home to me during the aftermath of Superstorm Sandy. The storm devastated parts of New Jersey; some areas are still struggling to recover, years later. I live approximately ten miles from the nursing home where I provide services. As a consequence of the storm, in my home we lost electrical service for about seven days, and TV, telephone, and cell-phone services were inconsistently available. My office is only about two miles from the nursing home. I was unable to provide services in my office for the same period of time because of problems with electrical power. However, during this time period I was able to practice in the nursing home. My usual fifteen-minute drive was completely disrupted. Huge fallen trees blocked my course, power lines draped across roads, and traffic lights were not working, making for tricky maneuvers at intersections. My formerly direct, leisurely drive became a harrowing, serpentine journey. When I got to the nursing home, however, it was business as usual. Powered by generators, the nursing home fundamentally was unfazed by the storm. Most of the town around the facility was dark throughout the week, but, charged with the responsibility to safeguard the residents, the nursing home was properly equipped and managing well.

That I was simultaneously existing in two very different worlds, one inside the nursing home and the other in the surrounding vicinity, was starkly evident in talking to residents. Two days after the storm hit, I felt able to make the trip safely to the nursing home. After surviving the trip in, I had one of my first therapy sessions with Veronica. A resident of the nursing home for several years at the time, Veronica was living in the room with her husband of fifty-four years, James. Veronica made several perfunctory comments about the storm and quickly moved on to more pressing matters—her complaint about having to deal with an aide with whom she was unfamiliar. Her usual aide was unable to attend work because of transportation problems. Veronica was angry and opined that if the nursing home really cared about its own workers, and its residents, it would provide transportation for the employees. It was bizarre and amazing to engage in such a discussion— and incredibly enlightening. The state had just survived a catastrophic storm. The devastation was visible from any of the many windows in the nursing home. The grounds were covered with large tree limbs and other organic litter. In addition, news reports on TV and telephone calls from family members and friends detailed the wreckage. Yet Veronica was carrying on in her usual manner. She was cognizant of the storm, but it had no more impact on her than a TV show about a hurricane in Miami. Her concerns centered on her personal, immediate situation, while the rest of the world around her quite literally had been all but blown apart.

I am retelling this story not to criticize Veronica for being self-centered; most of the other residents I spoke to had similar attitudes. In addition, conversations like the one with Veronica provided opportunities for valuable insights. The constricted focus that Veronica exhibited is not undesirable. It is enviable. The sequestered life of the nursing-home resident, free from the many obligations and responsibilities of daily life, can have the effect of narrowing a resident's attention to the immediate circumstances—the here and now. Detached from their pasts, and with futures of uncertain lengths and quality, the here and now is precisely where residents should place their attention. In fact, popular spiritual teachers, such as Eckhart Tolle and Ram Dass, as well as psychologists on the forefront of the positive psychology movement, such as Mihaly Csikszentmihalyi, extol the virtues of mindful awareness of the present moment.[1] The seemingly small details of daily existence in the nursing home have a pronounced impact on the residents' perceived quality of life. To the casual observer, a resident's fussing over getting chicken salad for lunch instead of a grilled-cheese sandwich might seem like silliness, because a suitable substitute meal was provided. However, if life is centered on the immediate circumstances, the importance of small details is magnified. Quality of life for residents like Veronica, who are mentally competent and astute, is a function of fidelity to the activity schedule, meal orders, and so on. Because it is best not to obsess over the past, or to dwell on a dubious future, the here and now better be good or a resident will be very unhappy.

Being fully absorbed in the present moment to the exclusion of broader concerns describes a basic formula for contentment for all of us. The attractiveness of being locked into the present by a single purpose accounts for the oddly positive reaction people have in dealing with crises. Many of my private patients have noted that an unexpected positive of addressing a crisis situation is that, because it is all-consuming, it allows them to ignore other negative or less interesting aspects of their lives. One might wonder if we can achieve this kind of exclusive focus without having to be in crisis or ready for a nursing home. I believe that a partial solution is to turn off, unplug, and drop out. Turn off the TV, unplug your devices, and drop out of the rat race, at least for brief periods of time. Temporary isolation can be good. We seem to have acquired a deep fascination with connection—to people, to devices, to people through devices, to games, to gadgets, and to information. And the faster the connection, the better—we can receive more information and stimulation per unit of time. We would do well to remember that the royal road to the brain is through the senses; the more we take in, the more this vital organ must process. We are over-taxing our brains and minds. Here again we can look at infants as a clear example; if a small child is brought from home to a busy restaurant with his family, the otherwise-calm infant can suddenly become irritable, fuss, and cry—all because of overstimulation. He is being bombarded with too many stimuli at once. This happens too, with adults, when we neglect to temporarily turn off, unplug, and drop out. Our psyches are not empty vessels to be relentlessly filled with stimulation from the outside. The mind is tasked with the considerable challenge of monitoring, analyzing, and integrating information from outside and inside our bodies.

We probably are all guilty of being seduced by the ever-present lure of titillation and activity. It seems as if the preferred American attitude has become extraversion, seeking stimulation, and acting on the world. Author Susan Cain has dubbed this cultural attitude the Extrovert Ideal, that is, a preference for and promotion of the traits of the extrovert—outgoing, gregarious, fast-moving and not given to contemplation or self-reflection.[2] The world around us is ready to support this mentality with continuous stimulation. However, we should not forget that symmetry and balance are the rules of nature: we do not expect to have one arm significantly shorter than the other, or to have one blue eye and one brown. The same rule applies to our mental functioning. Being out of balance in one way or the other is problematic. If we were almost exclusively outwardly focused, we would function like subhuman animals—our behavior would be determined primarily by external stimulation. So far as we can determine, we are the only beings capable of consciousness that allows for the reflexive study of our own minds. We throw this away when we pursue and respond to external stimuli like simple beasts. Yet if we were being completely inward-looking, we would be autistic, absorbed in our minds and unresponsive to the world. Some middle ground is advised whereby an individual has time and space to introspect, and is also actively involved in life at other times.

THE SIMPLE LIFE

In addition to the relative isolation from many features of the world, which allows for increased attention to the present moment, the nursing home is a relatively reduced, straightforward setting compared to a hospital, mall, business office, supermarket, or private home. For example, I usually provide services in the nursing home during the morning hours. A typical morning schedule for a resident includes waking up; being cleaned, groomed, and dressed; eating breakfast; and taking medications. Those residents who receive physical or occupational therapies are taken to the rehabilitation department; others are free to choose from a variety of activities, including the option to remain in their respective rooms. Just such a schedule will keep residents busy until lunchtime. Those of us capable of independent performance of the activities of daily life can accomplish these tasks prior to engaging in a full day's work. Clearly, the life of a resident is simplified, which is not to be confused with easy. Nevertheless, there are no complex problems to solve or major decisions to be made; and the goals are self-evident and achievable, providing for simple pleasure and satisfaction. To some, there may appear to be a whole lot of nothing going on: that is a correct perception. And that is the point. The aims that we pursue outside of the nursing home are often difficult to achieve, and the results are hard to assess. For example, how would we measure success in our careers, marital life, child-rearing efforts, and endeavors to be a good person? Sometimes a focus on getting out of bed, cleaning up, and eating a meal is a welcome counterbalance to ostensibly higher pursuits. The schedule I described above is strangely similar to the one I recently enjoyed on vacation, except that instead of receiving physical therapies I went to the hotel gym.

At times we need to be free from demands and heavy stimulation because we require relative quiet to study the contents of our minds. Freedom from the bombardment of stimulation allows for introspection, full attention to the present moment, and the pursuit of simple pleasures. Even temporary escape can be restorative.

Lesson: Retreat from the world is healthy and necessary in order to connect with your inner self and to find balance and serenity.

Applying the Lesson to Your Life

- Seek to escape in order to balance your mind. Whether you take a ten-day vacation to a remote cabin in the woods or simply take a long walk on your lunch break at work, you can make a conscious effort to seek out peace and solitude as a soothing counterbalance to the chaotic and complex daily lives we lead.
- Try these recommendations: practice daily meditation, schedule daily blackouts of electronica, take baths, exercise, engage in the regular practice of religion or other spiritual activities, and practice yoga.
- Engage in any activity that is engrossing and fully absorbs your attention and interest. Only you can determine the activities with the right amount of complexity and that require the proper level of effort to allow for your enjoyment.

CHAPTER 20

FAMILY MATTERS

C hanging trends in national values and behavior appear to be contributing to the destruction of American nuclear- and extended-family relationships. High divorce rates, increased mobility, an increase in out-of-wedlock births, the seeming endorsement of self-interest and total independence as a cultural ideal, and the valuation of career over family are some factors that appear to have radically changed the traditional family structure. The concept of home has even changed. The former model of home as a nest representing safety and security and a family base from which offspring can venture and return to is vanishing. Currently, a home is more likely to be perceived as an invest-ment property to be flipped rather than the sacred homestead it used to represent.

These changes create a greater sense of impermanence and even the belief that it is "every man for himself." The purpose of this chapter is not to judge or criticize this zeitgeist but rather to raise awareness of the consequences of choices we make. Many older people speak positively and longingly about their former neighborhoods and their connections with siblings, aunts, uncles, and cousins nearby, and with longtime neighbors who were like family. There was a deep sense of stability and support. The prior family structure provided security and permanence and formed the bedrock of society. Its disappearance comes at a cost.

One's choice of work or decision about where to live has major implications for one's quality of life. In fact, unintended negative con-sequences are perhaps most evident when older adults move to warmer climates in order to gain personal comfort but also unwittingly lose valuable support systems. This was the case for Suzanne, a retired elementary-school teacher, and Edward, a retired electrical engineer, who had decided to sell their home in Essex County, New Jersey, and move to a senior community in Florida. The climate and lifestyle suited them well for several years. Living around other seniors in a condominium with a pool and community center located on a golf course was idyllic. Sadly, however, Edward experienced a fatal heart attack after living there for six years. Both he and Suzanne were seventy-four years old at the time. After recovering from the loss of her husband, Suzanne reported managing acceptably well until about two months prior to coming to the nursing home. She recalled that, although she continued to derive some enjoyment from being with her friends and living in the beautiful community, she never felt quite the same happiness without her beloved partner. Even with gracious friends who attempted to include her in activities, she often felt like a misplaced third wheel.

Suzanne was diagnosed with a case of pneumonia, which landed her in a hospital near her home in Florida. Because her stay there was lengthy, she experienced significant deconditioning. She lost weight and became weak and unsteady on her feet; she was also emotionally shaken by the episode. Suzanne and her only son, who had remained in his home in Essex County, thought it best for her to receive rehabilitation at the care center where I provide services, due to its proximity to his home.

While in the nursing home, Suzanne began to report the experience of anxiety, despite making improvements in her physical rehabilitation, which generated a referral to me. She shared with me that the experience of temporary incapacity provided a frightening glimpse of future possibilities never previously considered: "What if I get sick again?" "Injured?" "What if I suffer more permanent disability?" "Who will take care of me?" "Who will manage my affairs (such as handling my banking, paying my bills, and so on)?" These and other troubling questions tormented her. She had developed good friends but none she trusted so much or felt comfortable burdening with these responsibilities. Her son was willing and able to assist her in New Jersey, but she had no social network here.

Suzanne felt caught between two worlds. Always well dressed and groomed, with piercing blue eyes and short salt-and-pepper hair, she had the appearance of a younger woman. She was in full command of her mental faculties and still enjoyed a variety of activities, so she was too youthful and vital for long-term placement in the nursing home. Although her son reported a willingness to support her remaining in the area, he could not accommodate her in his home. She experienced much angst before deciding to remain in New Jersey in an assisted-living facility following her rehabilitation in the nursing home.

Suzanne came to realize that when at such a vulnerable stage of life, it was not best to be far from loved ones. I have come to believe that, generally, it is never good to be isolated from the family support system. We not only need guidance and support when old or compromised in some way but also can benefit at virtually any time from assistance with marital advice, raising a family, or engaging in critical decisions related to career, investments, or major purchases such as an automobile or a home.

In my private practice, I have treated many young couples who moved away from their respective families for work or to live in a desired town, only to realize unexpected challenges. For instance, Jason, twenty-eight, and Amanda, twenty-six, came for treatment because of marital problems they were experiencing. They had moved together to northern New Jersey from Pittsburgh, Pennsylvania, where they both grew up. The couple relocated in response to an attractive career opportunity for Jason at a pharmaceutical company. Amanda was able to find work as a fitness instructor shortly after moving to the area. By their reports, the couple successfully navigated the challenges of moving to a completely unknown area, adjusting to new jobs, buying a home, and having their first child. The difficulties arose when Amanda became pregnant with their second child. A combination of factors—Amanda's feeling tired and sick, the demands of caring for a toddler, and Jason's increasingly long hours spent working—resulted in Amanda feeling overwhelmed and in the couple's mutual unhappiness.

The couple had not made it a priority to establish a solid social network. Without historical family ties to the area, they did not know anyone when they arrived. They were content to focus first on their careers, then on the family unit, and ultimately on nesting in their nice home. Although they reported being happy with their neighborhood, they knew the neighbors only well enough to exchange superficial pleasantries.

But the couple had a considerable support system in Pittsburgh. Both sets of parents were alive and healthy. In addition, Amanda had two older sisters and Jason had one, all of whom would have happily assisted them. Unfortunately, the distance between the couple and their respective families was prohibitive. The couple's problem could be summarized as follows: too much stress and too little support. Having Amanda's mother stay with them temporarily proved helpful. Also, since both Amanda and Jason were raised as practicing Jews, they accepted my recommendation to begin attending a local synagogue for spiritual and social support.

It can be very helpful to have nearby parents, siblings, or longtime friends to check out a home with first-time buyers, to give advice about landscaping, to have over to provide a respite for an exhausted mother who was up all night with a sick child, or to share a regular Sunday dinner.

Lesson: There are hidden costs to mobility and independence, which can increase insecurity and alienation.

Applying the Lesson to Your Life

- Remember that no man is an island. A strong support system consisting of family and longtime friends is as crucial to our success and happiness as are personal skills, achievements, financial opportunities, and attractive climates.
- When pondering options that may affect proximity to and availability of your support system, consider not just current circum-

stances but also future possibilities, including potential changes
of status in work, finances, health, and family.

- If you are presently alienated from your family, strongly consider
  reconciliation. Except in rare cases, we are better with family
  than without.
- If you do not have a family support system, make it a priority
  to construct a strong social network. You can do this by volunteering at a local soup kitchen or youth organization, attending
  religious services regularly, finding an exercise group, joining a
  book club, or attending a weekly cooking class, for example.

CHAPTER 21

MENTAL EXERCISE IS BRAIN SURGERY

Perhaps almost all residents in the nursing home recognize that they must exercise their bodies to keep them healthy, strong, and well functioning, especially in the subacute unit, where they come for rehabilitation after a hospital stay. Residents soon learn, to their dismay, that their body can become deconditioned very quickly. The evidence comes in the form of obvious changes, such as soft, sagging muscles, and in functional decrements—they simply cannot do things they could do effortlessly just weeks before illness or injury hit them.

It seems much more surprising to people that the brain operates on the same basic principle as the rest of the body: use it or lose it. And, just as a muscle requires exercise, so does the brain: it grows and changes in response to stimulation. Our brains are organs, not machines, and as such they are alive and plastic (they change). The notion of the brain as malleable is a relatively recent one. While I was earning my undergraduate and graduate degrees in the late 1970s through the mid-1980s, every psychology and biology textbook I read described the brain the same way: a complex and fascinating—but unchanging—organ. At that time it was thought that, like other organs of the body, any modification in structure or function could be due only to dysfunction or deterioration. Scientists also thought that we were born with a finite number of brain cells (neurons), a total that would diminish over time, leading to inevitable age-related decline and promising little chance of recovery from brain injury.

Current research, however, has demonstrated that the brain is capable of significant change—there can be new cell production and alterations of functional and structural relationships between existing neurons—processes referred to as *neuroplasticity*. The discovery of brain plasticity has been enthusiastically welcomed by clinicians because of the exciting potential it suggests for building and sustaining intellectual strength and mental health. This means that the relationship between brain and behavior is more complex than previously thought. We were accustomed to thinking of the brain as the determinant of behavior; it is now known, though, that behavior can remodel the brain.[1] Therapists have known for a very long time that adjustments in action and thinking are beneficial for an individual suffering from emotional and behavioral problems; most exciting is the new scientific evidence that behavior changes are reflected in modifications in brain operations. Psychiatrist Daniel Amen, through the measurement of brain activity using the technique of single-photon emission computed tomography (SPECT), reveals salutary alterations in neuronal functioning that result from traditional psychiatric and psychotherapeutic interventions.[2] Yet fervor must be tempered by a dose of reality: like the dual-edged sword, change can cut both ways.

The adaptability of the brain simultaneously holds the potential for improvement or for degeneration, depending on the choices an individual makes, as was exemplified by the case of Mario. At the time of my initial consultation with him, Mario had been a resident at the nursing home for about three months. After an apparently good initial adjustment, he had become increasingly isolated and uncooperative with staff workers, which prompted the referral to me. He was fully compliant in the interview, appearing friendly and eager to talk. His grooming was fair—he was unshaven and had a thick head of hair that he pulled back into a pony tail, giving him the look of a much younger man. Mario reported that he was widowed and had two daughters from whom he had been estranged for many years. Living alone, he had been convinced to seek a residential facility by a longtime female friend. Disability due to injury of his spine had progressed to the point of a complete loss of feeling and use of his legs.

During the interview, Mario exhibited symptoms of mild to moderate cognitive impairment. I noted a significant delay before he spoke, and once started, he sometimes stopped before completing a thought—a sign of anomic aphasia (also known as word-finding difficulty). He also exhibited impaired judgment, as evidenced in his response to my question, What would be the proper thing to do if you found a woman's purse in the grocery store? Instead of the expected responses, take it to the lost-and-found section or find a store employee, he answered, "I would go through it and look for ID. If I couldn't find her in the store, I would take it to her address." In addition to the noted problems with communication and judgment, Mario's memory was spotty, and he was prone to low moods and irritability.

One of four children, he was born and raised in West Orange, New Jersey. Mario quit high school during his senior year to enlist in the United States Marine Corps. Following an honorable discharge, he served an apprenticeship before becoming a journeyman member of the Plumbers and Pipefitters Union. Retired for fourteen years, he variously described himself as a pipefitter, a welder, or a construction worker. A seventy-nine-year-old Korean War veteran, he was a surprisingly powerful man. Mario always insisted on a handshake when I entered his room, which provided him with the entertainment of applying his pythonlike grip to my hand and challenging me to escape. A quintessential outdoorsman, he loved hunting, fishing, camping, and riding motorcycles. Because of incapacitation, he had been unable to participate in his favorite sporting activities.

When I asked about his adjustment to the nursing home, Mario explained that he had initially reconciled himself to the fact that his disability necessitated it. He felt that he had come into the facility with a positive mind-set, and staff observations supported his assertion. Shortly after moving in, however, he realized the permanence of his stay and became sharply aware of his difficulty in complying with the demands of institutional life—eating, bathing, toileting, and going to bed on *their* schedule. His response was to hunker down in his room and refuse to come out, except to be bathed twice a week; on most days, he even resisted the invitation to be moved from his bed to a wheelchair. It appeared that all he wanted to do was eat and watch old movies. Stacks of DVDs brought from home filled the bottom of the TV stand in his room.

When I entered his room for sessions, I sometimes felt as though I were going into a movie theater after the last show—if I visited him before housekeeping cleaned up, boxes of candy, bags of potato chips, and soda cans littered the area in and around his bed. Apparently fueled by excessive caffeine intake, he stayed up all night watching TV, much to the dismay of his roommate, who complained to staff workers. Mario slept most of the day. He ignored staff requests to turn his TV off during the night and advice to normalize his sleep schedule. His eating habits were also a concern of the dietician. Mario's response to my inquiries about his behavior was one of defiance: "If I want to stay in my room, who cares? I'm not hurting anyone." "Besides," he went on, "What am I missing? I tried going to all of the activities. They're boring. I used to bench press two hundred and fifty pounds. I don't think that doing arm lifts from my wheelchair is an activity that is going to build any new muscle—I'm stronger than you are. One day they had us playing balloon volleyball; another day, bowling on the floor with a plastic ball and pins. Those are baby games! And forget bingo. Half the people were asleep."

Mario's complaints seemed like self-defeating rationalizations. Was there any justification in challenging him? Since he was already showing signs of cognitive decline when he arrived at the nursing home, he was at risk for more intellectual degeneration. Mario's actions and comments disclosed his lack of acceptance and his negative attitude. He was preoccupied with a variety of behaviors that were encouraging brain damage rather than intellectual enhancement: maintaining poor sleep hygiene, engaging in little physical activity, creating social isolation, eating a poor diet, and staying in a monotonous environment.[3]

His sleep habits were problematic for many reasons: he was disturbing his roommate, putting himself out of phase with the routine and activities of the facility, and interfering with important brain functions. Staying up almost all night and attempting to sleep during the day, he was ensuring himself poor-quality sleep. Crucial maintenance activities are performed in the brain during sleep, including processes critical to an individual's abilities to maintain attention, learn new material, and consolidate memories.

Mario's refusal to leave bed except for a couple of times in a week guaranteed physical and social inactivity and constancy of his environment. Physical exercise promotes brain health through the increase of blood flow and oxygenation of the brain, and through the release of biochemicals that protect brain cells and augment their functioning.

Even though he had a roommate with whom he could interact from his bed, Mario ignored him. He kept the curtain drawn, and since he rarely left the bed, they hardly spoke. Social activity is beneficial, and a lack of it is harmful, for a variety of reasons. One way that it is helpful is in activation of areas of the brain that are stimulated by social contact, areas that will atrophy without sufficient stimulation. In fact, physical and social activity are recognized protective factors against dementia.

Sameness fosters boredom and fails to excite us emotionally or intellectually. Brain atrophy is hastened in a minimally stimulating environment. Researchers have found that training elders in specific cognitive skills, such as memory, problem solving, and perceptual speed, can prevent age-related decline in those and related skills.[4] Although it is yet to be established exactly what types of cognitive stimulation and training are best, it appears certain that the tasks must be sufficiently challenging to require sustained concentration and effort. Formal education is a good example of a brain-enhancing process and is a well-established protective factor that guards against dementing disorders. Some experts recommend that elders learn a new language or complex dance moves to maintain brain health.[5] Obviously, Mario had kept himself in an intellectually impoverished environment, which only encouraged further erosion of his cognitive functioning.

And his diet, dominated by simple carbohydrates such as candy, potato chips, and soda, not only was bad for his weight and general health but also could result in unstable blood-sugar levels and impairments in attention and memory.

Before I attempted to persuade Mario to consider making behavior changes, I had to address his low mood and poor attitude. He was forthright about his disinterest in the wishes of the staff workers— he perceived their recommendations as unwanted impositions rather than well-intentioned advice for his betterment. He had been troubled, though, by his memory problems and difficulty expressing himself. He told me, "That's half the reason I don't go out of the room—I feel stupid and embarrassed. I can't even talk right." His concerns about his worsening cognitive skills provided an inroad for discussion of his behavior.

Favorably impressed by the idea that he might be able to improve his mental functioning, he complied by adjusting his sleep schedule. He also agreed with my weekly recommendation to provide a "full movie review—plotline, main actors, and your favorite parts of the movie." By endorsing his interests, I endeavored to motivate him to work his attention and memory skills; the completion of these assignments also required him to speak extensively to me. Finally, since it was evident by his behavior and attitude that he enjoyed our time together, I requested that he meet with me outside, when weather permitted. He concurred with this suggestion, which ensured that he got into his wheelchair and out of his room. Although the changes Mario made could not realistically have resulted in a complete restoration of his brain functioning, they were successful in reducing excessive mental disability resulting from intellectual and emotional deprivation.

Current neuroscience research is finding hard, tangible scientific evidence confirming the value of mental stimulation in maintaining intellectual and mental health, or restoring it if lost. The important implications are more obvious for the vulnerable nursing-home resident, but the underlying principle applies to everyone—you can control and enhance your brain health.

*Lesson: Your brain is very plastic. You must properly
stimulate it for maximum benefit.*

Applying the Lesson to Your Life

- Recognize that the brain is a dynamic, ever-adapting organ.
- Use this knowledge to your advantage. Stimulate your brain for maximum development and protection against age-related deterioration. Enhancement is the result of an active process and cannot be achieved without effort or challenge.
- Remember the importance of the basics for good brain health: routine exercise, adequate sleep, sound nutrition, and regular social activity.

CHAPTER 22

ANIMAL MAGNETISM

I'm not Brad Pitt, but I could play him in the nursing home. Since most residents and staff workers are female, just about any male in the facility may be perceived as a movie star. Freud shocked the world over one hundred years ago by making the observation that some of children's behavior is sexual in nature. Not sexual in the adult sense, but rather in the way that behaviors involving love, intimacy, and affection toward parents are precursors to more mature sexual behavior. It is probably less shocking, but perhaps still unpalatable to some, to realize that elders remain sexual beings. A person's gender identity is formed as early as two to three years of age and is retained for life. In addition, there is evidence that libido (a drive to connect) is present throughout our entire life span. In other words, our sexual identity and sex drive are part of our lives from earliest childhood through our old age.

Matthew's behavior provides a prime example of how sexual interest remains on the mind even after sexual activity ceases. A seventy-four-year-old widowed resident of the nursing home, Matthew had been living in a two-family house with his daughter and her family, who occupied the other half of the home, prior to his admission to the nursing home. He informed me that his wife had died prematurely of cancer a number of years before he arrived at the care center, and he had attempted to carry on normally without her; for instance, he maintained his employment as an engineer for several years after her death. He was able to recover satisfactorily from the loss and was socially active, eventually dating several different women. He reported to me that he had had a healthy sex drive but experienced disappointing sexual-performance problems. Matthew was overweight and a chronic smoker with hypertension and diabetes. Persistently lax in the management of his diabetes, he suffered vascular damage with reduced blood flow to his extremities, which contributed to his sexual-performance issue. This problem was likely enhanced by cigarette smoking. The antihypertensive medication is another factor known to contribute to erectile dysfunction. While his wife was alive and healthy, Matthew felt comfortable and secure engaging in sexual behavior; his wife was gentle and understanding of any problems he experienced. However, with subsequent partners Matthew felt pressured and embarrassed, which only worsened his erectile dysfunction. He had become self-conscious of his physique and preoccupied with his performance to the point that sexual behavior lost its appeal to him. He continued to casually date until his health problems radically altered his life.

In some respects, the sexual issues Matthew described were more typical than we may care to think. Hormonal and other physical changes that both men and women experience as part of the aging process act to impair sexual performance. General health also greatly affects sexuality in the elderly. Medications, too, are notorious for interfering with sexual interest and performance. Absence of a partner is another factor affecting the sexual behavior of the elderly. Finally, mental-health issues can hinder sexual behavior. Matthew experienced anxiety and trepidation that ultimately worsened his sexual performance, even when he was still relatively healthy and living in the community.

Prior to his nursing-home admission, Matthew suffered a stroke on the right side of his brain and experienced paralysis on the left side of his body. He is now a long-term resident of the care center. Despite the fact that performance issues and embarrassment had caused him to cease sexual activity previously, I was asked to see Matthew because of sexually inappropriate behavior he was exhibiting toward female staff members in the nursing home. By their reports, Matthew was exposing himself, making explicit sexual comments about their appearance, and making frank propositions for sex with them.

Matthew's behavior was clearly unacceptable, and initial treatment interventions aimed at stopping his behavior. A fine line needed to be observed whereby firm limits were defined for the protection of staff members, who should not be expected to endure harassment of any kind (and which would also protect Matthew from rejection and humiliation), balanced by a concern to avoid snuffing out his strong drive. Regarding the latter, his behavior, though inappropriate, demonstrated passion. In the nursing-home setting I do not take such zeal for granted; more often than not the challenge is to find and encourage the life force. In Matthew's case, I wanted him to control himself better with staff members but not lose his libido altogether. In discussions, Matthew admitted to me that he did not expect to engage in sex with staff members but that he felt desperate for attention, affection, and love. I acknowledged and supported these more appropriate expressions of libido, and we discussed better ways to act in order to receive what he desired. For example, Matthew was encouraged to eat meals in the dining room, rather than alone in his room, to increase his opportunities for social contact and to reduce his seclusion. Also, he was advised to call his daughter when feeling the need for affection and comfort.

LADIES AND GENTLEMEN, BOYS AND GIRLS

If anyone ever doubted how important gender identity is to people, try identifying someone of any age by the wrong gender (e.g., refer to a little boy as a little girl); he will quickly inform you of your error. Many nursing-home residents have confided to me how invisible they feel when they are treated as undifferentiated, asexual beings rather than as a particular man or a woman. In the nursing home, as in other areas of life, it is important not to confuse social equality with biological and psychological equivalence. Men and women should receive equal rights and opportunities under the law, but to deny differences in gender is problematic, especially for children who are in the process of establishing their identities and elders who are clinging to theirs. Men and women reveal genetic, physical, hormonal, psychological, and behavioral differences. Whether sexually active or not, the nursing-home resident retains her gender identity.

Isabella has described to me the painful invisibility she feels. Once able to attract attention by merely walking into a room, she feels that nobody has any interest in her since she lost her youthful sex appeal. She is very clear that it is not that she feels like an unattractive woman—she has stated that she feels like an indistinct, characterless old person: "I didn't know what I had until I lost it. I thought everyone was just always nice to me because I was nice to them. I act the same way, but they don't anymore. Not that people are mean to me; they just don't seem to see me or care about me." Gender identity is important to us, whether we're young or old. It is part of how we perceive ourselves and how others view us.

The agonizing effects of having one's gender or sexual nature invalidated are not confined to the nursing home or the elderly. I commonly see the resulting tragic fallout in the suffering of gay and lesbian individuals, in my private practice. For instance, Gil, a twenty-eight-year-old broker at an investment bank in New York City reported to me that in his high-school years he suffered from depression and identity confusion "because my parents were disapproving of my nontraditional sexual orientation. At the time, I doubted if I was even a man." Fortunately, Gil found a strong support network in the gay community; within that community, he was able to accept the fact that he could be both gay and a man. He finally experienced comfort from this affirmation of his identity.

SEX AND AGGRESSION: DRIVE AND OVERDRIVE

The dual-instinct theory of motivation has existed since the early days of psychoanalysis. Stated succinctly, the theory asserts that our behavior is influenced by the dynamic combined action of two forces: libido (also known as the life instinct or sex instinct) and thanatos (also known as the death instinct). These instincts purportedly derive from the biological imperative to propagate the species. Libidinal drives motivate such behaviors as attachment, love, cooperation, and sex. Thanatos is the force behind aggressive behavior, which is necessary for defensive purposes. Interestingly, in terms of overt behavior, there is much more evidence of the presence of aggressive instincts in the nursing home. Hostile behavior is observed in some form every day. Residents curse angrily, yell, scream, threaten, and attempt to push or hit one another. Yet in all of my time in the care center I have never seen overt sexual acts—never even a kiss between residents. This observation includes married couples residing here. Libido as a motive force appears to be in neutral and thanatos in overdrive.

How can we account for this disproportionate expression of behavior in the nursing home? You might suggest that it is due to the greater modesty of the elder generation. I must remind you that the profane, threatening, and aggressive public behavior exhibited by some residents could make the proverbial drunken sailor blush. No, the control of sexual behavior is selective. I think that it reflects the influence of two factors: the perceived greater risk of expressing affection versus aggression; and the aim of the life instincts that has changed back to its original purpose. Anger, hostility, threatening statements, and belligerent gestures and actions express defensive intentions. We generally feel powerful and safer when warding off a perceived threat. Seeking to join others, we must let our guards down, bring the others closer to us, and render ourselves more vulnerable to rejection or hurt.

But the absence of libido in the nursing home is an illusion. No longer necessary to energize sexual behavior, the life instincts drive elders to seek attention, love, and affection, just as these instincts do for pre-adolescent children. Their libido does not vanish; it resumes old forms of expression, and although virtually no overt sexual behavior is observed between residents, their libido is still active. I believe that residents perceive that it is safer to express their affinity toward staff members than to other residents. I see this as acting in the service of attraction and bonding, not for sexual purposes per se. As seemingly out of control as Matthew was at his worst, he never showed any inappropriate sexual behavior with other residents. On a daily basis, I see many instances of residents making endearing comments, or reaching out to exchange tender touches with caretakers. These same individuals never display such behaviors with other residents. It is a puzzling fact that it appears easier for a resident to fight than unite with another resident.

WE HAVE A FAILURE TO CONNECT

Social connection is essential to the well-being of nursing-home residents, community-dwelling elders, and to all of us. The problem for nursing-home residents is that there are numerous barriers to affiliation. One obstacle is limited mobility. Some residents are bedridden, which requires others to come to them. Many other residents are wheelchair-bound and have difficulty moving about freely, even if they are capable of using their wheelchairs adequately. Rather than exert themselves, some choose to wait to be moved, or simply skip attendance at activities. Often there are psychological and emotional barriers to socializing as well. A resident contending with anxiety or depression, or who may be shy by nature, may need assistance interacting with other residents.

Yet sensory problems probably represent the most commonly occurring barrier to socializing. If you have ever been around two elders attempting to communicate directly to one another, it can appear to be a scene from the Tower of Babel—two people yelling at one another, misperceiving what is being said, and each understanding almost nothing. The communication requires the involvement of an interpreter with good hearing and the ability to project his voice loudly. The problem for nursing-home residents is plain to see: a dire need for human contact but abundant roadblocks. This is where libido comes in. Sexual attraction creates a force that can incline us to connect with one another. If it is devalued and viewed as unseemly, dirty, or inappropriate for the elderly resident, a legitimate tool for connecting and healing is wrongly dismissed. When I talk with residents, I neither instigate nor prohibit conversations containing sexual content.

The topic arises often, as Monica's case illustrates. Monica is meticulous with her things. From her wheelchair she carefully makes her bed and grooms herself. Her room is nicely adorned with personal belongings from her home. Decorations change to match the seasons. She is as careful with her appearance as she is with her room. Her morning routine is centered on brushing her hair, applying makeup, and dressing herself. When sharing some pictures from her youth, she commented to me that "people always said I was a Marilyn Monroe lookalike." She delights when I join her in admiring her old photographs. In our many meetings, Monica disclosed copious details of her life, starting with her childhood in Newark, New Jersey. The family endured financial hardship that compelled her to quit high school after the eleventh grade so that she could go to work in one of the city's factories. Charmingly, when Monica discusses her years of employment in the factory, the point she fixes on is not the work but the meeting of her husband, Arthur. A supervisor at the factory, Arthur was considered a very good catch—and Monica's marrying him was proof that she was one as well. Sharing the story of getting her man is Monica's way of making certain that I know she was once young and worthy. In addition to acknowledging that to her, I remind her that she is old and commendable, too.

Not only does Monica take care to present herself nicely, but she also evaluates others with her discerning eye, including residents, staff members, and me. Monica never fails to make a personal comment to me in the course of our discussions. Often her remarks are about my clothing—she might praise a tie, my jacket, or the shine of my shoes. However, the opinions can get even more personal, such as, "Tell your wife she's a lucky woman" or "You look nice today." I usually respond casually with a "Thank you" and with "You say such kind things" or "You have such a good eye for fashion." Inappropriate? Unprofessional? More like sweet and innocent. Professional boundaries are always maintained, so conversations are never allowed to become inappropriately personal or vulgar. Monica's statements reflect something important about *her* and have little to do with me or my appearance. Her graciousness and desire to connect and to please are what I hear and what I focus on when I talk with her. Such comments as those made by Monica provide a springboard to discussions about her late husband, her love of fashion, and the pride she takes in her appearance.

THE LAMB IN WOLF'S CLOTHING

Psychotherapy allows for a resident to express herself and to make human contact through words. An obvious cultural ageism exists in this country that deems the sexuality of the elderly utterly repellent. For a therapist to subtly support this bias by making such conversations taboo would be a disservice to that therapy recipient. Monica's behavior reflects the drive to connect characteristic of the libido-supported motivation of a child, except that it is cloaked in adult flirtation. *It is the lamb in wolf's clothing.* It is a healthy motive and one to which I respond positively. With so many barriers to social contact, it would be unwise not to use this natural bonding agent.

Lesson: Gender and sexuality are integral parts of identity; to deny or ignore them is annihilating.

Applying the Lesson to Your Life

- Keep in mind that a key to the understanding of others, and to good interpersonal relations, is sensitivity to all aspects of identity, including but not limited to gender, race, ethnicity, religion, social role, and occupation.
- Recognize and accept the omnipresence of libido as a healthy force of attraction for all of us, at any age.

CHAPTER 23

IT'S NOTHING PERSONAL

It is a self-evident truth that nursing-home residents comprise a very vulnerable population. Yet there is a certain irony present in working with them. Although residents may be helpless in certain ways, they can still be quite capable of hurting caretakers physically or with words. That is, a resident may be debilitated, but he may not be defenseless, and this places caretakers in a precarious position. Verbal behavior in the form of complaints or insults directed at staff members requires skillful responses in which a caretaker must act sensitively and undefensively (in order to protect the resident) yet simultaneously not be unguarded (so as to protect herself). The principles of superior customer service in the nursing home are the same as those that guide great human relations, and both customer and human relations depend on one's being able to depersonalize the behavior of others.

"What took you so long?" "You don't care about me." "I could hear you laughing in the hallway—you think that this is fun and games here?" "Don't be so rough! You toss me around like a sack of potatoes!" Such comments are commonplace in the nursing home. What do these complaints mean, and how should they be responded to? Should a worker insult the resident back or tell him off for complaining and being offensive? "Don't you take that tone with me—I work here. I'm not here for you to abuse!" Obviously not. Such responses from a worker would be wrong and would certainly result in disciplinary action if detected. The negative statements would also represent a gross misunderstanding of the professional role of caretaker and indicate that the caretaker is unaware of what is actually being communicated by the resident. Understanding the attributes of the professional role and awareness of certain aspects of communication are key components to effectively handle complaints or insults. Possessing these insights can improve service, enhance all our relationships—personal and professional—and protect us from experiencing unnecessary emotional duress.

When in a work or professional setting, we are not merely acting in a personal capacity. We are performing in a role. We represent the company or profession for which we work. Whether employed in retail or in healthcare, when we interact with customers, clients, or patients, we are perceived as agents of that organization or profession. A waitress, responding to complaints about the food served, would likely not feel personally upset. However, a complaint about the service might be experienced as more of an affront. How do you perceive your role at work? Excellent service involves being able to place a complaint in the context of the totality of who you are. A waitress, for example, may function also as a daughter, a student, a mother, a wife, a churchgoer, an athlete, and so on. A complaint is about one small aspect of who you are. At work you are known mainly through your job-related behavior. Your life outside of work remains unknown to most customers or clients. However, if you provide any service or make or sell any product and want to be great at what you do, then you want feedback. The ability to incorporate feedback in a nonthreatening way is a major source of learning and self-improvement.

Whether spoken or written, communication is based on the literal meaning of the words and the associated emotional interchange. In my work I typically consider understanding and responding to the emotional communication my top priority. Almost any comment can be shown to reflect at least one of the seven primary emotions, namely surprise, excitement, fear, sadness, anger, disgust, or happiness. My first order of business is to determine what emotion is driving a statement. In statements by nursing-home residents such as those above, I hear that they are frustrated, angry. Pay close attention to what I said: *they* are telling me that *they* are feeling frustrated and angry. It is not about me; it is about them. They are expressing *their* feelings to me. Even if their complaints involve my behavior, I understand that they are expressing *their feelings* about me. If I shift from thinking about me to thinking about their unhappiness, the situation feels less personal. This provides a degree of separation ("It's about them, not me"), rendering the information more objective and more easily accepted and dealt with.

Focusing initially on aspects of emotional communication, I can respond more purposefully instead of behaving in a reactive manner. I aspire to perform like any other good service provider: the customer is always right. In other words, I respond to the meaning of the emotional communication—if a resident says I don't see him frequently enough, I do not scold him for being too demanding. Before considering the possibility of unrealistic expectations, I address his emotional message: "I'm mad because you make me wait too long between visits." I might respond, "I understand that you are angry that I don't visit you more frequently. Sounds like I need to be around more" or "Having to wait even a minute probably feels too long. I think I need to come back more quickly." Recognizing the emotional level of communication also applies to positive statements. A statement of pleasure such as "You're great. Nobody else talks to me the way you do" might lead me to respond in recognition of their expressed sentiments, "I am so pleased that I can help you." Acknowledging the expression of positive, as well as negative emotions, deepens the connection between resident and provider of care. In the nursing home, negative sentiments predominate—a reflection of negative emotions generated by disability, pain, and loss associated with advanced age, illness, and incapacity. Understanding and applying the principles I discuss in this chapter can help prevent resident complaints from creating a toxic environment for staff workers and family members. The advantages of skillful emotional communication accrue equally well in any setting with any type of work, and in any human interaction, for that matter.

I find this approach to working with people effective in situations other than those encountered in the nursing home. In the popular book *The Four Agreements*, author Don Miguel Ruiz discusses agreements, or rules of life, that if we can keep, allow us to live a joyous life. The second agreement he identifies is, "Don't Take Anything Personally."[1] In his view, whatever a person says can be understood primarily as a statement about the person talking—her perceptions, motives, and opinions—rather than about the intended recipient. In my private practice I see the application of this principle in the context of the most intimate and personal relationships of all: parent-child. Some of our children's behavior is heavily determined by nature; although they are part of our small family, they are also part of the human family. As personal as our relationships are, there are impersonal aspects that parents may unwittingly and unnecessarily personalize to their dismay. A baby crying in the middle of the night is not acting to punish or manipulate you or to ruin your next day—although it might seem that way at times. A child grousing about doing homework for school is not torturing you any more than an adolescent is terrorizing you by testing the limits of tolerance with her fresh mouth. A young adult partying with friends is not trying to embarrass you or to drive you crazy. The behavior engaged in by the infant, school-aged child, adolescent, and young adult is age appropriate and requires parental intervention to guide development. The correct parental response is necessary to facilitate bonding and attachment, to develop a productive attitude about work and responsibility, to assist with self-control and separation from family, and to learn a healthy balance of the risks and pleasures of peer activities with safety concerns, respectively. If a parent is personally offended by each call to action, he will experience resentment and too much antipathy to enjoy the relationship or to parent effectively. In working with parents, I often attempt to normalize, or depersonalize, the behaviors of children in order to reduce negative emotions that only interfere with good parenting and healthy family relationships.

*Lesson: A key to superior service, and happiness,
is to avoid personalizing everything.*

Applying the Lesson to Your Life

- In providing any service, remember that you are acting in a role that only represents a narrow piece of your total identity. This allows for maintaining perspective and objectifying information. Do not allow yourself to be defined by any one piece of your complete personality. For instance, imagine that you work at a cash register and a customer complains that you take too long to scan and bag his purchases. Before responding to his comments in a negative, reactionary way, you should take the time to remember that you are much more than a cashier. Therefore, his complaint is not an attack on you as a person, since your cashier skills represent only a small part of who you are. You might be having an "off" day at work, or perhaps you really *are* not very good at your job. But regardless of whether or not his complaints are justified and his perspective accurate relative to your skills, his criticism of you does not mean that you are a failure overall. You are also, say, a doting father, a loving son, and one heck of a salsa dancer. Depersonalize his comments, and you will find that you are more at peace with yourself, behave more appropriately in the workplace, and are able to "leave work at work" rather than letting one dissatisfied customer destroy your whole day.

- Take the feedback. Learn and improve from what is said to you. Continue to perform behaviors that earn praise from others and consider ways to change in response to complaints.

- Listen to all communication with your ear tuned to the emotional component of what is being expressed to you. If you can discern the emotion(s) behind the words, you can capture the essence of any communication. Perhaps the grocery-store customer in the example above is feeling frustrated because he perceives your pace at scanning and bagging produce to be a detriment to his ability to get home to his sick child. Recognizing his emotions rather than reacting unthinkingly to his words will provide much better results for you personally and professionally.

- Remember that what is expressed to you in behavior or words is a reflection of the other person's thoughts, feelings and/or attitudes, and is not always an accurate reflection of yourself. Recognizing this can allow for another degree of separation from personal, knee-jerk responses to people and can enable you to behave more thoughtfully and intentionally and to experience less emotional upheaval.

CHAPTER 24

DISCONNECT

Cold water never quenches so well as when we come inside after strenuous exercise in the hot sun. Eating is most enjoyable when we feel strong pangs of hunger. We can drink or eat when not thirsty or hungry, but it is not quite so pleasurable. This is also the case with satisfaction of other bodily needs like urinating, defecating, having sex, sleeping, or releasing strong emotions. In other words, gratifying a bodily urge when it is keenly sensed provides for maximum enjoyment.

The relevance of responding in a prompt manner to bodily signals for the experience of pleasure was clearly illustrated in my work for a program dedicated to the care of people with diabetes. Evan, a twenty-eight-year-old single attorney, had "brittle" type 1 diabetes. That is, he had much difficulty maintaining his blood-glucose levels within the range recommended by his diabetologist. Because of the many factors that can and do affect blood-glucose levels, it is often helpful to maintain a regular routine involving exercise, food intake, blood-glucose monitoring, and the taking of insulin. Some individuals have more difficulty regulating their blood-glucose levels than others and therefore require adherence to a strict regimen of behavior. One factor Evan needed to control tightly was the timing of insulin injections with food intake. As a consequence, his eating behavior was determined more by the clock than by an internally determined need for nutrition. Evan's bodily signal of hunger lost meaning. For him, eating became more of a chore than a source of pleasure because it was driven by blood-glucose readings, insulin injections, and the passage of time, instead of a feeling of desire to eat. He complained of a loss of appetite and of the burden of eating. The disconnection of need and gratification resulted in displeasure even though he continued to eat.

The pressure for timeliness in the satisfaction of needs is ever present in the nursing home, where there is so often a delay between desire and satisfaction. Because of dependence of residents on caretakers, a lag exists between experiencing a need (to eat, to go to bed, to go to the bathroom, etc.) and satisfaction or relief. These situations lead to frustration and unhappiness. Instead of relief and pleasure, the pursuit of satisfaction of bodily needs becomes a source of misery.

When I walked into Mary's nursing-home room, she was livid. "You can ring this damn bell until you are blue in the face and it doesn't do any good! I'd like to bop someone over the head if they would ever get in here! I hate this place and everyone in it!" She told me that within a few minutes of pressing her call bell, an aide had come in to inform her that she would be back shortly. She did not return soon enough for Mary's liking.

The most common complaint that I have heard in my years in the nursing home is about having to wait for assistance. The inevitable frustration and stress universally experienced by nursing-home residents is an unfortunate but unavoidable product of the collision of two factors: the relative helplessness of residents and the staffing limitations of institutions.

Our bodies are designed to signal us when there is a condition of need. As infants, when disturbed by one of the signals, our distress is a call to our caretakers to satisfy the need. As we become more self-reliant, we can satisfy our own needs or use our verbal skills to gain the assistance of others. It is a system as old as humanity and one that usually works efficiently and happily. Nonetheless, being dependent on others to meet basic needs creates opportunities for trouble. The state of dependency is not so much the problem. With the assistance of a dedicated caretaker, the system can work well. Even as able-bodied adults, we do not necessarily mind being dependent on others for service if the help is readily available. I am certain that there are few complaints when receiving first-class service in an airplane. But how is dependency experienced if someone is receiving lousy service in a crowded, understaffed restaurant where the waiter disappears for long periods of time? The expected joy of being served food and drink becomes dissatisfaction. Whether we experience pleasure or something more negative turns on the quality of the assistance.

An unresponsive caretaker—a parent tending to the needs of a child or a waiter serving customers—not only frustrates needs but also generates deeper, more disturbing feelings: powerlessness and helplessness. This is when panic and rage set in. A mother's responsiveness to her child's cries forms the rudiments of two important aspects of development: a child's sense of capability and his general trust in people. If a mother is typically reliable and responsive to calls for assistance, a child develops a sense that he can make good things happen and that the world of people is a good one. If cries are met inconsistently, a child will generally feel ineffective and that his behavior is useless; he will also learn that people are untrustworthy and that the world is not a kind place. Mary's behavior was evidence that these feelings can be revived under certain circumstances no matter how old we are.

There is an additional dynamic at play that contributes to residents' emotional distress when they must wait for help: diminished frustration tolerance. Research on willpower by psychologist Roy Baumeister is relevant to this conversation.[1] His investigations demonstrate that we have a finite amount of willpower available to cope with challenges. On a typical day, we deal with situations that require willpower, leaving us less available to cope with other challenges for the remainder of the day. If enough willpower is consumed, we can reach a state of ego depletion resulting in low frustration tolerance and reduced ability to regulate thoughts, feelings, and behavior. Challenges that can deplete willpower include illness (energy is used to heal and to recover); chronic pain (energy is used to ignore and minimize the pain); fatigue (inadequate sleep and/or rest results in higher consumption of blood glucose); and hunger (low blood-glucose supplies). These conditions are regularly observed in the nursing home (hunger is a problem not because of a lack of available food but because of the inability to eat on demand). The negative impact of pain on mood and frustration tolerance can hardly be overstated. Pain is a signal from the body designed to alert us that something is wrong that requires our attention. Can you imagine what a strain it would be to try to concentrate at work with a fire alarm ringing all day long in your office? Instead of an external alarm, with pain there is an internal alarm sounding all day, which can be exhausting to cope with.

Baumeister's conclusion that each of us possesses a limited supply of willpower squares well with everyday observations. If you have had a rough day—you were stuck in traffic jams going to work and coming home, had a difficult discussion with a supervisor, and had to miss lunch for a mandatory meeting—there is little "left in the tank" to handle rambunctious children at home or to engage in a discussion about family finances.

Ego depletion was evident in Mary's behavior—she was highly emotional, angry, and threatening. She experienced chronic pain due to arthritis and at the time of the outburst was suffering from a cold that had kept her up throughout the previous night. Recognizing the state she was in, and the fact that I could not change any of the problematic circumstances (i.e., I could not cure her cold, alleviate her arthritis, or make staff members appear), I assisted her in several other ways. First, I made it clear to her that I understood how frustrated and angry she was. In effect, I communicated to her that "your message was received; your cries have been heard." In addition, I discussed specific coping strategies to reduce her dissatisfaction associated with waiting for assistance. The emphasis of my intervention consisted of acknowledging that neither she nor I could do anything about the staffing of the facility at the moment but that she had the power to change her feelings about the situation. I expressed concern about the distress she was experiencing and wondered if there was something she could do in her own self-interest. In directing the discussion in this manner, I was attempting to help her to participate in a solution, which would reduce the helplessness and powerlessness that were at the root of her aggravation. A practicing Catholic, Mary eventually decided that she would keep her rosary beads within reach at all times and would silently pray while waiting.

Lest anyone think that ego depletion with consequent decreases in self-control is confined to the elderly, I will quickly mention the example of the typical grade-school child after a sleepover. Following a night of minimal sleep and poor eating, and often with a bellyache or some other vague physical complaint, post-sleepover children return home as irritable monsters for parents to deal with. Young adults have their own version of this when they stay up much of the night playing video games, chatting online, texting and talking on their cell phones, and then attempting to write a school paper at 1:00 a.m. Ever try to wake one of these slumbering bears for school the next morning? Finally, many adults whom I treat in my office suffer the ill consequences of ignoring their own basic needs. Some of the more ambitious and diligent adults will ignore their needs for sleep and rest by working exceedingly long work hours; they skip meals and work when under the weather, as well.

No matter how old or accomplished we are, we never outgrow the necessity to satisfy our basic needs. Insufficient satisfaction of these needs, either because we are dependent on others to assist us or because we voluntarily ignore them in the process of pursuing other pleasures or obligations, comes at a cost. Our bodies signal us to behave so as to optimize our health and happiness, and we would do well to heed the calls. The timely satisfaction of bodily needs is pleasurable, and although it should be not be our highest priority, it should not be our lowest one either. Psychologists have established that a delay of gratification is critical to the achievement of many important goals in life, but they also recognize that daily satisfaction is integral to vitality and zest.

Lesson: Sensitivity to and timely satisfaction of needs will reduce frustration and increase pleasure.

Applying the Lesson to Your Life

- As a caretaker, be aware of the challenges of the individual whom you are taking care of. If there are some unusual hardships, some sensitivity and allowances are in order. For example, with a sick child, leniency is usually granted for irritable, angry behavior.
- Whenever possible, whether caring for someone else or ourselves, address any problems with practical solutions in order to reduce depletion of coping resources. For example, if an agitated baby appears tired or hungry, assist her in sleeping or eating.
- Do not ignore your own bodily signals for rest, nutrition, a bathroom break, affection, or other pleasures in deference to work or other demands. Dependent children and elders must contend with the hassles intrinsic to relying on caretakers; others should be careful not to surrender control of this satisfaction before they have to. Chronic frustration of our needs can contribute to a loss of vigor, feelings of unhappiness, and even pervasive depression. Enjoyment of the simple pleasures is life-affirming and helps us to maintain our connection to our bodies and to the comforts of the world.

CHAPTER 25

HARD LOVE

Sometimes love does not look like love. Love is not always beautiful, and at times, it can be downright ugly. Just ask the child who has the box of donuts taken away from her, the teenager who is required to leave a party to be home before everyone's 11:00 p.m. curfew, or the parent who must be placed in the nursing home. The role of caretaker often requires decisions that may be in the best interests of the person being cared for, but which generate unhappiness, protest, and anger.

Young children are accustomed to thinking only about what they want, not about the broader concerns that a competent, responsible parent must consider. Parents often report serious stress about enforcing healthy rules and limits when their children object. I believe that this stress results in part from unrealistic expectations and from a misunderstanding of one of the most important responsibilities as a parent. Should children feel happy when they are not getting what they desire? I know I am unhappy when I don't get what I want. Isn't everyone? Nobody can expect joyful thanks when denying others what they desire. Expecting such a response only adds to the tension and drama. Moreover, I consider it an essential duty of a good parent to assist children in coping effectively with negative emotions: anger, disappointment, sadness, frustration. Any parent can be a good-time Charlie when attending to a happy child. However, it takes a dedicated parent to effectively teach a child how to deal with negative experiences and emotions. Teachers, coaches, and other adults may take actions only to stop or limit the expression of these feelings; it is up to the parent to teach the child emotion management.

What is the best way to help our children deal with negative feelings? First, talk with them about their feelings just as if they were expressing positive sentiments, such as love and gratitude. Otherwise, the implicit message is, "I will only listen to you when you please me; if not, be quiet or go away." The classic scenario in which I see this dynamic played out in the nursing home is when a resident complains to a family member about having to go into the nursing home against his desire. Family members may talk endlessly about the advantages of being in the nursing home, but they will never convince their relative to be happy about his stay. Instead, everyone ends up angry, disgusted, and unhappy. Unfortunately, at times these conversations become so intolerable that residents will resort to forbidding family members from visiting. Sometimes, family members stop visiting on their own or, when they do visit, they try to enforce a "gag order" on the nursing-home resident. The net effect is unhappiness all the way around.

Lillian, an eighty-two-year-old widow with a daughter and a son, was extremely unhappy about moving into the nursing home. Her husband had died prematurely of a heart attack many years prior, and she expressed both pride and resentment about having raised her children alone. Because of the hard work and personal sacrifice she had endured, she found it unfathomable that neither child would care for her at home. Her children felt that Lillian's placement in the nursing home was necessary because of recent falls that she had experienced in her apartment; although she did not sustain any serious injuries, they decided to move proactively, fearing that she would be harmed if she remained home alone. The practical obstacles to keeping Lillian in her home, or taking her into one of their homes, were considerable. Financial resources were reportedly not available to provide sufficient care in Lillian's home, and neither child's home was suitable: her son was in the process of divorcing his wife, and her daughter's husband was experiencing serious health problems and they were struggling financially.

Lillian's daughter, Ann, had a meeting with me and Lillian because she was very upset about her mother's persistent complaints and insistence that she be taken out of the nursing home. To put it plainly, it was an intense encounter. Lillian expressed to Ann all her misgivings about, and disapproval of, her placement in the nursing home. She implied that Ann and her brother were behaving selfishly, wondered if they really cared about her, and questioned the handling of her belongings and money, insinuating that their motivation for placing her in the nursing home was based on personal gain. Although Ann and I had discussed what to expect from Lillian in the meeting, as well as the best ways to respond, Ann was defensive, argumentative, and threatened to avoid visiting her mother. Sadly, she followed through on her threat. Despite having heard all the complaints before, she was no longer able to tolerate them or to work productively with her mother. Ann later told me that she felt too upset seeing her mother so unhappy, and that her complaints and accusations were too painful to endure. Lillian remained disgruntled for the remainder of her stay at the nursing home. She refused psychotherapy and psychiatric care, expressing the sentiment that her only problem was that she had ungrateful children who had forced her into the nursing home.

In my opinion, the most effective way to deal with an unhappy nursing-home resident is to have their loved ones work with her in the same manner that I advise parents of young children and adolescents. Family members should expect disappointment, frustration, and unhappiness, and need to assist the resident to express these feelings verbally; in addition, they must maintain their commitment and availability. In order to reduce their own stress and to increase acceptance of the situation, family members must learn to feel comfortable with the knowledge that they did what they thought was best, just as their elder family member must be allowed, without threat of retaliation or abandonment, to have her own thoughts and feelings about the situation. The message that "I love you so much that I'll do what is best for you even if you hate me for it" is a very powerful communication of love and one that usually wins the day. Residents who do not feel abandoned or that they must avoid expression of their feelings generally adjust better to the nursing-home environment. Unfortunately, in Lillian's case, Ann was unable to tolerate her mother's complaints and had to withdraw completely in order to protect herself.

In most cases that I have seen, the complaints of residents usually soften after an initial period of acclimation. Sometimes, however, family members need to set verbal limits on residents so that they do not engage in verbal abuse. To allow for one-sided, harsh verbal attacks would benefit no one; engagement in civil discourse, especially around touchy subjects, is beneficial to all parties. Just as children need limits, so do elder adults.

A number of years ago, when I worked in a substance-abuse treatment facility, I was repeatedly reminded of the value of providing strong parenting in the face of resistance. I listened to scores of thirty-year-old men and women express regret that their parents had not set firmer limits on them when they were younger. Why hadn't their parents done more when they were staying out late at night, neglecting school-work, associating with sketchy characters, or coming home obviously intoxicated? Many commented that at the time they thought it was amusing that their parents either had turned a blind eye or responded meekly, ineffectively. To the individuals seeking recovery, their parents' behavior was seen in retrospect as neglect or incompetence. They would have benefited at the time from one or both of their parents standing up to them. Seeing that someone is stronger and determined to do what is best is comforting, even if it's frustrating in the moment. That kind of committed parenting communicates the message that the child is valued; dangerous, self-defeating behavior does not go unchallenged because the child's well-being is worth the fight to the parents. Acting decisively and with conviction communicates the same message to elder parents. Not unlike adolescents, many elders whom I have seen in the nursing home minimize risks, overestimate their abilities to function safely and independently, and are clueless about the costs and practical obstacles to getting competent, trustworthy care in their homes. And, as with adolescents, someone will have to fill the role as the guardian who will not tolerate dangerous arrangements, will make tough decisions, and will remain involved to deal with the emotional fallout.

Being a caretaker is a tremendous responsibility. The rewards are often not immediate, or obvious. Maintaining interest in and contact with a disgruntled loved one, young or old, can be the ultimate expression of compassion, acceptance, and commitment.

Lesson: Good caretaking sometimes means acting in ways that may not feel so loving to the recipient of the care.

Applying the Lesson to Your Life

- When in the role of caretaker, act with certainty. This is especially important when you will be challenged about your decisions. If uncertain, seek guidance. There are many available resources, including family and friends, literature on virtually any problem from child rearing to elder care, and professional assistance, if necessary.
- Understand and accept that decisions will need to be made that will be unpopular with the person you are caring for. Children do not like to do homework, adolescents do not like to do chores or go to bed before they feel ready to, and elder adults do not like to live in institutions.
- Embrace the unhappy individual just the same as you would a happy person. An especially potent expression of love is to be available when things get tough. From this behavior, the dependent will learn that he is being watched and cared for by a strong, reliable caretaker, a situation that enhances the dependent individual's sense of safety and security. Whether you're caring for a child who wants to eat nothing but cookies, a teenager whose promiscuity is threatening her health and safety, or an elder who needs around-the-clock care by professionals, you should anticipate negative reactions to your tough-love decisions and try to plan for your own response to those reactions.
- Recognize that "sticking to your guns" has its own rewards for caretakers. The idea of doing the "right thing" in spite of hardship raises self-esteem. Parents who give in to a child in a misguided attempt to keep her happy fail to prevent unhappiness and often feel bullied and ineffective.

CHAPTER 26

ACT NOW!

Ever notice how every elderly man is a kind and friendly gentleman and every older woman is a sweet, loving soul? Me neither. One quick stroll through the nursing home confirms this: the personalities of senior citizens are as diverse as for any other demographic because the qualities of a child tend to persist into adulthood. For example, a person who is shy, cautious, and introverted will likely remain that way into old age. There is no magic to aging: an obnoxious, stubborn young man usually becomes an obnoxious, stubborn old man. Despite popular notions, not every woman or man ages gracefully. In fact, if anything, the physical and mental stresses of aging may accentuate certain negative behaviors and personality traits.

I make this point as a call to action. I have seen old age "sneak up" on almost every person in the nursing home. What has become painfully clear to me is that the person you are in earlier stages in life will be the person you are in old age, unless you make explicit efforts to change. The longer you wait, the more difficult it will be to change. I want to say to people, "What are you waiting for?" Make improvements NOW in health, relationships, finances, and mental health. It only gets tougher later.

A classic example of the perils of ignoring or putting off addressing health matters was illustrated by the case of Marlene, a gentle, timid woman. Seventy-four-years-old, widowed, and a mother of three children, she received ample attention from her family while at the nursing home. She was in the short-term wing (subacute care unit) of the care center for rehabilitation, services made necessary by an ankle injury. While in the nursing home, the physical-therapy staff workers expressed concern that Marlene was excessively fearful of participating in therapeutic exercises, which was impeding her progress.

In my initial interview with Marlene, she described herself as a lifelong "worry wart," which was a dramatic understatement. Her reported history described the experience of chronic anxiety, as well as periodic panic disorder. Panic episodes are characterized by the experience of intense fear and physical symptoms such as excessive perspiration, trembling, dizziness, rapid heart rate, nausea, tingling or numbness in the extremities, shortness of breath, and tightness in the throat. Hardly subtle symptoms, yet Marlene had never sought mental-health treatment for them. Especially with undiagnosed panic symptoms, people typically seek emergency medical services for fear that they are having a heart attack or suffering some other serious medical problem. To complicate her rehabilitation further, Marlene was a longtime cigarette smoker, and she had mild respiratory problems; whenever she exerted herself physically, she tired easily and experienced shortness of breath, which frightened and inhibited her.

Marlene informed me that she had managed the daily anxiety at home by occupying herself with enjoyable activities, such as gardening or needlepoint projects. She would quell more acute "nervous spells" (panic symptoms) with tranquilizers that she was given by her regular doctor many years prior. Marlene was a much more complicated case than she otherwise would have been if she had sought mental-health treatment at a younger age. When she left the nursing home, she needed to continue with psychotherapy, psychiatric care for medication management, and smoking-cessation services, in addition to the appropriate medical care. How much better would her life have been had she sought assistance sooner? How much better would your life be if you addressed problems in your career, health, or finances today rather than at some later time?

HUMAN-RESOURCES MANAGER

The circle of life inevitably results in the youth in our society taking care of the elders. The child essentially becomes the father to the man. If all goes according to plan and the natural order of things is preserved, there will be a reversal of roles. On both ends of the life cycle we need caretakers. At the beginning of life, our parents are our caretakers. Toward the end of life, our children, spouse, or perhaps our siblings, provide our care. Our parents are our caretakers by fate, and as infants we have little choice or influence over them. In contrast, as older adults, the loved ones who will assist us have been part of our lives for a long time. We have shaped our relationships with spouses, siblings, children, nieces, nephews, and other family members over many years. The family and social environment we create and nurture will be what surrounds us when we are at our weakest and most vulnerable times. If we have treated the people closest to us with respect, compassion, and thoughtfulness, these sentiments are likely what we will receive when we require help and support from them. If, however, we have maintained troubled, unsatisfying relationships with our family members, that, sadly, is what we will get back. I have seen how children's responses to their aging parents reflect the quality of the relationships they have shared over the course of their lives together.

We read and hear much about preparing for retirement. This talk typically refers primarily to financial planning; however, human-resource planning is also critical. Financial hardship can ruin the retirement years. Poor relationships and loneliness can destroy the quality of old age as well.

We need to assume responsibility for our lives and take necessary action, *today*, to secure a better future. As adults, we have control and choices about how we live our lives and conduct our relationships. We can improve ourselves personally, and we can be sure to have good relationships.

Lesson: Act now to improve yourself and your life, and consider human resources, not just financial ones, in planning your future.

Applying the Lesson to Your Life

- Take a mental inventory of yourself and your life as they are now. Are things as you would desire them to be with your physical health, mental health, career, and finances? If not, take corrective action now. Waiting usually only allows for problems to get worse or to multiply. For instance, if you find yourself living paycheck to paycheck because of outstanding credit-card debt, don't continue to pay off old credit cards with new ones. Cut up the plastic cards, organize a budget, and start paying off your debt with your income. Although you might not be able to go out to dinner every other day, buy the latest fashions, and shower your friends and family members with lavish gifts right now, you will be setting yourself up for a much more successful and stable future.

- Focusing on your relationships, do you see them as the gifts and valuable human resources that they are? Make having great relationships a priority in your life. It should be your mission to enjoy time and activities together with family members and friends. If there are obstacles and conflict, vow to remove and resolve them immediately. Happy, healthy relationships will not only enrich your life in the present but also serve as the foundation of your future "social security."

- General intentions are difficult to act on. Set a specific date for taking your personal and relationship inventories and develop clear behavioral goals. Share the plan with a trusted family member or friend in order to increase accountability and to improve your chances of following through on the pursuit of your objectives.

CHAPTER 27

ONE MOTHER CAN TAKE CARE OF FIVE CHILDREN, BUT FIVE CHILDREN CAN'T TAKE CARE OF ONE MOTHER

T he above statement, a frequent lament of the nursing-home resident, points to a regrettable change in family dynamics. In the opinions of many nursing-home residents to whom I talk, the shift in our country has occurred over the last generation or two. Often, attention, energy, and resources are focused on children—their development, comfort, and happiness—at times, to the neglect of building aspects of personal character and responsibility. It was not this way for most of the current elder generation. When they were young, many provided assistance to their families. Young children helped with chores around the home and were generally expected to contribute to the greater good— their parents, family, church, temple, school, and community. We seem to need to reemphasize the values of mutuality in relationships and contribution to the greater good as part of a child's growth, family life, and social development.

In prior generations, children were expected to serve their parents. As parents aged, children cared for them as a natural extension of this relationship. Nowadays, parents serve children, sometimes neglecting to inculcate a sense of reciprocity in relationships. When aging parents need assistance, children may be ill prepared. Providing support for elder parents calls for a complete role reversal. Consider a fairly typical family evolution. A child is born and, by necessity, attention is focused on the newborn. Parents sacrifice sleep, energy, time, and money for their new arrival. In the current spirit of the times, this mentality tends to project forward so that parental sacrifice and hard work are endured in order to provide the child with the best of everything: fashionable clothes, camps, vacations, and birthday parties, as well as electronic entertainment and communication devices, prom outfits, automobiles, and college educations. After their education is completed, children are assisted to find jobs and homes, and after marriage, grandparents often provide child-rearing and babysitting services. The elder generation is a necessary element of the success of the entire family. But when elders are in need, where does the help come from? Their own parents are either very old or have passed away, and for their children, the elders pose both practical and emotional challenges. Practically, the children must draw on their own resources to assist their elder parents. Emotionally, the adult children must accept that they no longer have parents, at least not the parents who took care of them.

Acknowledging and accepting the sea change in family roles requires a difficult adjustment for elder parents and their children. For the elder parent, going from being a caretaker, advisor, and authority figure to being a recipient of care often feels like a demotion in life. It can be an ugly reminder of losses of status, independence, youth, and purpose. For the adult child, the role reversal is a challenge as well. If the parent requires his assistance, then he has lost that person in his life to go to when he is in need. Your parent cannot be both your caretaker and your dependent at the same time.

In addition to changes in family dynamics, cultural factors also weigh against giving our elders their proper attention, respect, and relief. Residents often complain to me about what they see as the overvaluation of money and material enrichment. Their families' pursuits of this kind require long hours of work and usurps time that could be available for family, including aging parents. This point is obvious to residents in the nursing home. A common grievance of nursing-home residents is that their children's pursuit of "the almighty dollar" is the reason residents have been unable to stay at home with their adult children. To make matters worse, aging parents who are no longer functionally or financially independent are seen as threats to the bottom line because their care requires the investment of time that many younger adults prefer to spend at work earning money or enjoying material pleasures. Furthermore, it is costly to find caretakers able to attend to elderly family members in the home.

An additional trend in the United States exacerbates the problem for the elderly: the celebration of youth (and devaluation of elders). Youth tends to be associated with beauty and perfection; things that are older tend to be perceived as worn-out, broken-down. Wisdom and experience are devalued. There appears to be little appreciation for what was done in the past. We have become a culture of "What have you done for me lately?"

Few of us realize that we will either die prematurely or live to be an older American. What kind of fools are we to perpetuate a system that seems to ensure that if we live a long life, we will eventually become human burdens without value in our society? The disproportionate pursuit of material wealth and vanity can lead to spiritual impoverishment. When we were young, long before we produced anything of value for anybody, many of us were fortunate to be loved, respected, and admired just for existing. We were rich in the original and best currency of life: affiliation and related feelings of love, security, and affection. We need to foster these values in our appreciation of every individual, not just children.

Rebecca, an eighty-one-year-old widowed mother of one son, had an upbringing representative of her era. She spent her early years in Pennsylvania before moving to northwest New Jersey when she was sixteen years old. The family that moved together consisted of her mother and father, sister, brother, and maternal grandmother. Feeling no particular attachment to the local high school or other students there, and growing up at a time when formal education was not a priority, especially for young women, she dropped out of school before her senior year.

Rebecca fondly recalls the years she spent at home with her family before moving out, marrying, and starting her own family. She was occupied by full participation in family life. Work at home in those days was distributed along traditional gender lines: Rebecca and her sister assisted their mother with the domestic chores of cooking, cleaning the home, sewing, doing laundry, and helping in the care of their younger brother and grandmother. She affectionately described her memories of her grandmother, who remained in their home until she passed away. Endeavoring to maintain her sense of dignity and belonging, they would give her grandmother certain "jobs"; she would peel potatoes for dinner, or from her "post" on the front porch, she would alert the family when the mailman was coming. Rebecca's father worked a job with then-traditional hours and, with rare exception, the family ate dinner together seven days a week. Even recreational time was spent with family, listening to the radio, later watching TV. Religious worship was engaged in together every Sunday.

To most children of today, this lifestyle may read like a horror story, but, although there was an unmistakable emphasis on work and other responsibilities, there were some perhaps subtle benefits. With the primacy of the family unit came a sense of belonging and protection. Everyone in the family had his role, and fulfilling his responsibility provided a sense of purpose and value. The obligation to contribute as well as to receive from the family served as an excellent antidote to a more selfish preoccupation with personal needs and desires. Everybody contributed and everyone benefited.

PROMOTE GRATITUDE

Although the family model of Rebecca's youth may be gone irretrievably, teaching virtuous behavior does not have to be. Without completely resorting to an early-twentieth-century lifestyle, children can be taught the importance of family, of having a clarity of purpose, and of altruistic contributions to benefit family and community. Through modeling and promoting these values, we can enrich our children's lives and better prepare them for their adult years, including the meeting of obligations to the elder generation.

The concept of gratitude nicely captures the spirit of the old-school values described above. With gratitude there is not only thankfulness but also acknowledgement of what was done and a sense of obligation. Through child-rearing practices, parents can foster gratitude in their children.[1] Some recommended practices for young children include involving them in local community giving. For example, they can assist parents in volunteer work at animal shelters or participate in clothing drives or food collection for a food pantry. Modeling grateful behavior by thanking children when they are behaving in a helpful manner is also advised. Establishing traditions, such as starting a weekly dinnertime ritual of having each family member identify something she is grateful for, is another option. Parents can also inculcate gratitude practices by engaging in personal rituals such as a daily reflection on a gratitude list. These practices can also be taught in school and as part of religious instruction.

To a young woman currently in her adolescent years or young adulthood, being neither a child nor having children herself, there may be some questions about what she might gain from giving back to family or community. Practicing gratitude and engaging in service to others can function as good preventive behaviors that support mental health. Service to others is potent medicine for the self-centeredness that typifies these stages of life. Unfortunately, the late teen years and early twenties are a time when serious mental-health challenges exist that commonly result in presentations of anxiety, depression, or substance abuse. Whenever we are suffering, our attention naturally turns inward and can reinforce an unhealthy focus on the self. A beneficial practice to reverse this tendency consists of doing for others. The recommendation to engage in service to others is a staple of religious practice, nonreligious spiritual practice, mental health, and recovery from drug or alcohol abuse.

In addition, service to others is an honorable endeavor that is a potent countermeasure to cultural and personal malaise. Through service we can express respect and recognition of the value of human life, not just for the direct recipients of our efforts, but for all humanity.

Lesson: Teach your children to practice gratitude and to value service to others by direct education, reinforcement of good behavior, and modeling it yourself.

Applying the Lesson to Your Life

- If you are raising children, promote behaviors that support the family. Provide family dinners. Engage in recreation together. And require blackouts of electronica during family time in order to minimize distraction and intrusion.

- Support your children's involvement in service activities, whether through formal organizations such as Boy Scouts or Girl Scouts, or religious institutions, or in more personal, informal ways. Sharing in chores with other family members is a good way to start.

- If you are an adolescent or adult, volunteer your time and services. Again, consider formally sponsored programs as well as informal opportunities, such as shoveling snow for the elderly couple down the street, offering to cut the grass, or babysitting at no cost for the single mother next door.

- Practice gratitude. Engage in a simple, easy custom of spending several minutes every day generating and meditating on three to five things you are grateful for that day.

- Teach gratitude to your family by modeling it yourself and by supporting their practice of gratitude rituals.

CHAPTER 28

OUTSIDE IN

Human development is essentially a process of internalization, an absorption of products of life experience generated by interaction with others. In the typical course of events, through interchanges with an ever-expanding circle of people, an individual acquires information and skills, allowing for progressively greater degrees of independence and competence in motor, cognitive, emotional, and social functioning. That which is inside us was originally outside, or better stated, between us and those with whom we associated. Just as the nutrients we consume provide the raw material necessary to build and maintain our physiques, social interaction supplies the substance for our mental structures. The coexistence of a suitable environment and normally maturing body are required for proper development to occur. Because a well-functioning, healthy brain is necessary to retain the remnants of our life experience, normal age-related retrogression and deterioration due to illness or injury of the brain can result in a need for external support for a once-independent, declining elder.

With a developing child, much of the evidence of her advancement is plain to see. Her achievement of the traditional milestones of sitting up, crawling, standing, and walking are self-evident. Cognitive development, as indicated by an increasing memory capacity, the acquisition of speech, and improving problem-solving ability, also proceeds in the open. One of the less obvious, but arguably most important changes, occurs in the social-emotional sphere. Sometime in the second to third year of life, as brain maturation permits, children symbolically represent images of their caretakers in their minds, and these representations provide a feeling of security and also serve as the basis for self-control and social relations. If brain functioning is diminished, as may be the case with some elders, there might be not only memory and other cognitive decrements but emotional and behavioral regression as well.

As I approached the second-floor nurse's station in the care center, I spotted Rosa sitting in her wheelchair next to a nurse who, while busily entering information into a computer, engaged in a friendly repartee with Rosa. Once in the nurse's station, I could see that Rosa was holding a stuffed animal in her arms. She smiled at me, appearing calm and content. Although Rosa is not my patient, I am familiar with her because I evaluated her about a month prior to this encounter. I determined that she was not able to benefit from psychotherapy because she was cognitively impaired. In order to benefit from psychotherapy, a prospective patient minimally must be able to communicate and retain the contents of our conversations in memory.

A diagnosis of dementia and the decision not to treat her with psychotherapy were based on facts gathered from Rosa's medical records, staff reports, and my clinical interview of her. Information found in her medical records indicated that Rosa had a history of minor strokes resulting in the condition of multi-infarct dementia. She was referred to me for evaluation because of behavior problems of restlessness, verbal agitation, confusion, and low mood. When I interviewed Rosa, she was seated in her wheelchair in her room and was casually and appropriately dressed, appearing well groomed. She was friendly and compliant for most of the interview. Rosa correctly reported that she was an eighty-eight-year-old widowed mother of three children. But she was restless and repeatedly asked to get out of her wheelchair, making several attempts to do so while asking permission. She was responsive to my appeals to remain seated, which needed to be restated multiple times.

Rosa exhibited no difficulty with comprehension or speech articulation. However, she did demonstrate word-finding difficulty, resulting in halting, erratic speech. Despite the noted difficulty with verbal expression, Rosa was able to communicate effectively. Rosa reported the consistent experience of unhappiness, crying, sleep difficulty, diminished appetite, and reduced energy and motivation. She lacked insight and was unable to account for her low mood. Rosa's history, as recorded in her chart, described a pattern of progressive deterioration at home. She lived alone and over the prior year had required the increasing involvement of her children for cooking, shopping, cleaning, laundering, and paying the bills—most of the classic activities of daily living (ADL). In addition, her memory lapses were becoming more frequent and obvious, as were disturbances in her behavior and mood. By her children's accounts, Rosa was an excellent and caring mother whom they loved dearly.

During the interview, Rosa was confused and disoriented; she thought she was in a different facility than the nursing home and she incorrectly reported the date. Her long-term memory was preserved, however, as she was able to accurately share details of her personal life and historical facts. Rosa performed poorly on screening items for short-term memory, a telltale sign of dementia. I observed some irritability in response to frustration she experienced when attempting to answer some questions. Rosa was aware that she failed to provide correct answers to some queries, prompting spontaneous questions from her such as, "Why do you need to know all of this?" and "Haven't you gotten enough?"

So what accounted for the improvements in Rosa over the month or so since I had evaluated her? One factor was that the passage of time allowed for increased familiarity with the facility, including the physical environment, routines, and people. In addition, the psychiatrist had recommended psychotropic medication that Rosa had been taking for several weeks. Finally, the positive impact of human intervention was conspicuous. The proximity of a familiar staff member, combined with affable interaction and the soothing touch of the stuffed animal, were beneficial.

From British researcher John Bowlby's seminal studies on human attachment, we know that we are biologically programmed to respond to certain situations with fear: being in strange situations; being with unknown people; being without familiar people; hearing loud noises; experiencing pain; and being in darkness.[1] The impact of any of these conditions can be mitigated by possession of familiar objects, proximity to a trusted person, or both. Developmentally, until about three years of age, the physical presence of a caretaker is required to soothe a frightened child. Thereafter, the presence of a caretaker is internalized, symbolic. In Rosa's case, such a presence was well established but lost due to brain damage. With dementing disorders, there is not only a loss of cognitive skills and related functional incapacity that some individuals experience. The loss of internal representations can leave an individual feeling alone and fearful unless someone is physically present with her. Rosa has been participating in a program for residents with dementia in the nursing home. However, because she is still vulnerable to acute distress from time to time, she requires one-to-one contact such as she was receiving when I saw her at the nurse's station. There is simply no better medicine for emotional distress than proximity to a familiar, properly responsive human.

The importance of the internalized caretaker for security is most dramatically illustrated in cases of childhood separation anxiety. Kiersten was brought to treatment in my private office by her parents, primarily because of behavior at school. She was a student in a three-morning-a-week preschool program and, at four years old, was the youngest of three children in her family. This was Kiersten's first attempt at preschool; her parents intended to start her a year earlier but had been persuaded by her pediatrician to wait another year. Kiersten was shy and uncomfortable when out of her home, and her parents had agreed with the recommendation to give her more time to mature. On the first day of school, serious issues emerged: Kiersten refused to let go of her mother's leg, cried loudly, and only relented when her teacher personally escorted her into the classroom. Kiersten's teacher reported that even after Kiersten stopped crying, she was difficult to entice into interaction with the class. She would not make eye contact with other students who attempted to speak and play with her. When they persisted in their pursuit of her, Kiersten became agitated—she cried, yelled "Leave me alone!" and crawled under a desk. Kiersten was having a very difficult time separating from her mother and getting comfortable at school.

Similar behaviors were observed outside of school. On multiple occasions, when her parents had attempted to take her to soccer practice, Kiersten had refused to get out of the car, insisting they take her home. Even in her house, Kiersten insisted that either a sister or a parent be present in a room with her or she would panic. Kiersten was a product of a stable, intact family, and her developmental history was unremarkable except for the separation issue. Her reported history was negative for prior psychotherapeutic treatment, family mental-health treatment, learning difficulties, and medical problems. Kiersten was described by her parents as happy, kind, and affectionate when comfortable and relaxed.

When I met Kiersten, she separated from her parents in the waiting room slowly and cautiously. Presented with a variety of material, she chose to play with a toy house and human figures. She made no eye contact while she played and positioned herself with her back to me. Kiersten appeared to ignore my questions and initially offered no responses. At first content to watch and respect her space, after about ten minutes, I sat nearer to her and began to comment on her play, eventually asking to join her. Soon she was interacting with me through the human figures, and I could see that she was verbally precocious and smart. Her self-control in the office was good, perhaps too good—she was initially inhibited and withdrawn. Although she was guarded, she did not exhibit sadness or low mood. Except when challenged by separation from her parents, Kiersten appeared a happy, normal child.

The focus of treatment was to assist Kiersten in improving her ability to tolerate separation from her family, principally from her mother. She had a superior memory and ability to represent thoughts and feelings in words. The requisite skills existed, so the challenge consisted of helping Kiersten to increase her mother's symbolic presence in her mind. We employed several interventions for this purpose. Kiersten and her mother met with the teacher after school, which helped to establish the teacher and the classroom as "Mom-approved," more familiar, and safe. Kiersten started carrying a picture of her family in her backpack that she referred to at will. She drew a picture for her mother every day at school, helping to keep her central in Kiersten's thoughts. Her mother also made a playdate in her home with a little girl from Kiersten's class. Finally, a reward system was implemented to support the desired behavior change. The goal was to increase Kiersten's security and comfort, not to break her of a bad habit. Her behavior was clearly fear-based and not reflective of cunning manipulation. As such, the aim was to assist her, not punish her for misbehavior.

Fortunately for Kiersten, she had a solid foundation, with excellent cognitive skills and responsive parents. Some minor tweaking of the system was enough to effect significant improvement. On the other hand, because of brain injury, Rosa can no longer sufficiently retain a soothing internal presence in mind and always will require the calming physical presence of a familiar caretaker when distressed.

The stuff of our minds is the result of an interplay of our native endowment and social environment. Traces of our early relationships become internal models for feelings toward self and others and basic attitudes about, and expectations of, life. This is why primary relationships are critically important. As we age, these internal models are refined by life experience. You do well to remember that your social environment continues to influence you throughout life. When you are very young or old, you have relatively little influence over your social world; in the many intervening decades, however, you have much control over the people with whom you spend time and how you interact with them. If you want to make changes in yourself or your life, you should strongly consider whom you choose to associate with and the quality of the relationships you maintain. Seek information to help yourself or find experts with whom you can work, whether you desire to make changes in your health habits, spiritual practices, career, relationships, or feelings. If you want to soar like an eagle, you must fly with eagles and avoid the turkeys as much as possible.

Lesson: Good relationships, external and internal,
are keys to security and success in life.

Applying the Lesson to Your Life

- If you are a caretaker, recognize the awesome power and responsibility of your position.
- Accept that the need of others for support is legitimate and natural.
- Adjust your level of support to others as development and independence allow.
- Remember that good relationships are vital ingredients for health and happiness; we all need them.
- If you want to make life improvements, find the right people to associate with. Being in the company of people who model the behavior you aspire to facilitates your adoption of desirable attitudes and habits. If you wanted to improve your fitness level, for example, you would not seek advice from the guys who visit the local tavern nightly to smoke cigarettes and drink beer. Rather, you would identify someone at the gym or yoga studio who exemplifies the habits and physique you desire.

LESSONS LEARNED

When psychologists discuss termination, they are usually referring to the end of treatment. Ideally, it is a decision arrived at by mutual agreement, in which both patient and therapist feel that satisfactory progress has been achieved. In the nursing home, many of my cases end in this traditional manner, with improvements in a resident's mood or adjustment to the facility, for example. Sometimes, however, treatment ends when a resident is no longer able to benefit from therapy because of worsening physical or mental conditions. It is a special challenge and honor to work with individuals in their final stage of life. Because of the uniqueness of the work environment, where I essentially coexist with residents in their living space, I am able to observe and interact with them in a way that has proven exceptionally fruitful for revealing lessons about life and humanity. In this book, I have documented twenty-eight simple lessons from this endeavor. Below is a summary of the lessons, with discussions of some of the individuals who helped me develop these invaluable insights.

Lesson: Although suffering in life is inevitable, we can mitigate it.

We are confronted by the unavoidable encounter with adversity and its emotional ramifications. A confluence of catastrophic factors bore down on Jonathan, generating suffering: he was ill, with respiratory and cardiac conditions; he had endured premature losses of his only two children; and he was facing the impending loss of his wife. Jonathan's tragic experiences engendered feelings of sadness, anger, hopelessness, and helplessness. And yet I assisted him to experience less anguish by compassionate intercession. Helping Jonathan illustrated that even when sources of pain are unalterable and cataclysmic, sorrow can be relieved by the empathetic response of another. When we are experiencing heartache and distress, the receipt of consolation is restorative. Similarly, we can assuage others in such need. The capacity to heal requires only the most natural and basic acts of kindness—which we can all furnish.

Lesson: Love is an irreducible, lifelong requirement for health and well-being.

During World War II, astute mental-health practitioners observing children from London who were housed in foster homes and orphanages established that loving human relationships are a vital necessity, on the order of food and water. With satisfactory relationships we can flourish; without them we wither and suffer.

Frank and Angelo were two nursing-home residents whose situations illustrated the principle that the quality of an individual's relationships is a leading determinant of his quality of life. Both gravely ill, Frank with ALS, and Angelo with Parkinson's disease, they had dramatically different relationships with their respective families. Frank maintained affectionate relations with his children and his spirits were high. Angelo, on the other hand, expressed anger and hostility to his children and was very unhappy most of the time. Moreover, Frank's sour disposition pushed other residents away, only adding to his loneliness and torment. Fortunately for Frank, compassion provided by staff workers and me ensured that he received the essential emotional sustenance he required. That Frank was responsive to caring interventions of professional staff workers illustrates the general principle that humaneness is a powerful nutrient, regardless of the source.

*Lesson: Pain, injury, illness, or setbacks of any kind involve
distress and demoralization; recovery requires trust and courage.*

A setback can cause a crisis of faith—we may wonder if we are up for
the challenge to bounce back. Physical and psychological problems
are particularly daunting and can result in demoralization, a loss of
fighting spirit. Tim was in the nursing home following hip-replacement surgery. His negative attitude and halfhearted efforts in physical
therapy were symptomatic of a problem with morale. Tim had no faith
in his surgeon, the nursing home, and worst of all, himself. He questioned if he were worth fixing and if he had the fortitude to endure the
effort and pain required to recover. Tim also lacked a sense of purpose—
he wondered why he should improve himself, just to live in a nursing
home. Restoring Tim's morale consisted of instilling hope, bolstering
his self-efficacy, enhancing his family connections, and defining a clear
and meaningful purpose. Once his motivation increased, he participated
more earnestly in his rehabilitative services and achieved improvements
in his physical and emotional functioning. The nursing home always
had provided the way, but Tim needed to find his will.

*Lesson: The anguish associated with loss is necessary to help
with separation from the lost person, image, or belief;
to promote affiliation for comfort; and for emotion regulation.*

Loss is a necessary evil. A clearing away of the old or obsolete is required
to make room for the new and improved. Even emotional responses that
accompany loss—sadness and dejection—serve positive purposes. Our
experience of sorrow pushes us to move forward by detaching us from
lost people or things and to seek the support of others. Our distress also
encourages our friends and family to console us. By acting as a point of
contrast, our emotional suffering also allows us to appreciate the highs
of life when they occur.

Because they present similarly, grief and depression are sometimes confused. The nursing-home resident Jill demonstrated the normal grieving process following the passing of her sister. Jill reported feeling sadness and anxiety and experienced difficulty sleeping. She was eager to talk about her thoughts and feelings, maintained her usual level of participation in nursing-home activities, and recovered in about two months. By comparison, Linda, a sixteen-year-old patient in my private practice, exhibited signs and symptoms of depression. She experienced the failure to earn a position on a softball team as a humiliating personal defeat. She also expressed sadness, but, unlike Jill, she withdrew from the potential support of family and friends and rejected assistance when offered. Linda angrily devalued herself and reported feeling worthless. Linda's treatment was lengthier and more intensive than Jill's. Grief is a normal, healthy reaction to loss, requiring only comforting responses from others; depression is abnormal and often requires considerable professional assistance.

*Lesson: Longtime companions maintain a presence
in our brains when they go,
which renders our whole world different and incomplete.*

The psychological and emotional reactions to loss are familiar to most of us: sadness, crying, confusion, disbelief, guilt, anxiety, disturbances in sleep and appetite, to name several. Some of the suffering response is the result of cognitive processes: the strong mental association between the lost person and activities we shared with him.

Robert lost his wife, Ruth, just months prior to his admission to the nursing home. He had completely withdrawn from life and was languishing in his home. Every activity in which Robert engaged not only failed to provide enjoyment but also evoked punishing memories of Ruth. Through sixty-one years of marriage, they did almost everything together. Robert attempted to cope with his grief by doing virtually nothing at home. Fortunately for Robert, he was rescued by a nephew, who brought him to the nursing home. Initially, Robert was as passive and uninvolved in the nursing home as he had been in his house. He responded to the knowledge that his missing of Ruth would be abated by re-engaging in life and generating fresh, new associations and memories. We cannot fix a vacancy in our mind left by a lost loved one by wishing it gone, or other passive means; we must actively immerse ourselves in life. When we act, we modify our brains and can fill mental gaps with new memories.

Lesson: You can be an active architect of your own good health plan.

We can do much more for our health than enroll in an insurance plan and find good doctors when we are sick. Although national health statistics tell us that too many people fail to take advantage of the information, we know that adherence to certain behavior practices will promote vigor and increase longevity. Regina's habitual mistreatment of her body and lack of acceptance of responsibility for her health produced unfortunate consequences of obesity, diabetes, and heart disease. The success of her treatment in the nursing home turned on my convincing her that she could make behavior changes that would have a positive impact on her recuperation. Once she changed her attitude, she was willing to comply with recommendations involving diet, exercise, and participation in physical therapy.

There are no iron-clad guarantees of wellness. We know enough, however, to improve our hardiness. Avoidance of smoking, excessive alcohol intake, and overeating is beneficial. Regularly participating in family activities, exercising, engaging in spiritual/religious practice, and socializing are good for our health. Getting sufficient sleep, effectively managing stress, moderately consuming red wine, and achieving higher education are also associated with positive health outcomes.

Lesson: Exhibit unmistakable beneficence when in a superior position.

With the privileges of rank, position, or superior personal attributes, come greater responsibility. Nursing-home workers, performing with the authority of staff membership, and the personal power that comes from being strong and healthy relative to residents, must behave with extraordinary awareness and care to prevent perceptions of maltreatment. The dynamics of power are such that the more powerless a recipient of care, the greater the potential for fear, anxiety, and a sense of victimization. Roseanne, a thin, weak, eighty-three-year-old resident with exquisite sensitivity to any stimulation, had to be handled with kid gloves. If not, she was rattled, upset, and agitated; she experienced normal encounters as sensory assaults. Her case stands as a clear reminder of the moral obligation we all have to act with sensitivity and kindness to the less able among us.

Lesson: We can modify our environment to our benefit.

We are immersed in the information age. Noting the undeniable advantages that computers, satellites, smart phones, and other electronic innovations confer, we must also acknowledge that an unlimited influx of information from around the globe into our homes and minds can leave some of us feeling overwhelmed and insignificant. This chapter illustrates the point that even small changes in our microenvironment, the people and things we interact with on a daily basis, can yield big results. We need not change the whole world to improve our quality of life, just our piece of it. The reclusive nursing-home resident Carmen's transformation of her living space, and other improvements, were proof of the benefits of effective management of those aspects of life closet and most meaningful to us. Carmen was originally withdrawn and unhappy, engaging in many self-defeating habits (i.e., consuming low-quality snack foods and watching or listening to negative TV and radio programs, being physically inactive, and allowing her room to remain messy and her body to become unkempt), but ultimately I was able to convince her to make beneficial changes. She uncluttered and beautified her room, increased her physical and social activity, improved her diet, varied the forms of entertainment she consumed, and practiced meditation on a gratitude list. She showed that by acting to ensure positive interaction with people and things nearest to us, we can create our own happiness.

Lesson: Words are potent forms of energy that you can wield wisely to promote good for yourself and others.

Residents often arrive at the nursing home sick and dispirited. Medicines and physical therapies are used to address their physical/medical needs. Psychological interventions are necessary to assist residents with their emotional recoveries. The verbal expression of thoughts and feelings has demonstrated effectiveness in promoting physical and mental health. By talking in therapy, individuals in the nursing home can gain hope, develop appropriate expectations for their recovery, benefit from venting their emotions, experience elevated self-esteem, and strengthen their sense of self-efficacy.

Craig, a polio survivor with post-polio syndrome, experienced impressive gains in his mental status from talking in therapy. Expressing previously buried feelings about childhood trauma (teasing and social rejection), Craig was able to rewrite his personal narrative to one of triumph and pride, supplanting the long-carried shame he experienced. Craig also learned how to cope effectively with repetitive, self-defeating thoughts. His case showed that psychological ailments can and must be addressed by psychological interventions, through the healing power of words.

*Lesson: The capacity to give loving care is unlimited,
under the proper conditions.*

If we are not cautious, caretaking may be hazardous to our health. Certain factors must be present to maintain our capacity to serve, as well as to safeguard our physical and mental well-being. In the nursing home, getting to know a resident personally promotes intimacy and reduces the perceived burden on a caregiver. The quality of life that a caregiver experiences outside his professional duties is another important variable to consider. If a caretaker manages stress well and has an ample supply of personal support, he will be able to brook the many challenges of caregiving. The attitude of the recipient of care is another relevant factor; when caretaking efforts are well received, it is mutually gratifying and effortless for the caretaker. If they are met with resistance, caretakers must maintain their professionalism and employ coping skills to protect themselves and the recipients of their care. When we act as good caretakers of ourselves, we ensure our personal well-being and our ability to care for others.

Lesson: Good news: you can choose happiness.

Forgiveness, acceptance, and attitude are unrelated concepts linked by one unifying theme: they represent choices we can make to improve our lives. With our natural inclination to experience life as happening to us, it is good to remember that, although people and events may be out of our control, we can maintain command of our mind-sets and moods. Blaming others, idly complaining about unfavorable developments, and acting as if our attitudes were determined by external factors may provide some consolation to us when we are upset, but these choices and behaviors relegate us to passenger status in our own lives.

Brooke was unhappy about her admission to the nursing home. She was initially engaged in a fight against everyone and everything. Her general antagonism and external focus resulted in her unwittingly handing over her personal power and experiencing unnecessary aggravation. Eventually choosing to forgive her perceived offenders, accepting her need for help, and adopting a positive attitude toward the nursing home, she regained control of her emotions and her life. Important for building personal agency and serenity, deliberately assuming responsibility for our states of mind allows us to achieve independence from the fickleness of people and happenstance.

Lesson: Resist the temptation to act in haste: your intellectual faculties and judgment are at their worst in a crisis.

People often seek psychotherapy services in the midst of a crisis. Although it is a common tendency to act impulsively in the pursuit of immediate relief from distress, it is risky. This is one reason why therapists traditionally request that patients wait six to twelve months from the start of treatment before making life-altering decisions. Resolving emergent situations and calming feelings permits the engagement of all our mental faculties, which is necessary for exercising good judgment and achieving the effective execution of plans.

William reported a nearly irresistible desire to be home with his wife, Edith, who had been diagnosed with dementia. Even though she was receiving appropriate in-home care, William was so determined to watch over Edith that he was prepared to sacrifice his own recovery from leg surgery. From the combined influence of psychotropic medication and psychotherapy, as well as intervention by his daughters, William was able to discuss the pros and cons of his options more rationally. Deciding to remain in the nursing home, he was able to successfully complete his rehabilitation and return home in the best condition possible, which demonstrates the advantage of resisting the temptation to quickly appease your impulses.

*Lesson: Material loss clears the way for spiritual gain
(but why wait?).*

Freed from the many responsibilities and obligations that occupy them in earlier times of life, elderly nursing-home residents appear to find more time for the practice of religion or spirituality. Residents who regularly participate in spiritual practices (whether through prayer, meditation, and other value-laden practices) gain a reprieve from loneliness, experience an abatement of suffering, and find enhanced meaning in their lives. Disabled by obesity and respiratory and cardiac conditions, Tina was a devout Catholic. Often physically uncomfortable and preferring solitude, her only pleasures came from reading Christian literature, praying, and attending services in the nursing home on Sundays. With her severely restricted lifestyle, these religious activities made the difference for Tina between a tolerable acceptance of her life and the experience of unendurable misery. The benefits of spiritual practice are available to us all, and we need not wait until negative circumstances prompt us to pursue such interests.

*Lesson: Despite the close interaction, mind and body are
separate entities; a loving attitude toward the body is
the basis of good personal caretaking and well-being.*

Seeking to avoid illness or disease may not be the most effective motivational approach to encourage the development of healthy habits. If we consider mind and body as separate, it is possible to contemplate the relationship between the two. Taking time to foster a healthy love of our body can serve as a positive motivational strategy that can lead to good personal caretaking. In this chapter, different aspects of the mind-body relationship are discussed: thinking of your body as a receiver of pleasure, a machine to execute your will, the physical representation of your essence, and a gift from its creator can help you view it as the deserving object of your affection.

*Lesson: Your body is generic, with exchangeable parts;
your mind is unique and irreplaceable.*

By attacking the brain, dementing disorders reveal the specialness of our minds. Victims may be recognizable by sight but represent only hollow shells of the persons they once were. For instance, Norman's decline followed a classic course of slow, progressive deterioration of intellectual faculties and functioning, culminating in an absence of volition, inability to communicate, and a loss of identity. His case is a clarion call for early identification and intervention. The quality of the lives of afflicted individuals and their caretakers can be significantly improved if detected and treated when the first signs of trouble are observed. Especially since screening methods are quick and noninvasive, there is no risk for seeking an evaluation for anyone whose mental status is in question.

*Lesson: A good attitude and positive behaviors
will encourage excellent care from others.*

The best way to assure your good treatment by others is to give good treatment to them. We have been taught this fundamental principle since grade school: what goes around comes around. Being a gracious recipient of assistance encourages good caretaking from others. Joyce's naturally generous spirit made spending time with her in the nursing home a pleasure. She was sure to offer a warm greeting and fond farewell and always made her gratitude known. Although she faced all the same challenges of other nursing-home residents and was frequently unhappy, her likeability made working with her easy. This simple formula for good human relations, also known as the golden rule, can work anytime, anywhere.

*Lesson: An understanding and skillful management of feelings
are necessary for health, effective behavior, and good relationships.*

Long undervalued, even by the social sciences, feelings used to be con-sidered irrelevant subjective experiences. Our emotion system is now rightly recognized for its vital roles in communication and motivation. To achieve happiness, we aspire to maximize the experience of positive emotions and minimize the negative. In order to behave effectively, we need to know how we are feeling. And recognizing the emotional state of another is the basis for competent social interaction. In four brief sce-narios, Edgar, Lynne, Sean, and Marina expressed emotions of happiness, anger, sadness, and fear, respectively. The vignettes demonstrated how easy it is to identify emotions when we attend to the pertinent clues.

A list of our primary emotions includes surprise–startle; interest–excitement; enjoyment–joy; anger–rage; fear–terror; distress–anguish; and disgust–contempt. Learning this list of primary emotions, the cir-cumstances that evoke each, the function each serves, and the char-acteristic facial expressions associated with each emotion, we can become excellent at feeling recognition, which allows for greater per-sonal understanding, more effective emotion management, as well as improved communication and social relations.

*Lesson: The young and the elderly have much in common,
which generates insights into caretaking.*

Young children and older adults share many similarities. Enhanced understanding of these individuals at the extremes of the life spectrum can encourage our sensitive handling of our most vulnerable citizens. With the aging of the American population, our encounters with the elderly in the community and residential facilities will increase. It is to everyone's benefit to be well informed and effective in our interaction with elders.

Commonalities between the young child and the older adult to which I have become sensitive through my work in the nursing home are: helplessness and dependency; focus on the body and internal states; the primacy of emotions over intellect; detachment from the environment and responsibility; fragility and sensitivity to change; limited communication skills; surplus of negative emotions; levels of competence differ; women most often serve as caretakers.

Lesson: Retreat from the world is healthy and necessary in order to connect with your inner self and to find balance and serenity.

Although confinement in an institution may seem unquestionably bad, the relative seclusion and simplicity of the nursing home environment has its advantages. With many of the larger hassles of life relegated to the background, residents can direct efforts to the achievement of concrete, easy-to-reach goals—having a nice meal, reading, or winning a bingo game, for example.

In the aftermath of Superstorm Sandy, conversation with Veronica exposed a complete lack of regard for anything other than the satisfaction of her personal and immediate needs. Veronica's attitude provided a lesson in the value of escape from the troubles of the world and concentration on simple pleasures. Taking a page from Veronica's book, we can pursue peace of mind by practicing meditation, scheduling blackouts of electronica, and practicing yoga, to name some activities.

Lesson: There are hidden costs to mobility and independence, which can increase insecurity and alienation.

The availability of a solid support system is a precious asset at any stage of life. We may take this resource for granted, or perhaps be lured away from family and friends by attractive job opportunities or climates. In calculating the costs and benefits of relocation, we should recognize that there may be unexpected risk incurred when separating ourselves from our primary support system.

A New Jersey native, Suzanne was doing well in a Florida retirement community until her husband died and she became sick with pneumonia. She experienced an intense sense of vulnerability and loneliness while in the hospital. Wisely, she came to the nursing home in New Jersey for rehabilitation because of its proximity to her son. The comfort and security Suzanne felt by being close to her family formed the basis of her decision to permanently move back to New Jersey following her discharge from the nursing home.

Lesson: Your brain is very plastic.
You must properly stimulate it for maximum benefit.

Our brains are dynamic, malleable organs. They change and grow in response to stimulation and demand. Just as we can condition and strengthen our muscles through vigorous exercise, we can build brain power with training. The brain's plasticity represents a classic good news–bad news scenario—if you work your brain to sharpen your faculties, you will enjoy enhanced performance. Neglecting your brain, however, will produce a wasting of intellectual skills.

Mario's self-imposed sequestration meant that he was choosing a minimalist lifestyle in the nursing home. Already showing signs of cognitive decline when I met him, his seclusion could only hasten his intellectual degeneration. Because he was bothered by difficulty with memory and communication, Mario agreed to institute changes in his sleep schedule, physical exercise, food consumption, and social activity. In addition to lifting his spirits, the behavior changes helped to provide sorely needed stimulation to act as a hedge against further cognitive decline.

Lesson: Gender and sexuality are integral parts of identity;
to deny or ignore them is annihilating.

We are sexual beings virtually our entire lives, born with a drive to attach to others that impels us to connect, first to caretakers and family members and later to others. We also develop a gender identity in our formative years, which we retain for life. By adulthood, our interest in connection becomes frankly sexual. In our elder years, we continue to require social contact and appreciate being addressed as gendered individuals, even after sexual behavior ceases.

Matthew was at times crude and inappropriate, and Monica, demure and coquettish, but despite their outwardly different behaviors, they demonstrated our universal need for attention and emotional intimacy, and our desire for the pleasure and security of human connection.

Lesson: A key to superior service, and happiness,
is to avoid personalizing everything.

If you provide any type of service, you will be the recipient of criticism. This is especially so in the nursing home, where residents, displaced and unhappy, are prone to grumble about services. It is a matter of self-preservation and professionalism to learn to avoid personalizing complaints. One way to neutralize complaints is to remember that when performing services, you are acting in a professional role; it is only a small piece of who you are. It can also be helpful to recognize that when a grievance is made against you, the complainer is actually talking more about himself and his feelings than about you.

Lesson: Sensitivity to and timely satisfaction of needs
will reduce frustration and increase pleasure.

We are most content when our needs are satisfied immediately. Our independence usually permits us to gain satisfaction for hunger on demand, for example. If we are dependent on another for need fulfillment, however, we will experience more disappointment and dissatisfaction. Being repeatedly thwarted in our desires wears down our coping skills and makes us vulnerable to decreased self-control, excessive emotionality, and anger.

Her coping skills already threadbare because of chronic pain and a poor night's sleep, Mary was in a rage when I found her in her room on one particular day. Having experienced what appeared to be a minor disappointment with an aide, she required considerable time and attention to regain her composure. We all have limits to our frustration tolerance and willpower, and Mary found hers on that day. Her behavior reminds us of the importance of satisfaction of basic needs to maintain our equanimity—getting sufficient rest and adequate nutrition, and satisfactorily addressing pain and illness when present.

Lesson: Good caretaking sometimes means acting in ways that may not feel so loving to the recipient of the care.

Few experiences eclipse the bliss of shared pleasure with loved ones or the intolerable heartache of conflict and disharmony with these same individuals. Although the joys of caretaking usually outnumber the sorrows, responsible caretaking sometimes requires that we act in ways that evoke frustration, disappointment, and anger in our dependents. How we handle these negative reactions can have far-reaching implications for the overall quality of our relationships with our children or reliant elders.

Lillian was furious about being placed in the nursing home by her children. Resentful that they could not provide acceptable assistance in her house, or in either of theirs, she was relentlessly hostile toward them when they visited her. Sadly, because her children were unable to bear her anger, they broke off contact with her, leaving all three embittered. Luckily, in most cases, resistance mounted by residents usually softens after an initial adjustment period, requiring less forbearance by family members and allowing for better results than those experienced by Lillian. Generally speaking, dependents derive a sense of trust and love when caretakers remain available to them even when they are unhappy.

Lesson: Act now to improve yourself and your life, and consider human resources, not just financial ones, in planning your future.

Planning for a comfortable future should encompass more than financial considerations. Other resources are necessary to enjoy our lives, including sound physical and mental health and wholesome relationships. Just as we dare not wait until our later years to begin saving money for retirement, we should not put off the development of our personal or social capital.

Marlene was in the nursing home for rehabilitation of an injured ankle. Fearful and unable to participate in her physical therapy, I discovered that she had experienced longstanding anxiety and panic symptoms for which she never sought mental-health treatment. Her intense fear was a major obstacle to her participation in her rehabilitation; allowing her anxiety to go untreated made her mental-health treatment more difficult and unnecessarily complicated and limited the treatment of her ankle.

Ignoring problems usually allows them to worsen over time. We should assess our physical and mental health, personal finances, and relationships, and take corrective action where necessary, sooner rather than later.

Lesson: Teach your children to practice gratitude and to value service to others by direct education, reinforcement of good behavior, and modeling it yourself.

Compared to prior generations, a disproportionate allocation of time, attention, and resources goes to our youth. By devoting so much backing to our children, ironically, we may not be preparing them adequately for certain aspects of adult life. Rebecca contentedly shared details of her childhood in the 1930s. Her life revolved around family and home, and although much of her time was spent performing daily domestic duties, significant benefits to her lifestyle were evident. Rebecca acquired a deep sense of security and purpose, a healthy respect for work and responsibility, and an appreciation of the value of mutuality—giving as well as receiving.

Although the traditional family model of Rebecca's youth is no longer the norm, we can still provide experiences for our children to help round out their development by modeling and promoting gratitude practices in the home, encouraging service to others, and enjoying regular family time.

Lesson: Good relationships, external and internal, are keys to security and success in life.

With all due respect to nature, we are largely products of our social environments. Satisfactory relationships are necessary for normal emotional, behavioral, social, and mental development, and for success and happiness throughout life. Judiciously choosing whom we befriend, and carefully cultivating high-quality relationships, is crucial to our personal prosperity.

NOTES

CHAPTER 1: SUFFERING IS OPTIONAL

1. Antonio R. Damasio, *Descartes' Error: Emotion, Reason, and the Human Brain* (New York: Avon Books, 1994), p. 266.

2. Allan N. Shore, "The Experience-Dependent Maturation of a Regulatory System in the Orbital Prefrontal Cortex and the Origin of Developmental Psychopathology," *Development and Psychopathology* 8 (1996): 59–87.

3. Krzysztof Kaniasty, "Social Support and Traumatic Stress," *PTSD Research Quarterly* 16, no. 2 (2005): 1–8.

CHAPTER 2: SOCIAL SECURITY

1. Anna Freud and Dorothy T. Burlingham, *War and Children* (rpr., Westport, CT: Greenwood Press, Inc., 1973).

2. John Bowlby, *Attachment and Loss*, vol. 1, *Attachment*, 2nd ed. (New York: Basic Books, 1982), p. 314.

3. Jeree H. Pawl, "The Therapeutic Relationship as Human Connectedness: Being Held in Another's Mind," *Zero to Three* 15, no. 4 (1995): 2-5.

CHAPTER 3: HUMPTY DUMPTY OR BIONIC MAN?

1. E. Allessanda Strada, "Grief, Demoralization, and Depression: Diagnostic Challenges and Treatment Modalities," *Primary Psychiatry* 16, no.5 (2009): 49-55; Randy A. Sansone and Lori A. Sansone, "Demoralization in Patients with Medical Illness," *Psychiatry* 7, no. 8 (2010): 42-45.

2. Strada, "Grief, Demoralization, and Depression."

CHAPTER 4: LOSS: SUBTRACTION AND ADDITION

1. Judith Viorst, *Necessary Losses* (New York: Fireside, 1986).
2. Erick H. Erickson, *Childhood and Society*, 2nd ed. (New York: W. W. Norton, 1963).

CHAPTER 5: PHANTOM PAIN

1. V. S. Ramachandran, *A Brief Tour of Consciousness: From Imposter Poodles to Purple Numbers* (New York: PI Press, 2004).

CHAPTER 6: BEST DAMN HEALTH PLAN

1. CDC, "Deaths and Mortality," http://www.cdc.gov/nchs/fastats/deaths.htm (accessed August 2, 2014).
2. CDC, "Sleep and Sleep Disorders," http://www.cdc.gov/sleep/ (accessed August, 2, 2014).
3. CDC, "How Much Sleep Do I Need?" http://www.cdc.gov/sleep/about_sleep/how_much_sleep.htm (accessed August 2, 2014).
4. Dan Buettner, *The Blue Zones: 9 Lessons for Longer Living from the People Who've Lived the Longest*, 2nd ed. (Washington, DC: National Geographic Society, 2012).
5. George E. Valliant, *Aging Well: Surprising Guideposts to a Happier Life from the Landmark Harvard Study of Adult Development* (New York: Little, Brown, 2002).
6. Buettner, *Blue Zones*.
7. Valliant, *Aging Well*.
8. Dean Ornish, *The Spectrum: A Scientifically Proven Program to Feel Better, Live Longer, Lose Weight, and Gain Health* (New York: Ballantine Books, 2007).
9. Charles E. Dodgen, *Nicotine Dependence: Understanding and Applying the Most Effective Treatment Interventions* (Washington, DC: American Psychological Association, 2005).

CHAPTER 7: NOBLESSE OBLIGE

1. Stanley Milgram, "Behavioral Study of Obedience," *Journal of Abnormal and Social Psychology* 67 (1963): 371–78.
2. Craig Haney, Curtis Banks, and Phillip Zimbardo, "A Study of Prisoners and Guards in a Simulated Prison," *Naval Research Reviews* 30 (1973): 1–17.

CHAPTER 9: I TOUCH THEM ALL AND NEVER LIFT A FINGER

1. Irvin Yalom, *The Theory and Practice of Group Psychotherapy* (New York: Basic Books, 1975).

2. James Pennebaker, *Opening Up: The Healing Power of Expressing Emotions* (New York: Guilford, 1990).

CHAPTER 10: THE ULTIMATE RENEWABLE RESOURCE: LOVE

1. Ellen F. McCarty and Charles Debring, "Burden and Professional Caregivers: Tracking the Impact," *Journal for Nurses in Staff Development* 18, no.5 (2002): 250–57.

2. Richard S. Lazarus and Susan Folkman, *Stress, Appraisal, and Coping* (New York: Springer, 1984).

3. Sebastian Eriksson and Gunvor Gard, "Physical Exercise and Depression," *Physical Therapy Reviews* 16, no. 4 (2011): 261–67.

CHAPTER 11: THE MOST IMPORTANT DECISIONS YOU WILL EVER MAKE: FORGIVENESS, ACCEPTANCE, AND ATTITUDE

1. Fred Luskin, *Forgive for Good: A Proven Prescription for Health and Happiness* (New York: HarperCollins, 2002).

2. Viktor E. Frankl, *Man's Search for Meaning: An Introduction to Logotherapy*, 3rd ed. (New York: Touchstone, 1984).

CHAPTER 12: PUMP THE BRAKES

1. Paul Ekman, *Emotions Revealed: Recognizing Faces and Feelings to Improve Communication and Emotional Life*, 2nd ed. (New York: Holt Paperbacks, 2007), p. xxi.

CHAPTER 13: FINDING MY RELIGION

1. Barbara L. Frederickson and Thomas Joiner, "Positive Emotions Trigger Upward Spirals Toward Emotional Well-being," *Psychological Science* 13, no.2 (2002): 172–75.

CHAPTER 15: THE GHOST IN THE BROKEN MACHINE

1. CDC, "Caregiving for Alzheimer's Disease or Other Dementia," http://www.cdc.gov/aging/caregiving/alzheimer.htm (accessed September 25, 2014).

2. CDC, "Alzheimer's Disease," http://www.cdc.gov/aging/aginginfo/alzheimers.htm (accessed September 25, 2014).

3. Richard L. Strub and F. William Black, *The Mental Status Examination in Neurology*, 2nd ed. (Philadelphia: F. A. Davis, 1985).

4. Christopher M. Clark and Douglas C. Ewbank, "Performance of the Dementia Severity Rating Scale: A Caregiver Questionnaire for Rating Severity in Alzheimer Disease," *Alzheimer Disease and Associated Disorders* 10, no. 1 (1996): 31–39.

CHAPTER 17: FEELINGS: OUR TRUE COLORS

1. Daniel Goleman, *Emotional Intelligence: Why It Can Matter More Than IQ* (New York: Bantam Books, 1995).

2. Stanley I. Greenspan, *Developmentally Based Psychotherapy* (Madison: International Universities Press, 1997).

3. Silvan S. Tomkins, *Affect, Imagery, Consciousness*, vol. 1, *The Positive Affects* (New York: Springer, 1962). (Although there are fine distinctions in the professional literature among the terms *affect*, *emotion*, and *feeling*, for this discussion I use *emotion* and *feeling* interchangeably and do not refer to the term *affect*.) Silvan S. Tomkins, *Affect, Imagery, Consciousness*, vol. 2, *The Negative Affects* (New York: Springer, 1963). Silvan S. Tomkins, *Affect, Imagery, Consciousness*, vol. 3, *The Negative Affects Anger and Fear* (New York: Springer, 1991). Paul Ekman, *Emotions Revealed: Recognizing Faces and Feelings to Improve Communication and Emotional Life*, 2nd ed. (New York: Holt Paperbacks, 2007)—please note that Tomkins and Ekman describe a similar, but not identical, list of primary emotions. The menu presented for discussion is a blend of the two lists.

4. Ekman, *Emotions Revealed*.

CHAPTER 18: CIRCLE OF LIFE

1. CDC, "Nursing Home Care," http://www.cdc.gov/nchs/fastats/nursing-home-care.htm (accessed September 25, 2014).

2. Harold R. Ireton, *Child Development Inventory* (Minneapolis: Behavior Science Systems, 1992).

CHAPTER 19: TURN OFF, UNPLUG, DROP OUT

1. Eckhart Tolle, *The Power of Now: A Guide to Spiritual Enlightenment* (Novato, CA: New World Library, 1999); Ram Dass, *Still Here: Embracing Aging, Changing, and Dying* (New York: Riverhead Books, 2000); Mihaly Csikszentmihalyi, *Flow: The Psychology of Optimal Experience* (New York: Harper Perennial, 1990).

2. Susan Cain, *Quiet: The Power of Introverts in a World That Can't Stop Talking* (New York: Broadway Books, 2012), p. 29.

CHAPTER 21: MENTAL EXERCISE
IS BRAIN SURGERY

1. Norman Doidge, *The Brain That Changes Itself: Stories of Personal Triumph from the Frontiers of Brain Science* (New York: Penguin Books, 2007).

2. Daniel G. Amen, *Change Your Brain, Change Your Life: The Breakthrough Program for Conquering Anxiety, Depression, Obsessiveness, Anger, and Impulsiveness* (New York: Three Rivers, 1998).

3. John B. Arden, *Rewire Your Brain: Think Your Way to a Better Life* (Hoboken, NJ: John Wiley & Sons, 2010).

4. Florian Schmiedek, Martin Lovden, and Ulman Lindenberger, "Hundred Days of Cognitive Training Enhance Broad Cognitive Abilities in Adulthood: Findings from the COGITO Study," *Frontiers in Aging Neuroscience* 2 (2010): 1–9.

5. Doidge, *Brain That Changes Itself*.

CHAPTER 23: IT'S NOTHING PERSONAL

1. Don Miguel Ruiz, *The Four Agreements* (San Rafael, CA: Amber-Allen Publishing, 1997), p. 47.

CHAPTER 24: DISCONNECT

1. Roy Baumeister and John Tierney, *Willpower: Rediscovering the Greatest Human Strength* (New York: Penguin, 2011).

CHAPTER 27: ONE MOTHER CAN TAKE CARE OF FIVE CHILDREN, BUT FIVE CHILDREN CAN'T TAKE CARE OF ONE MOTHER

1. Zero to Three, "Raising a Thankful Child," http://www.zerotothree.org/child-development/social-emotional-development/raising-a-thankful-child.html (accessed September 27, 2014).

CHAPTER 28: OUTSIDE IN

1. John Bowlby, *Attachment and Loss*, vol. 2, *Separation-Anxiety and Anger* (New York: Basic Books, 1973), p. 96.

BIBLIOGRAPHY

Amen, Daniel G. *Change Your Brain, Change Your Life: The Breakthrough Program for Conquering Anxiety, Depression, Obsessiveness, Anger, and Impulsiveness.* New York: Three Rivers, 1998.

Arden, John B. *Rewire Your Brain: Think Your Way to a Better Life.* Hoboken, NJ: John Wiley & Sons, 2010.

Baumeister, Roy, and John Tierney. *Willpower: Rediscovering the Greatest Human Strength.* New York: Penguin, 2011.

Bowlby, John. *Attachment and Loss.* Vol. 1, *Attachment.* 2nd ed. New York: Basic Books, 1982.

———. *Attachment and Loss.* Vol. 2, *Separation-Anxiety and Anger.* New York: Basic Books, 1973.

Buettner, Dan. *The Blue Zones: 9 Lessons for Longer Living from the People Who've Lived the Longest.* 2nd ed. Washington, DC: National Geographic Society, 2012.

Cain, Susan. *Quiet: The Power of Introverts in a World That Can't Stop Talking.* New York: Broadway Books, 2012.

Centers for Disease Control and Prevention (CDC). "Alzheimer's Disease." http://www.cdc.gov/aging/aginginfo/alzheimers.htm (accessed September 25, 2014).

———. "Caregiving for Alzheimer's Disease or Other Dementia." http://www.cdc.gov/aging/caregiving/alzheimer.htm (accessed September 25, 2014).

———. "Deaths and Mortality." http://www.cdc.gov/nchs/fastats/deaths.htm (accessed August 2, 2014).

———. "How Much Sleep Do I Need?" http://www.cdc.gov/sleep/about_sleep/how_much_sleep.htm (accessed August 2, 2014).

———. "Nursing Home Care." http://www.cdc.gov/nchs/fastats/nursing-home-care.htm (accessed September 25, 2014).

———. "Sleep and Sleep Disorders." http://www.cdc.gov/sleep/ (accessed August 2, 2014).

Clark, Christopher M., and Douglas C. Ewbank. "Performance of the Dementia Severity Rating Scale: A Caregiver Questionnaire for Rating Severity in Alzheimer Disease." *Alzheimer Disease and Associated Disorders* 10, no. 1 (1996): 31–39.

Csikszentmihalyi, Mihaly. *Flow: The Psychology of Optimal Experience.* New York: Harper Perennial, 1990.

Damasio, Antonio R. *Descartes' Error: Emotion, Reason, and the Human Brain.* New York: Avon Books, 1994.

Dass, Ram. *Still Here: Embracing Aging, Changing, and Dying.* New York: Riverhead Books, 2000.

Dodgen, Charles E. *Nicotine Dependence: Understanding and Applying the Most Effective Treatment Interventions*. Washington, DC: American Psychological Association, 2005.

Doidge, Norman. *The Brain That Changes Itself: Stories of Personal Triumph from the Frontiers of Brain Science*. New York: Penguin Books, 2007.

Ekman, Paul. *Emotions Revealed: Recognizing Faces and Feelings to Improve Communication and Emotional Life*. 2nd ed. New York: Holt Paperbacks, 2007.

Erickson, Erik H. *Childhood and Society*. 2nd ed. New York: W. W. Norton, 1963.

Eriksson, Sebastian, and Gunvor Gard. "Physical Exercise and Depression." *Physical Therapy Reviews* 16, no. 4 (2011): 261–67.

Frankl, Viktor E. *Man's Search for Meaning: An Introduction to Logotherapy*. 3rd ed. New York: Touchstone, 1984.

Frederickson, Barbara L., and Thomas Joiner. "Positive Emotions Trigger Upward Spirals Toward Emotional Well-being." *Psychological Science* 13, no. 2 (2002): 172–75.

Freud, Anna, and Dorothy T. Burlingham. *War and Children*. Reprint. Westport, CT: Greenwood, 1973.

Goleman, Daniel. *Emotional Intelligence: Why It Can Matter More Than IQ*. New York: Bantam Books, 1995.

Greenspan, Stanley I. *Developmentally Based Psychotherapy*. Madison: International Universities Press, 1997.

Haney, Craig, Curtis Banks, and Phillip Zimbardo. "A Study of Prisoners and Guards in a Simulated Prison." *Naval Research Reviews* 30 (1973): 1–17.

Ireton, Harold R. *Child Development Inventory*. Minneapolis: Behavior Science Systems, 1992.

Kaniasty, Krzysztof. "Social Support and Traumatic Stress." *PTSD Research Quarterly* 16, no. 2 (2005): 1–8.

Lazarus, Richard S., and Susan Folkman. *Stress, Appraisal, and Coping*. New York: Springer, 1984.

Luskin, Fred. *Forgive for Good: A Proven Prescription for Health and Happiness*. New York: HarperCollins, 2002.

McCarty, Ellen F., and Charles Debring. "Burden and Professional Caregivers: Tracking the Impact." *Journal for Nurses in Staff Development* 18, no.5 (2002): 250–57.

Milgram, Stanley. "Behavioral Study of Obedience." *Journal of Abnormal and Social Psychology* 67 (1963): 371–78.

Ornish, Dean. *The Spectrum: A Scientifically Proven Program to Feel Better, Live Longer, Lose Weight, and Gain Health*. New York: Ballantine Books, 2007.

Pawl, Jeree H. "The Therapeutic Relationship as Human Connectedness: Being Held in Another's Mind." *Zero to Three* 15, no. 4 (1995): 2–5.

Pennebaker, James. *Opening Up: The Healing Power of Expressing Emotions*. New York: Guilford, 1990.

Ramachandran, V. S. *A Brief Tour of Consciousness: From Imposter Poodles to Purple Numbers.* New York: PI Press, 2004.

Ruiz, Don Miguel. *The Four Agreements.* San Rafael, CA: Amber-Allen, 1997.

Sansone, Randy A., and Lori A. Sansone. "Demoralization in Patients with Medical Illness." *Psychiatry* 7, no. 8 (2010): 42–45.

Schmiedek, Florian, Martin Lovden, and Ulman Lindenberger. "Hundred Days of Cognitive Training Enhance Broad Cognitive Abilities in Adulthood: Findings from the COGITO Study." *Frontiers in Aging Neuroscience* 2 (2010): 1–9.

Shore, Allan N. "The Experience-Dependent Maturation of a Regulatory System in the Orbital Prefrontal Cortex and the Origin of Developmental Psychopathology." *Development and Psychopathology* 8 (1996): 59–87.

Strada, E. Allessanda. "Grief, Demoralization, and Depression: Diagnostic Challenges and Treatment Modalities." *Primary Psychiatry* 16, no. 5 (2009): 49–55.

Tolle, Eckhart. *The Power of Now: A Guide to Spiritual Enlightenment.* Novato, CA: New World Library, 1999.

Tomkins, Silvan S. *Affect, Imagery, Consciousness.* Vol. 1, *The Positive Affects.* New York: Springer, 1962.

———. *Affect, Imagery, Consciousness.* Vol. 2, *The Negative Affects.* New York: Springer, 1963.

———. *Affect, Imagery, Consciousness.* Vol. 3, *The Negative Affects Anger and Fear.* New York: Springer, 1991.

Valliant, George E. *Aging Well: Surprising Guideposts to a Happier Life from the Landmark Harvard Study of Adult Development.* New York: Little, Brown, 2002.

Viorst, Judith. *Necessary Losses.* New York: Fireside, 1986.

Yalom, Irvin. *The Theory and Practice of Group Psychotherapy.* New York: Basic Books, 1975.

Zero to Three. "Raising a Thankful Child." http://www.zerotothree.org/child -development/social-emotional-development/raising-a-thankful-child.html (accessed September 27, 2014).

INDEX